Client/Server and
Open Systems

Client/Server and Open Systems

Technologies and the Tools That Make Them Work

Rand Dixon

John Wiley & Sons, Inc.

New York • Chichester • Brisbane • Toronto • Singapore

Publisher: Katherine Schowalter
Editor: Robert M. Elliott
Associate Managing Editor: Angela Murphy
Text Design & Composition: Integre Technical Publishing Co., Inc.

Designations used by companies to distinguish their products are often claimed as trademarks. In all instances where John Wiley & Sons, Inc. is aware of a claim, the product names appear in initial capital or all capital letters. Readers, however, should contact the appropriate companies for more complete information regarding trademarks and registration.

This text is printed on acid-free paper.

This publication is designed to provide accurate and authoritative information in regard to the subject matter covered. It is sold with the understanding that the publisher is not engaged in rendering legal, accounting, or other professional service. If legal advice or other expert assistance is required, the services of a competent professional person should be sought.

Library of Congress Cataloging-in-Publication Data:

Dixon, R. M., P.E.
    Client/server and open systems: a guide to the technologies and
the tools that make them work / R.M. Dixon.
        p.   cm.
    Includes bibliographical references and index.
    ISBN 0-471-05007-5 (paper: alk. paper)
    1. Client/server computing.   2. Open system interconnection.
    I. Title.
    QA76.9.C55D59   1995   95-32268
    055.2–dc20

Printed in the United States of America

10 9 8 7 6 5 4 3 2 1

Preface

Everybody's talking about it. The mainframe is dead. It's been over-thrown by something called "client/server." But has it? Are companies really unplugging their big computers and replacing them with net-works of desktop machines? You might easily conclude that they are, judging from all the publicity surrounding client/server computing.

The truth is, however, client/server and mainframe computing aren't directly pitted against each other as some would have us believe. Nothing is more secure, or processes information better, than the mainframe. It's not about to disappear anytime soon.

Client/server is a model of computing, just as mainframe computing is. Its attraction is that it can blend information from multiple sources (servers) and present it to the user (client) in ways that are easier for us humans to understand. This can lead to increased end-user productivity. But it comes at a cost. Client/server is generally not cheaper than the style of computing we've known in the past. Its inherent heterogeneous nature, a shortage of skills, demanding maintenance requirements, and a lack of tools necessary to put it all together make client/server an expensive undertaking—if it even works at all. Estimates place the odds of a client/server development failure at about 50/50.

Client/server and open systems cover a lot of ground. They're dif-ficult subjects to come to terms with quickly. In this book, I've tried to stick to a practical, no-nonsense approach. If you've ever wondered what client/server is, what it has to do with open systems, whether it's something you, or your organization, should be involved with, how it's built, or what the risks are, this book is for you.

But before we get to it, I would like to express my appreciation to the people at John Wiley and Sons, Inc., and to Bob Elliott in particular. He has been helpful and patient throughout this demanding writing process. I would also like thank Fred Bevan, friend and exponent of the object-oriented arts, for his review of selected pieces of this work. His clarity of mind was helpful on more than one occasion.

R.M. Dixon, P.E.
rdixon@passport.ca

Contents

**Chapter 1 Gluing It All Together:
Client/Server and the Quest for Open Systems**   1

Introduction   1
The Standards Makers   4
Enter Middleware   6
Notes   9

Chapter 2 Data Communications: The Basics   11

Introduction   11
Protocol Soup   12
Layers Upon Layers   14
The Lower-Level Protocols   19
   Ethernet 19
   Token-Ring 25
   FDDI 29
Wireless LANs   33
Wrap-up   35
Key Terms and Ideas Appearing in This Chapter   36
Notes   39

**Chapter 3 Network Operating Systems:
First Stop on the Road to Client/Server**   41

The Client/Server Protocol of Choice?   41
NetWare: File Serving for the Masses   42
The Internetwork Packet Exchange   45
The Sequenced Packet Exchange   47
The NetWare Core Protocol   48
NetWare 4.x   50
Windows NT Advanced Server   52
NetWare Loadable Modules   53
Wrap-up   56
Key Terms and Ideas Appearing in This Chapter   57
Notes   61

Chapter 4   WANs: Bridging the Great Divide   **63**

Introduction   63
Circuit-Switched WANs   65
  Dial-up Analog Lines 65
  Switched-56 69
  ISDN 69
  The T-Carrier Facility 70
Packet-Switched WANs   72
  X.25 73
  Frame Relay 75
  SMDS 75
  ATM 76
  SONET 78
Wrap-up   79
Key Terms and Ideas Appearing in This Chapter   80
Notes   82

Chapter 5   The Internet Protocol: TCP/IP   **85**

Introduction   85
The Net   87
TCP/IP from the Ground Up   89
The Internet Protocol   91
IP Addressing   92
Addressing on the Internet   96
  Accessing the Net 98
The Transmission Control Protocol   99
The Application Layer   100
  Internet Applications 103
Doing Business on the Net   108
  Internet Security 110
Classical SNA   112
The New SNA   114
Wrap-up   118
Key Terms and Ideas Appearing in This Chapter   119
Notes   123

Chapter 6   UNIX: On the Way to Open   **125**

Introduction   125
UNIX: Under the Hood   126

X Windows   128
The UNIX Vendors: a Who's Who   130
Why Is UNIX so RISC-y?   131

   Digital's Alpha 133
   The PowerPC 136
   Intel's Pentium 137
   The P6 138

Windows NT: The New UNIX?   139
POSIX: In Pursuit of Openness   141
The Distributed Computing Environment   143
Wrap-up   146
Key Terms and Ideas Appearing in This Chapter   147
Notes   151

Chapter 7 Client/Server Computing: Information for the People   **153**

Client/Server Is . . .   153
Models of Computing   155
What's Good About Client/Server   158
What's Bad About Client/Server   160
Client/Server: Who's Using It   161

   Banking on Client/Server 161
   A World-Class Event 163
   Taking the Cure 165
   Keeping Their PROMISe 166

Wrap-up   168
Notes   169

Chapter 8 The Client, the Middle, and the Server   **171**

Introduction   171
The Client Side   172

   Microsoft's Windows 173

The Middle   183

   Structured Query Language 183
   ODBC 185
   It's Everyware 186

The Server Side   189

   Serving Up Data 189

Wrap-up   193
Key Terms and Ideas Appearing in This Chapter   194
Notes   198

Chapter 9   Client/Server Development   201

Introduction   201
Software Development   202
   PowerSoft's PowerBuilder   209
   Gupta's SQLWindows   210
   Visual Basic   211
Putting It Altogether: System Integration   212
Wrap-up   217
Key Terms and Ideas Appearing in This Chapter   218
Notes   220

Chapter 10   Client/Server Management   223

Introduction   223
NetView/390: The Top-down Approach   224
SNMP: The Bottom-up Approach   227
   SNMP-based Management: The Big Three   230
Client/Server Security   232
   Assessing Your Risk   233
   Layers of Client/Server Security   235
   Fault Tolerance   238
   Defending against Intruders   240
   The Devil Only Knows   245
Wrap-up   246
Key Terms and Ideas Appearing in This Chapter   247
Notes   252

Chapter 11   Some Final Words   253

A Few Words of Advice   253

Vendors Mentioned in This Book   257

Glossary   271

Index   299

Client/Server and Open Systems

Chapter 1
Executive Summary

Client/server systems often bring together hardware and software from various sources. The challenge is to get it all working together. To succeed, client/server needs standards. Client/server needs open systems.

But we don't have open systems today. On the contrary, we're far from it. Client/server implementors must simply make do with what they've got. Even then, often it's not enough. Client/server projects have an alarming failure rate. According to Standish Group International, a Massachusetts-based market research group, 31.1 percent of all information technology (IT) projects are canceled prior to completion for one reason or another. Of that, 40 to 50 percent involve client/server technology.[1]

What is client/server anyway? There are plenty of definitions. Put simply, it's a model of computing in which the requester of some action resides on one system and the provider resides on another. As it is a model that's largely defined in software, however, there's no reason that the "system" can't be the same computing device.

In most of its incarnations, client/server means client/*data*/server with a personal computer (PC) at one end and a database server at the other. Because we don't have truly open systems, getting these two—and the applications residing on them—to talk is the real issue. This is where middleware makes its stand. Middleware is third-party software that links up clients and servers. It can be a bit slow, but at least it's a solution.

With all the attention client/server is receiving in the press, it's easy to conclude that it is the solution to all our computing woes. It's new. It's exciting. But newer doesn't necessarily imply better. While the client/server model can improve end-user productivity under certain circumstances, it isn't as secure or as easy to manage. The client/server model is harder to develop applications for and generally not as cheap as the computing models we've used in the past. Following this theme, this book is intended to equip readers with the knowledge necessary to decide where, when, and how (and if) to best deploy client/server within their organizations.

CHAPTER 1

Gluing It All Together: Client/Server and the Quest for Open Systems

Introduction

Question: What do client/server, open systems, and reengineering have in common? Answer: They're all very hot right now. But on a more useful note, the client/server often is a solution to some reengineered business needs. And those who've tried client/server unanimously state that their success largely resulted from a near-religious adherence to available standards. Standards make systems "open," and for client/server to work, we need as many of them as we can get.

But alas, open systems are but a dream. Competitive forces conflict with the level of vendor cooperation required to make them a reality.

Vendors may talk "open," but the concept means different things to different people.

X/Open Ltd., an independent company that makes its money testing third-party products for standards-compliance, defines open systems this way: "a computer or communications system that conforms to agreed international standards and is available from more than one independent supplier."[2]

Definitions are great, but it's what open systems can do for us that matters. For starters, they can make our lives easier. Want to move a program from the Mac to DOS 6.2/Windows 3.x? No problem. And while we're at it, who—besides vendors—cares about DOS *this* and Windows *that* anyway? You shouldn't have to take a crash course in "compuspeak" in order to run a spreadsheet. But there's more.

Imagine this scenario: You need some stats from marketing to combine with your financials for a presentation to senior management. The problem is, the marketing folks run on a Dinglehoffer 5000, and you're using a Wingnut 86. They don't speak. In a completely open systems world, it would be possible not only to get the two talking, but to get your presentation application, your spreadsheet, and marketing's database all working together seamlessly as well. With open systems, the spotlight moves from data to the application. People stop worrying about where the data is, and what format it's in, and simply get on with their jobs.

System administrators would benefit from open systems too. They could order hardware and software from anyone they wished, knowing it would work with the installed base. Staff skill sets would be easier to maintain; people wouldn't need networking experience with Dinglehoffers *and* Wingnuts; they'd both network the same way.

How would vendors differentiate themselves in an open systems world? Already we're seeing that the quality of service sets some vendors apart from the rest of the pack. In the future, this will be perhaps *the* major vendor differentiator.

Connectivity, commonality, and vendor independence: That's what open systems boils down to. We want the ability to pick our products from . . . whomever. But there's a down side, one that comes in the form of a hidden cost—one many of us are already encountering in our trek toward opentopia.

Remember when we used to deal with just a single vendor? That company handled everything. Whatever it dropped off on our loading docks (usually) worked with whatever was already on site. It was that company's stuff too, after all. But if you ever found yourself pining for some "best-in-class" product that your vendor didn't support, you just had to buck up.

In those univendor days, our supplier was our pal—although, arguably, the relationship often felt more like a hostage situation. Still, if something broke, at least we knew whom to call. That's changing. In heterogeneous environments, when something breaks, it's always the other guy's fault. Today we find ourselves dealing with a profusion of suppliers, each offering its own piece to a quiltwork we call our computing infrastructure.

To make things worse, standards—standards that would help everything work together—unfold at a pace that's nothing short of glacial. But users sometimes can't, or won't, wait. And when that happens, there's always someone around to step in and sell them something; standards be damned. The result is usually a divergence of standards. Consider the optical storage market. WORMS (Write-Once Read-Many) disks and drives come in a plethora of sizes and capacities. Unable to work out a compromise, each manufacturer has come up with its own proprietary file system. As these systems become entrenched into our workplaces, the hope of a single, unifying standard becomes more and more unlikely.

Okay, so the computing world as a whole isn't open, but what's all the commotion about UNIX? you might ask. Isn't that supposed to be the great open environment? At first glance you might think so. Practically every hardware and software house has a UNIX offering in its product line. Lotus, IBM, WordPerfect, HP, Digital—everybody "speaks" UNIX. There's even a version of PKZIP, the popular PC file compression utility, for UNIX. The problem is, like some modern-day Tower of Babel, they're all different dialects. There are at least 30 different versions of UNIX in circulation (possibly more). So then what defines their UNIXness? How can all these versions exist and still call themselves UNIX? As we'll see later when we examine the operating system in depth, from a user perspective, one UNIX does look pretty much like another. That's because at their core, they are all alike. But in an attempt to differentiate each version, each vendor has added proprietary "value-added" features to the base operating system. While users see no significant difference, these features are enough to make the various UNIX versions incompatible when it comes time to move programs around.

In spite of this, the similarities between the different versions of UNIX do outweigh their differences. AIX, IBM's version of UNIX, and Solaris, Sun Microsystem's rendition, have a lot more in common than does, say, AIX and MVS, IBM's mainframe operating system. So it *is* a step in the right direction. A rash of related technologies that, for the most part, help define the open systems movement have evolved: POSIX (Portable Operating System Interface), DCE (Distributed Computing Environment), NFS (Network File System), and SNMP (the Simple Network Management Protocol). These one-time UNIX fixtures are now spreading to many non-UNIX operating systems as well. So while UNIX may never directly lead to the open systems promised land, it will have played an important role, if we ever do finally get there.

The Standards Makers

Who's pushing for open systems? You and I may think they're a good idea, but neither of us is probably doing much to make them a reality. The biggest beneficiaries from the move to open systems would be large organizations that possess stacks of operating systems and platforms—organizations such as the U.S. federal government, for example. One of the world's largest purchasers of hardware and software, it's quite interested in getting everything working together—simply and cheaply. And when a customer that big says that it would like something done, vendors listen. A number of large North American organizations have also banded together to form Corporations for Open Systems International (COS). More than just pushing for usable standards, COS actually steps in to help define them.

There's a slew of formal standards-setting bodies too, including the IEEE, the American National Standards Institute (ANSI), the International Organization for Standardization (ISO), the SQL Access Group (SAG), and X/Open Inc. These are the de jure standards makers.

The IEEE has strongly influenced the definition of local area networks (LANs). Its "802 group" contains specifications for Ethernet and Token Ring. ANSI and X/Open are standards-for-profit organizations; they're funded through the development of standards. Among other things, ANSI concerns itself with computer languages such as SQL, C, and FORTRAN. It represents the United States at the ISO, which is sort of a United Nations for standards making. SAG is a consortium of companies interested in advancing standards for the SQL language. We'll run into these standards-setting bodies, and others, many times throughout the pages of this book.

Just as valid are the de facto standards makers. De facto standards occur along product lines; a particular product becomes so popular that other vendors start to provide value-added services to it in order to make a sale. WordPerfect, Lotus, and Borland's dBASE—each has held this coveted position at one time. But now they're all at the mercy of Microsoft, the most successful de facto standards maker in modern times. As we all know, Microsoft produces the world's most popular operating system, DOS, and an environment that wraps around it, called Windows (both just now being replaced by Windows 95). People like Windows. Businesses like Windows. So if you're a software vendor, you have to like Windows.

Owning the world's most popular operating system can be very gratifying—not only for the profits that it provides. The reason is because in addition to making operating systems, and operating system add-ons, Microsoft produces application software ranging from e-mail systems to databases. Many believe that this gives Microsoft an advantage; it's inconceivable that their word processor designers, for example, aren't forewarned of impending DOS/Windows upgrades. As a result, the company is in a better position to bring new application software to market faster than the competition. Each time it does, it grabs a little more of the potential sales. Microsoft Word is steadily eating into WordPerfect's piece of the word processor pie. Excel has Lotus 1-2-3 on the ropes. And there's no end in sight. Windows 3.x is just now going through a radical upgrade to Windows 95, and Windows NT's planned successor looms just over the horizon.

De facto, de jure, formal, informal: There are a lot of people working on standards out there. Unfortunately, many of them are working on conflicting standards. If we didn't need some form of order—especially in development of client/server systems—so badly, the situation would be funny. But we're not completely without options; we can invoke a middleman to help tie our systems together. While doing so costs a bit more, it's worth it.

Enter Middleware

Try this sometime: Take the very next computing magazine that lands on your desk, and open it anywhere. Scan the two exposed pages. Chances are good that you'll find the term "client/server" somewhere. The concept has literally galvanized the industry. But that's all it is, a concept, a computing "model." By itself, it's of little value. It's what you do *with* client/server that matters.

Client/server is attractive because it enables us to split the computational load of some application between a device on the desktop and some other box locked away in a room somewhere. (See Figure 1.1.) In the process, the desktop machine can add value to the whole operation—even if it just presents things in a more attractive format.

The key word in the last paragraph is "between"—between the desktop device and some other one. That other device is, of course, the server—usually a *data* server—at least as that is popularly defined.

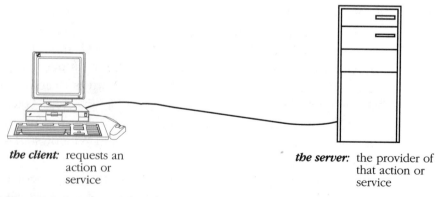

the client: requests an action or service

the server: the provider of that action or service

Figure 1.1 What is client/server anyway?

In this very same way, there could be servers for computational purposes, fax servers, and others. In an open systems world, connecting up clients and servers would be a snap. As it stands, however, doing so can be tricky. Both have to "speak" the same communications protocols, and the application running on the client must be appropriately hooked up to the database engine running on the server. That's an issue of interoperability: Enter middleware, to the rescue.

As its name implies, middleware stands between the client and a server. Acting somewhat as a gateway, middleware products convert information and allow two otherwise noncooperative entities to get along. Doing so is big business. Add a few other things that organizations need, such as work routing features, and you have a workflow manager, an especially hot application for client/server computing these days.

At the heart of the client/server philosophy is the notion of enterprisewide data access. Employees access whatever data they need, whenever they need it. With the right information at their fingertips, they can make better, and faster, decisions. Making all this possible is the network. Without it, there is no client/server. So it's logical then that our exploration of open systems and client/server should begin there. In Chapter 2, we take a brief tour of networking and focus on local area networks (LANs): Ethernet, Token Ring, and Fiber Distributed Data Interface (FDDI). We'll also see how wireless networking is changing the face of the office.

From there we'll move on to Network Operating Systems. Novell's NetWare dominates this slice of the business, but it's steadily losing ground to Microsoft's Windows NT, which many now regard as a better platform for client/server applications. We'll see why in Chapter 3.

From LANs to WANs: In Chapter 4 we examine Wide Area Networking technologies. WANs have two undesirable features—from the point of view of client/server deployment—they're slow and they're expensive. Most installed Wide Area Networks operate at the 56 kbps (thousands of bits per second) level. That might not sound too bad until you realize that on average, LANs operate at speeds of more than 200 times that. But we stand on the verge of a networking renaissance. While today WANs and LANs are supported by separate, and very different, technologies, a homogenizing force promises to provide organizations with a single (very high-speed) networking fabric. As corporations become more global, this shift will have a profound effect on how they run their businesses.

Rounding out our study of data communications, in Chapter 5 we explore Transmission Control Protocol/Internet Protocol (TCP/IP), the basis for the now-famous Internet. Able to run over most LAN and WAN technologies, TCP/IP's nonproprietary stance is attracting hordes of organizations. It has become their leading choice for internetworking communications.

In spite of some claims to the contrary, openness does not equal UNIX. In Chapter 6 we'll take a look at the operating system and all its trappings. Companies are increasingly choosing UNIX as the server operating system in the client/server relationship. But their choice may have as much to do with the types of platforms UNIX runs on as with the operating system itself.

Client/server may be relatively new, but newer isn't always better or the best fit. There are times when the good old mainframe model, or even the standalone computing, is the better choice. In Chapter 7 we turn our attention to the client/server model and attempt to put some definitions to it, discuss what's good about it, and identify its risks. We'll also walk through several case studies of organizations that have successfully deployed it.

In Chapter 8 we move from computing in business to the business of computing, and take an under-the-covers look at the client/server model. At a high level, there are only three components to a client/server application: the client side, the server side, and something standing between them that connects the two. In practice, there are many ways to implement each. Getting the right mix is essential to success.

Client/server development challenges are quite different from what we've known in the past. Start with system design and configuration, add application partitioning and network load balancing, database design, and a whole new series of object-oriented development tools, and you quickly understand why development skills are in short supply. In Chapter 9 we explore the client/server development process.

Client/server is a distributed computing model. It owes its success to the health and dependability of the network. Unfortunately, network management is an evolving field. As yet, no stable, comprehensive toolsets satisfy all corporate network management needs. In Chapter 10 we take a look at what's available and speculate as to where the market's going. We follow this up with a related review of network security practices. Client/server's "data when it's needed, where it's needed" credo directly conflicts with traditional security practices. Many cite this as a leading reason to choose client/server with caution.

In total, Client/Server and Open Systems will be a grand tour of computing. If you thought ATMs were only machines that dished out cash, BLOBs were something that chased Steve McQueen around in the movies, and RAID was a bug spray, you ought to find it an informative read. And if you're trying to come to grips with client/server, to determine what's good about it, what's bad about it, and how it is built, the pages to come will prove interesting reading.

Notes

[1] L. G. Paul, "User Input: Key to Avoiding Failure in Client/Server Development Projects," *PCWeek*, Jan. 23, 1995, 74.

[2] Charles T. Clark, "What Is Open", *Digital News & Review*, Sept. 26, 1994, 11, 25.

Chapter 2

Executive Summary

In the past, a knowledge of networking technologies and practices wasn't a requisite for software development. However, that all changes when organizations "go distributed"—when they adopt client/server.

Client/server computing is a significant step toward distributed processing. The desktop (client) device is usually responsible for presenting information to the user; the server holds and controls the data. Applications that manipulate that data must be carefully split between the client and the server in order to optimize system response time. Lying between the client and the server lurks what is fingered most often for bringing linked systems to their ruin: the network. If its importance is disregarded in any of the aspects of the client/server development process, failure is practically guaranteed.

Getting networked devices to communicate is no small matter however. And traditionally, when faced with complex tasks, we try to simplify them by breaking them down into more easily handled chunks. Such is the case with data communications. It leads to the notion of the seven-layer communication model. The top layer deals with user applications, the bottom with rules regarding the hardware used to transmit the data physically. Each of these layers is a protocol, a standard way of doing something. Three dominant protocol "stacks" are in use today: Transmission Control Protocol/Internet Protocol (TCP/IP), systems network architecture (SNA), and Novell's Sequenced Packet Exchange/Internetwork Packet Exchange (SPX/IPX).

SPX/IPX, TCP/IP, and SNA share one thing in common: They can all use the same low-level protocols—those charged with actually putting data out onto the line. There we find three main choices in the local-area arena: Ethernet, Token-ring and Fiber Distributed Data (FDDI). All are baseband protocols, meaning that only one signal (transmitting machine) can dominate the network at a given time.

The concept of a "network" doesn't necessarily involve something you can physically touch. Today you can purchase both Ethernet and Token-ring supporting products that allow users to set up quickly and to move about a given area freely, all the while accessing other devices within the corporation—without a wire in sight.

CHAPTER 2

Data Communications: The Basics

Introduction

This is a book about client/server computing. So why then are we beginning with a discussion of data communications? By its design, client/server computing is a distributed computing model; no network, no client/server. Client/server computing is also fundamentally heterogeneous in nature: serving computer from vendor A, client access device from vendor B, database software from vendor C, and so on. This, of course, is where open systems comes in, but something else rides along on its coattails. If we're no longer relying on a single vendor, and we employ bits and pieces from a variety of them, who's going to ensure that everything works together? In most cases, *we* have to. Even if we employ a systems integrator, we're still forced to become at least somewhat conversant in the language of data communications.

Protocol Soup

To the uninitiated, linking up devices for the purpose of information sharing doesn't sound like a big deal: "Just adhere to the prevailing communication standard, and everything should interoperate." But that's precisely the problem: which standard? As someone once said, the best thing about computing standards is that there are so many to choose from. If, for example, you wanted to network a DOS PC, a UNIX workstation, a Mac, and a mainframe, you'd be facing four different communication protocols. Getting them intercommunicating dependably would be no small trick.

Fundamentally speaking, data communications is easy to understand. Just as with a common telephone conversation, there's a series of rituals, or protocols, that we have to go through before we can get down to the reason for the call. But they have to be steps that both parties understand and expect. The same is true when two computers intercommunicate; unless both adhere to the same communication protocol, not much can happen.

One of the most daunting aspects of data communications is the literal existence of protocols upon protocols—many with tongue-twisting acronyms. This is where we run into TCP/IP, SPX/IPX, CSMA/CD, FDDI, IEEE 802.X, and a veritable phalanx of others. Client/server planners and developers require, at the very least, a basic understanding of these protocols.

Most LANs operate in a baseband fashion. In baseband networks, only one transmission can dominate the network at a given time. And while you may have never heard of the term "baseband," you've probably heard of its two leading manifestations: Ethernet and Token-ring. Ethernet, Token-ring, and FDDI—another, lesser-known baseband technology—are protocols that stipulate the physical arrangement of the LAN and how data is to traverse it. They take care of the low-level stuff. But there's more to data communications than that. Error checking must be done, and some means of insuring that transmissions reach their intended destinations must exist. These areas are addressed by higher-order protocol groups, such as TCP/IP, Novell's SPX/IPX, and IBM's SNA.

On baseband networks, messages travel in "packets." Packets are electrical pulses that contain both the actual data, sometimes referred to as the "payload," and information about the source and destination nodes —"tombstone information." If the data being sent is larger than the maximum allowable packet size, it's broken up into a number of pieces. Because of changing network conditions, packets being transmitted might not all follow the exact same route between sender and receiver, so it's possible for them to arrive in a different order from that in which they were sent. Using information contained in each packet, the receiving node must reassemble the message as it was intended. Data transmission speeds in baseband LANs currently range from 50 kbps (thousands of bits per second) to less than 20 Mbps (millions of bits per second). Ethernet, for example, operates at a top speed of 10 Mbps. At speeds like that, an average page of text (about 7,000 bytes [7K]) screams by any point on the LAN in milliseconds. The physical transmission speed is approximately 60 to 80 percent the speed of light.

Baseband isn't the only way LANs can operate. It's also possible to stratify the transmission capacity (its "bandwidth") of the carrier (the actual wire or fiber) so that a number of conversations take place at the same time. Known as "broadband," such as a cable television signal, transmissions are multiplexed (or interleaved) from several sources across a single carrier. Multiplexing is done on a time, or frequency, division basis. Time division multiplexing shuffles a number of transmissions and ushers them down the line. Frequency division multiplexing slices up the available data path and makes it available to several sources at the same time. These techniques are sometimes used to connect departmental LANs into a corporate network. The signals of several baseband networks can share a single (possibly fiber) line, often referred to as the "backbone." Requiring signal manipulation at

CLOSE-UP

What is a "bit" again?

Bits are binary digits. They are the smallest unit of information handled by a computer. By themselves, bits aren't very meaningful to us humans. But taken in groups of eight, they can be used, in accordance with the American Standard Code for Information Exchange (ASCII), for example, to represent letters, numbers, and punctuation marks. A group of eight bits (used to represent a single character) is called a byte.

both the sending and receiving ends, broadband networks are more expensive, and more complicated, to operate than baseband nets.

Limitations in the connecting cable and within the network adapter cards present in each participating node restrict physically networked LANs to departmental or, possibly, office-building size. Multiple LANs can be strung together into what's sometimes called a campus-size network. This could involve one or more buildings spaced over a distance of several miles. This is called "internetworking." TCP/IP and IBM's new version of SNA are regarded as superior internetworking (high-end) protocols because of their ability to cope with sprawling networks of networks. Beyond the scope of campus-size internetworks, we move into the domain of the wide area network.

WANs are garnering a great deal of attention at present. Who among us hasn't heard of "the Internet," model for that now most threadbarren of concepts the "information superhighway"? The Internet is a massive global network of networks. By some accounts, there's more than 1 million nodes directly attached to it with as many as 1,000 new ones being added daily. The Internet uses the TCP/IP protocol group for data communications. But apart from happenings on "the Net," new technologies such as video teleconferencing and imaging are pushing the envelope of corporate WAN implementations. The vendor community is answering the challenge with Integrated Services Digital Network (ISDN), frame relay, and the emerging holy grail of communication technologies, asynchronous transfer mode, capable of transmission rates greater than 10 times that of Ethernet or Token-ring. As companies extend their reach and become truly global in nature, some are already feeling pressures to scale the client/server model to levels not yet realistically practical with today's technology.

Layers Upon Layers

If you've ever read about or taken a course on basic data communications, you'll recall incessant reference to something called the seven-layer OSI model. The first few times you see it, it appears to be a frustratingly abstract concept. You're trying to learn how to make machines intercommunicate, and they're presenting you with pictures of stacked boxes.

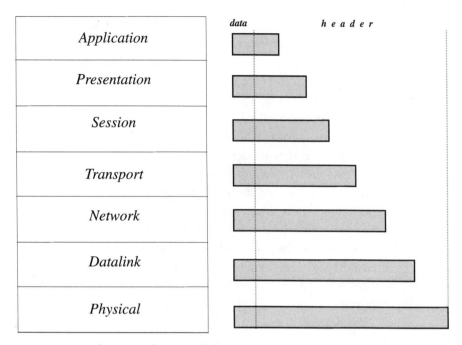

Figure 2.1 The OSI 7-layer model.

But the model is a useful one (and so yes, we're going to talk about it too!). It takes the job of moving data over a network and busts it up into seven discrete tasks. (See Figure 2.1.) Tasks near the bottom of the model address the actual job of putting electrical pulses onto a communication line. The stuff at the top makes sure that transmissions get to where they're going and determines what to do if they don't.

Over and above the seven discrete tasks, making up the model, it's helpful to cut the stack into two larger pieces: the low-level (physical) stuff—taken care of by standards such as Ethernet and Token-ring—and the higher-level, error-checking tasks, addressed by agglomerations of software "protocols" such as TCP/IP, SNA, and SPX/IPX (among others). As evidence of at least some degree of openness, it's possible to mix and match most of the popular higher-level protocol groups with the lower-level standards.

Each layer of the model, shown in Figure 2.1, is seen as a separate communication protocol (usually a piece of software). An outgoing transmission, starting at the top of the stack, is handed from one layer to the next, until it hits the actual (physical) communication line. As it moves down this stack, a data packet is assembled, with each protocol contributing its own chunk of bits (such as some to take care of error-checking or to perform data encryption) to the whole.

Briefly, from the top, network software performing the Application layer function commonly takes care of things such as file transfers, terminal emulation, and security. You might also see e-mail and database management software here. It's the only layer in the model that end users can interact with directly.

Below the Application layer sits the Presentation Services layer. From it's name, you'd figure that software operating here would have something to do with data presentation to end users. But not so. (That's higher up, as we just saw.) Not all real communication protocol stacks directly support this layer—TCP/IP doesn't, for example. Those that do often address things such as data translation between ASCII (on PCs) and Extended Binary Coded Decimal Interchange Code (EBCDIC) (on mainframes) encoding schemes there.

The Session layer can be a bit murky in its intended function too, and once again, not all real protocol stacks support it (at least in this exact modular fashion). Generally, it's supposed to handle network management functions such as password recognition.

The Transport layer is represented by software usually concerned with making sure that data packets get to where they're supposed to; it deals with error recognition and recovery. TCP, the Transport Control Protocol, not surprisingly, sits at this level. Novell's SPX, the Sequenced Packet Exchange, on the other hand, sort of straddles both this layer and the one above it, in terms of its functionality.

The Network layer is responsible for packet routing. To do this, most Network layer software maintains routing tables indicating where things (LANS, hosts, etc.) are and how to get packets to them. Novell's IPX (Internetwork Packet Exchange) and TCP/IP's IP (Internet Protocol) serve this function in their respective protocol stacks.

The Datalink layer is closely associated with the layer below it. (In fact, together, these bottom two define the low-level protocols.) It takes the packets and assembles them into data frames (codes for pulses) suited for the physical transmission medium being used. It adds bits to indicate the beginning and ending of data frames, drops some error-checking bits into outgoing frames, and checks the same bits on incoming frames to make sure nothing was corrupted en route. It hands this all over to the Physical layer, which actually puts the frames out onto the line (in the form of electrical or optical pulses).

While there's a lot of interaction between the layers, from another perspective, each layer can be seen as communicating with the corresponding layer on a peer (target) machine. The Network layer protocol on a receiving machine "speaks" only to the Network layer protocol on a sending machine, for example. This measure of modularity is what allows selected high-level protocols to run over different low-level ones.

It's important to understand that the seven-layer model is just that, a model. Some actual networking protocol suites follow it rather closely. Others don't. But all tend to take a modular approach. One of the most widely used actual protocols, TCP/IP, employs a five-layer stack (when the low-level protocol layers are counted), as shown in Figure 2.2.

Either Ethernet or Token-ring can appear at the Datalink layer and below. TCP/IP has a long-standing relationship with Ethernet, however, so usually it occupies the lower levels. We'll take a closer look at TCP/IP in Chapter 5.

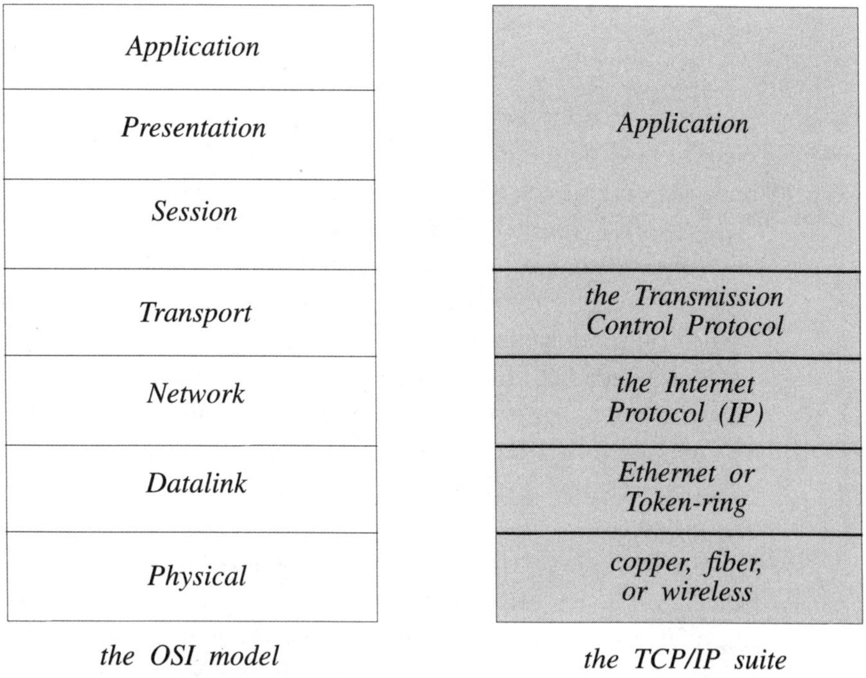

the OSI model	the TCP/IP suite
Application	*Application*
Presentation	
Session	
Transport	*the Transmission Control Protocol*
Network	*the Internet Protocol (IP)*
Datalink	*Ethernet or Token-ring*
Physical	*copper, fiber, or wireless*

Figure 2.2 The OSI model compared to TCP/IP.

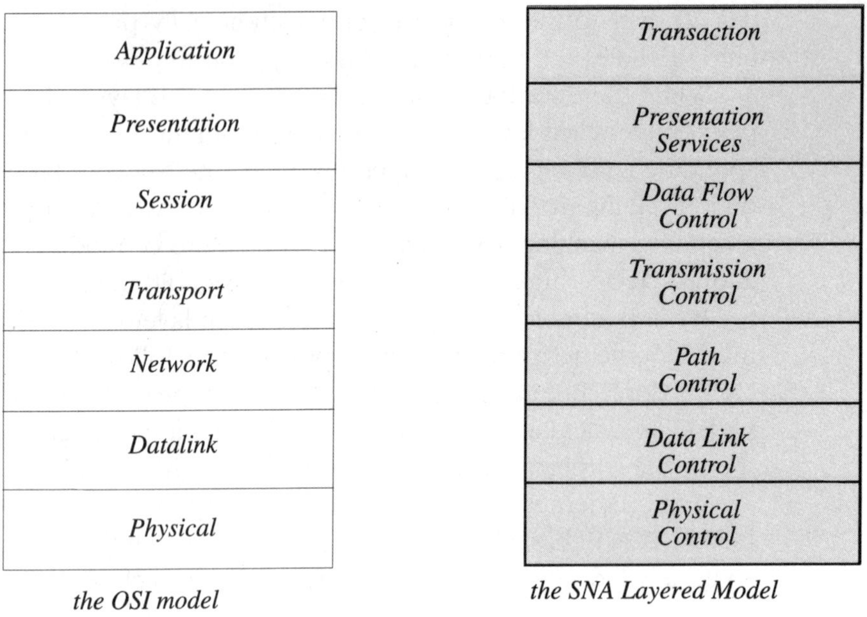

the OSI model	the SNA Layered Model
Application	Transaction
Presentation	Presentation Services
Session	Data Flow Control
Transport	Transmission Control
Network	Path Control
Datalink	Data Link Control
Physical	Physical Control

Figure 2.3 The OSI model compared to SNA.

SNA also adheres to a layered approach to data communications. It was, in fact, defined a number of years before the seven-layer model and, depending on whom you talk to, has either four, six, seven, or eight layers. (The confusion arises because some combine functionality that others see as distinct (Figure 2.3). It is just software, after all; most of it isn't something that you can actually touch.) Due to the popularity of the OSI model, though, lately seven seems to be the favorite.

SNA's Data Link Control layer (and below) is supportable by Token-ring, Ethernet, and some proprietary IBM stuff. Like TCP/IP, SNA has its favorites too; IBM's interest in Token-ring has resulted in a close relationship between the two. It's rare to see SNA running over Ethernet, though.

The lower-level protocol groups such as Ethernet, Token-ring, and FDDI are so pervasive that it's virtually certain that one will form an essential part of any client/server implementation you field. But high-speed upstarts, such as high-speed Ethernet and ATM, are starting to elbow their way onto the desktop; the additional bandwidth they offer could provide some welcomed maneuvering room for client/server designers. But, on the down side, it also presents them with more decisions.

The Lower-Level Protocols

As designers and implementors of a client/server solution, should you care which low-level protocol it runs over? If they were all equal, perhaps not. But they aren't. Basic Ethernet is the slowest and least dependable under variable network traffic. With even just a modest number of end users, you could find your client/server application gasping for bandwidth. Then what? But basic Ethernet is fast being superseded by high-speed, switched, and full-duplexed versions that greatly (and often cheaply) extends its capabilities. Switched Ethernet, in particular, is seen as a migration step toward really high-speed/high-bandwidth data transmission mechanisms such as ATM (We'll examine ATM in depth in Chapter 4.)

When it comes to LANs, currently Ethernet reigns (primarily because of its low cost). It holds about 70 percent of the market. Token-ring, a more expensive but faster option, has about 28 percent.[1] With all the activity in Ethernet camps these days, many wonder about the future of Token-ring. While sales of its adapters have increased steadily since the introduction of the LAN protocol in the late 1980s, sales are expected to flatten out by 1996.[2] ATM and fast Ethernet are expected to take the lead then.

In order to make sound technical decisions as to the right low-level protocol to use, we need to briefly examine how they work. We begin with Ethernet.

Ethernet

Ethernet employs what is referred to as a contentious networking method. All machines connected to the network have equal access to it. But as pointed out earlier, in baseband networks, only one signal actually can dominate the network at a time. That's the contentious part.

The network is traditionally "bus shaped" when used with the Ethernet protocol. When a station is ready to transmit something, it "listens" to its portion of the network to see if it's in use. If so, it waits and tries again later. If the network is free, the computer waits a small amount of time (9.6 microseconds), to ensure proper message spacing, then it transmits. The packets put out onto the network contain the data plus the header information. The maximum amount of data that can be stuffed into an Ethernet packet is 1,500 characters. If the message to be sent exceeds this amount, it's sliced up before transmission. If everything works as it should, the receiving station captures the packet(s) meant for it and reassembles the original message. The network is then "grabbed" by the next waiting station. (See Figure 2.4.)

There are some problems with this scheme. Because of the physical distances separating stations on the LAN, there is a propagation delay between the time a packet is transmitted and the time it reaches a given point in the LAN. Signals travel at about 70 percent the speed of light over the cable; nevertheless, even at such speeds, it's possible for a station to poll its portion of the LAN and conclude that the network's free even though a packet is actually en route. It's also entirely possible for two (or more) stations to poll the LAN at exactly the same moment, conclude the line is free, and begin transmitting. In both cases, the result is the same: a data collision.

Sending stations continue to monitor the line after transmission. When a collision occurs, they're able to detect it. The first transmit-

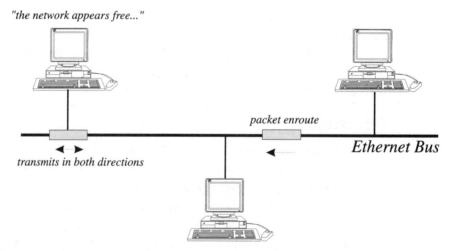

Figure 2.4 Ethernet uses a bus structure.

ting station involved in a collision that detects it sends out a jamming pulse. This tells other nodes waiting to use the line to back off for a while. Meanwhile, the colliding stations wait random time intervals before polling and transmitting again. In theory, they should end up retransmitting at different times. If they don't (since the wait period is really only pseudorandom), and a collision occurs again, the random time-out range is doubled, and they try a third time.

In networking circles, this is all called Carrier Sense with Multiple Access and Collision Detection: CSMA/CD. And while it sounds as if Ethernet may not be all that efficient, it's actually pretty good—at least under moderate load conditions. Therein lies the problem: When an Ethernet LAN becomes heavily loaded, performance becomes unpredictable.

Ethernet can be "run" over several media types, though it's commonly believed that it's fastest when run over fiber (glass) cable. Nope. Ethernet always operates at the same transmission speed no matter what medium it uses: 10 Mbps. This is a function of the Ethernet protocol.

Copper is the most popular transmission media for Ethernet. It generally comes in three styles: 10BASE5 (thick coaxial), 10BASE2 (thin coax), and 10BASET (unshielded twisted pair). The protocol stipulates literally heaps of rules for the use of each (how many machines can be hooked up, distance between machines, overall length of the network, etc.). It's pretty dry stuff, and we don't need to go into all that here. But unshielded twisted pair (UTP) is probably worth discussing, the emerging choice for Ethernet cabling, since its use carries some important side effects for users of the Ethernet protocol.

Worldwide estimates of LAN installations demonstrate the rise in popularity of UTP cable. Even a few years ago, it held about a quarter of the market. Thick coaxial, the one-time Ethernet favorite, accounted for slightly less of the installations at that time. By 1996, the UTP is expected to be approaching half of the overall LAN media market, and the reason is simple: It costs less and is easy to work with.

UTP is made up of four twisted copper wires (two twisted pairs). One pair is used for transmission, the other for packet reception. Twists in the cable are required to help cancel out each wire's electromagnetic (secondary) emissions, which always accompany electrical current flows in metal conductors. Without the twists, the electromagnetic emissions produce noise, possibly corrupting the data path.

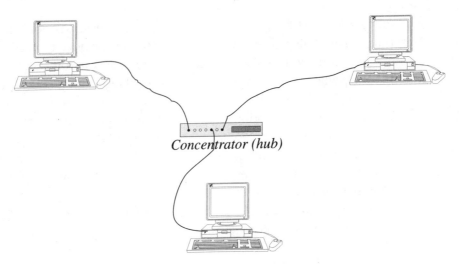

Concentrator (hub)

Figure 2.5 A star topology offers a number of advantages.

Both Ethernet and Token-ring commonly use UTP. As shown in Figure 2.5, the savings offered by this lower-cost cabling alternative has, in turn, led to some important changes in popular Ethernet wiring designs. Instead of the traditional bus shape, a star layout now is often used. In a star topology, each node is individually wired. This isolates cable breaks. It also allows for the placement of LAN diagnostic equipment in wiring hubs (concentrators). The expense of additional cable (stars require more wiring than a bus design) and wiring hubs is somewhat offset by the lower cost of the UTP cable.

The hub connects the wiring so that logically, the network still behaves as if it were a bus. The CSMA/CD model still applies.

As mentioned earlier, Ethernet is a contentious networking scheme. With only a few machines on the network, contention is usually negligible under normal circumstances. But as the number of nodes increases, or as the type, and frequency, of information exchanged over the network goes up, problems can develop. To put this into the terminology of the business, the available "bandwidth" drops; each transmission still monopolizes the 10 Mbps Ethernet maximum transmission rate, but systems have to wait longer to obtain transmission rights.

Numerous studies have shown that the number of networked nodes is steadily rising; being "on the LAN" is increasingly becoming a required part of an employee's workday. And the move to client/server is expected to place further demands on networks. Ethernet switching is an emerging solution to both of these needs. Instead of a passive hub, switched Ethernet networks employ switching hubs that can establish a number of simultaneous communication channels between pairs of senders and receivers—all operating at 10 Mbps. Effective bandwidth is increased, and network contention is reduced; problems become more a function of the switching capacity of the active hub. Switched networks are an attractive option that buys additional bandwidth for a minimal investment. And a star-shaped wiring topology makes this kind of upgrade much easier than the older bus-shaped topology once popular with Ethernet LANs.

Beyond Ethernet switching, there have been a number of moves to increase Ethernet base transmission speeds. There currently appears to be three options for upping the Ethernet speed limit: full-duplex Ethernet, 100Base-T, also referred to as "fast Ethernet," and Hewlett-Packard's 100VG-AnyLAN.

High-Speed Ethernet

As we've seen, standard Ethernet allows a node to receive or transfer, but not both at the same time. If the networked node isn't running a multitasking operating system such as UNIX, OS/2, or Windows NT, it isn't really an issue. But if it is, full-duplex Ethernet can boost overall bandwidth for only a small price. In fact, in some implementations of this simultaneous send- and receive-version of Ethernet, only the server

CLOSE-UP

Client/server and Ethernet switching

There are actually two emerging switching hubs. One type, generally referred to as a cut-through switch, is a low-latency (fast-acting) device. It just checks the header portion of the packet, grabs the destination address, and then sends it on its way. The other type is called a store-and-forward switch. It queues and error-checks entire packets before shipping them along to their destinations—unless they've been corrupted, in which case they're discarded. Store-and-forward switch is slower than a cut-through switch, but it can reduce network congestion by queuing transmissions to heavily targeted devices such as servers.

needs to be outfitted with a new full duplex card and switch to achieve a 20 Mbps burst throughput.

If 20 Mbps still isn't enough—and many tell us that it soon won't be—we have 100 Mbps Ethernet, the subject of an ongoing feud. Hewlett-Packard and friends are pushing something they call 100VG-AnyLAN. It's a from-the-ground-up rebuild of Ethernet that supports direct connection to both standard Ethernet and Token-ring networks. In the other corner, there's the Fast Ethernet Alliance. Its product, 100Base-T, remains true to Ethernet's CSMA/CD heritage by adjusting system timing and limiting network sizes to attain the tenfold speed increase. Of the two, 100Base-T appears to be simpler and cheaper to implement; for this reason, it has gained the upper hand. The altercation cost both camps, however; while the industry waited for a clear direction to emerge, 155 Mbps Asynchronous Transfer Mode (ATM) extended its reach to the desktop much sooner than anyone predicted. Many now view 100 Mbps Ethernet as just an interim solution.

HP's 100VG-AnyLAN is intriguing in that it promises to blur the line between two longtime baseband networking adversaries: Ethernet and Token-ring. Right from the beginning of networking, these two low-

CLOSE-UP

Will client/server pose a serious threat to existing network performance?

Of course, client/server computing will further tax our existing local area networks. But how much? Do you need to necessarily consider full-duplex or other high-speed networking solutions if you intend to implement client/server? No two networks are the same, but there are a couple of general statements that can be made about client/server network impact. Providing us with choices, the client/server model allows us to decide how best to split applications between the server and the desktop client. So in theory at least, we can minimize system response times and network activity. But beware: it's often very difficult to estimate client/server system usage beforehand. That's because most systems are deployed for decision support; if the system is very helpful to workers, it may get used more than initially thought. Also, once a client/server system is set up successfully in one area, pressures will arise to set up others throughout the organization.

level protocols have struggled for market dominance. Today Ethernet retains the largest installed base, but the gap is narrowing. As we're about to see, in many respects Token-ring is a much more elegant approach to networking. And if it were not for its higher cost, it's very possible that it would have displaced Ethernet some time ago.

Token-Ring

In contrast to Ethernet, Token-ring is a noncontentious networking scheme. There's no scrimmage for the right to use the transmission medium here. Things are much more orderly, due to the use of a token, a special group of bits containing tombstone information and the data to be transmitted. There's only one token on the ring at any given moment, and it's in continuous motion—no one network node can commandeer it. (See Figure 2.6.)

When a station wishes to transmit a data frame, it must wait and grab the token, if it's not already in use. Stations (actually the adapter card in the stations) determine if a token is free by examining its "T-bit,"

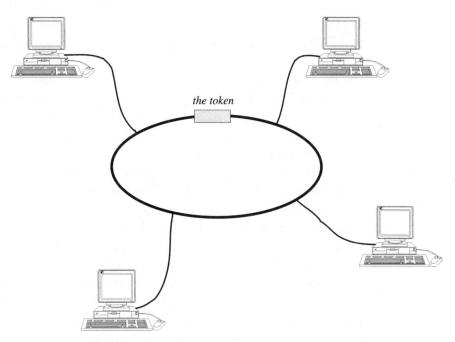

the token

Figure 2.6 Token-ring.

a special bit field in the frame header. If it's set to 1, the token's free. A transmitting station can capture the free token, change the T-bit to a 0 (indicating the token's now in use), stuff in the data, and put it out onto the transmitting medium. As with Ethernet, if the message to be transmitted is larger than the allowable frame size, it's broken down into pieces. Once a sending station traps the token, it transmits until all the frames are sent or until a timer expires. In either case, it must relinquish the token.

Token-ring stations operate in one of four modes: transmit, listen, bypass, or receive. If a station is on-line and it's not transmitting, it's in the listen mode. As the token zips around the ring (at about 60 percent the speed of light), each station in turn examines the destination address in the header. If it corresponds the address of the listening station, that station flips into the receive mode. In receive mode, the node copies the data frame to its local memory, sets a flag in the token's header indicating the data was received, and allows the token to continue on its way around the ring. Eventually it makes its way back to the sending station. It checks to see that the data was received and, if so, it strips off the header, generates a fresh token, and either transmits another frame or puts the token out onto the network for another node to use.

In a Token-ring, each node is a link in a chain. As the token circles the ring, it passes through each node, being copied from the incoming side to the outgoing side of the network interface card. But what if a station is off-line? The answer requires us to clarify something first. In practice, a Token-ring isn't ringlike—like the preferred emerging Ethernet topology, it's a star shape. Logically, it behaves as if it were a ring, however. That's one of the jobs of a central concentrator called a Multistation Access Unit (MSAU). Another of the MSAU's jobs is to watch for off-line stations. If it detects one, it establishes a bypass around that node to preserve the ring. (See Figure 2.7.)

Okay, that's taken care of, but what happens if a station goes down immediately after transmission? Recall that only the sending station can release the token. As before, the MSAU sets up the bypass, but when the token returns to the sending station to be reissued, it simply goes right by—and, in theory, circles forever. Well, Token-ring has to safeguard for that too. In every Token-ring LAN, one of the nodes—any station on the ring—is designated as the "active monitor." The job of the active monitor is to watch for runaway tokens. When the token makes its first traverse

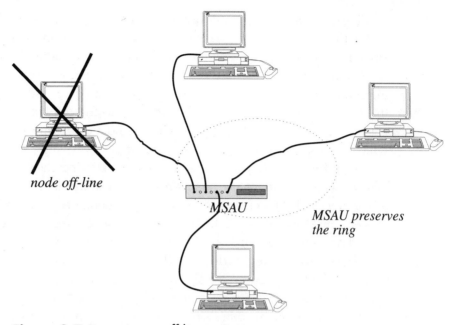

node off-line

MSAU

MSAU preserves the ring

Figure 2.7 Bypassing an off-line station.

of the LAN, the active monitor flips a bit field (the so-called M-bit) in the token header. If all goes well, the next time the active monitor node sees the token, the M-bit will have been reset (since a new token will have been generated). If the M-bit hasn't been reset, the active monitor "knows" that something went wrong with the transmitting station. It traps the token and re-issues a new one. Should the active monitor ever go off-line, another (and another and another..., if necessary) node on the LAN steps in to assume the role.

An MSAU can accommodate either eight or 16 LAN nodes. Two additional ports allow the nodes to be connected in series to other MSAUs, if necessary. Connections often are made with shielded twisted pair (STP) cable. The IEEE, which refers to Token-ring as IEEE 802.5, sanctions both STP and UTP, for the original (4 Mbps) and (16 Mbps) operating speeds. There is also an emerging Token-ring-over-fiber standard.

Companies like IBM have come along with a "full-duplex" version of Token-ring, similar to full-duplex Ethernet. The full-duplex version allows nodes to send and receive data simultaneously, effectively increasing Token-ring speed by 100 percent. The enhancement requires modifications to both the MSAUs and Token-ring cards in each node. So far, the user community hasn't shown much interest in the idea (possibly because the networking focus is in the Ethernet camp these days). As with full-duplex Ethernet, full-duplex Token-ring is more of a holding action. Newer and much higher speed technologies are just around the corner. It doesn't cost much to upgrade to full-duplex Token-ring, gets you a bit more needed bandwidth, and buys some time to see which high-speed technology will dominate.

Over the past few years, Token-ring has been increasing in performance, while its price has been dropping steadily. In no small part, this is due to IBM's efforts to standardize operation over unshielded twisted pair cable. Because the price advantage once held by Ethernet is eroding, some have predicted that Token-ring may overtake Ethernet installations sometime this decade. That seems unlikely. It's more probable that, in the short term, we'll see an increase in high-speed Ethernet installations as companies prepare to migrate toward ATM.

Whatever happens, there's no doubt that Token-ring has set a standard of sorts for highly reliable baseband LAN transmission. In fact, its

CLOSE-UP

Ethernet versus Token-ring

Although standard Ethernet has a maximum transmission speed of 10Mbps, signal control overhead (checking for collisions and all that stuff) effectively limits the speed to about 8Mbps. By its design, Token-ring requires even greater control than Ethernet. Therefore, the difference in their transmission speeds is less than the raw numbers would lead us to believe. At moderate network loadings, this difference usually doesn't justify Token-ring's higher cost. As loadings (traffic) increase, however, Ethernet's CSMA/CD scheme runs into difficulties and network predictability falls off. This situation favors Token-ring. But there are other considerations in the Ethernet versus Token-ring debate. Currently, market activity is focused on faster versions of Ethernet. Token-ring's smaller installed base simply doesn't attract the same level of vendor interest. This fact may afford Ethernet users a quicker, and probably cheaper, migration path to higher-speed local data communications.

style of transmission was adopted as the model for the last low-level protocol in our discussion—one generally employed for high-reliability backbone service: FDDI.

FDDI

When people talk about "fiber," often they really mean the Fiber-Distributed Data Interface, FDDI. Like Ethernet and Token-ring, FDDI is a protocol that deals with the two lower layers of the OSI model—one that just happens to primarily run over fiber optic cable. Although it can be implemented as a high-speed alternative to Ethernet or Token-ring, because of its higher cost, most often FDDI is deployed for fast, dependable backbone service.

The FDDI protocol limits communications to 100Mbps. To reach these speeds and to sustain them over significant distances, FDDI needs glass or plastic fibers to transmit pulses of light. But there's more to FDDI than just speed. Dependability was just as important to its creators.

FDDI uses a token-sharing scheme, much as does Token-ring. Devices on the network are allowed to use the token for a set interval of time—a value often preset by the FDDI vendor. Once the time is up, the token has to be released. FDDI implementations follow a dual counterrotating ring design (as shown in Figure 2.8). The primary ring is used for data passing, while the secondary ring is a fallback in case the primary one fails in some way. Devices on the ring are either single-attached or dual-attached to both rings. Dual attachment offers a higher level of fault resilience; if a fault occurs in the primary ring, the secondary ring "wraps" to preserve the data path. The two rings then collapse into one.

Two data paths are expensive—especially if they're fiber. (Actually, the cable itself isn't that expensive; it's installation that's costly.) Cost is one reason FDDI rarely directly reaches the desktop. As it is used primarily for backbone implementations, it's a wise practice to connect only the most reliable, and critical, units to it—bridges, routers, and FDDI concentrators, for example.

FDDI concentrators are similar to Token-ring's MSAUs. Often an enhanced personal computer, they're more active than MSAUs, frequently checking the line integrity between themselves and any devices attached to them, such as workstations and servers.

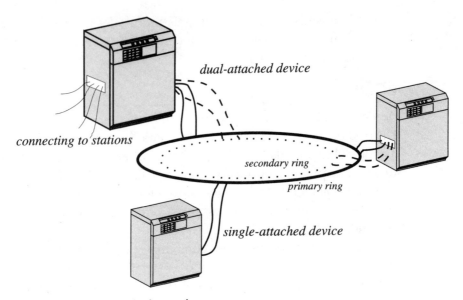

Figure 2.8 FDDI's dual-ring design.

Mission-critical platforms, such as transaction and database servers, can be wired to the concentrators using a technique known as dual-homing. (See Figure 2.9.) Instead of connecting to a single concentrator, these high-availability nodes can be dual-attached (with cheaper, copper cabling) to two different concentrators. This provides an alternate route should one concentrator fail for some reason.

The preferred and so far only recognized transmission medium for FDDI is glass or plastic fiber. Plastic is cheaper but doesn't transmit light as well. For transmission paths less than 2 km, ANSI has specified that the filaments (cores) be 62.5 microns in diameter—that's 62.6×10^{-6} meters!

There's more to optical cable than just a core of glass or plastic. Next comes the cladding. The cladding plus the core makes "a fiber." (See Figure 2.10.) The cladding reflects stray light rays back into the filament as the signal travels along. Optical transmission, by the way, requires two fibers: one for transmitting, and another for receiving.

What surrounds the cladding depends on what the cable is used for. If the cable will be used indoors, it's common to wrap many fibers together into a jacket, in a style referred to as "breakout cable." Outside use demands a more rugged covering. In an arrangement known as

FDDI concentrator
secondary
primary
transaction server
FDDI concentrator

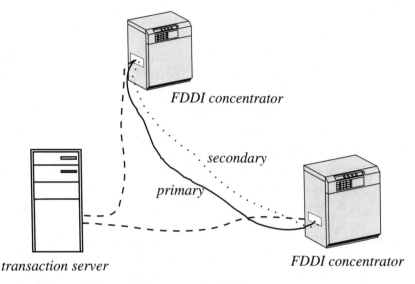

Figure 2.9 Dual-homing for improved reliability.

"loose tube," a number of fibers are floated in a gellike substance, which is, in turn, wrapped in an insulating cladding. Several of these loose tubes are then wrapped together to form thick cables. Loose tube can be messy, so it isn't popular.

As the FDDI protocol physically isn't limited to running over glass or plastic, although that's the media specified in the standard, vendors have begun offering FDDI over copper. They call it CDDI. It's cheaper (actually, this depends on the type of copper cable being used. Shielded twisted pair is actually a bit more expensive than fiber optic cable), and copper is much easier to work with. CDDI isn't really an alternative to FDDI, however. One of the beauties of optical is its immunity to differences in building electrical potential. Equipment, a building's in-

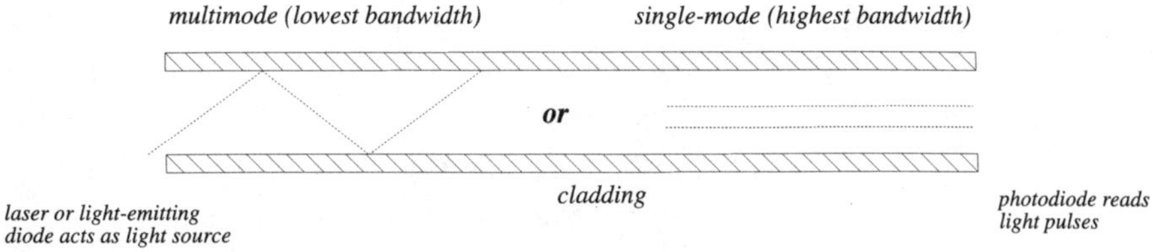

multimode (lowest bandwidth)
single-mode (highest bandwidth)
or
cladding
laser or light-emitting diode acts as light source
photodiode reads light pulses

Figure 2.10 Modes of light transmission in fiber.

ternal activities, and the human comings and goings from a building all dictate its electrical state. No two buildings are exactly the same in this respect. Glass and plastic aren't affected by the electrical state of a building, but copper is. This makes fiber more attractive for running backbone services between buildings.

Security concerns also favor fiber. It's harder to tap. And if you're going to go through all the trouble of laying a backbone today, it just doesn't make a lot of sense to select copper—in spite of the higher installation costs associated with optical. There's little doubt that future communications loads will demand fiber backbones.

FDDI is changing. As we saw earlier, it uses a token-passing scheme analogous to Token-ring. Each network node can hold the token for only a set period of time. While in its possession, the node can transmit all the data it can get onto the line. Then it has to hand the token over. This approach to token sharing doesn't lend itself to continuous data transmissions, however. Digitized voice and video can't be sent over the existing version of FDDI—at least not continuously. So FDDI II has been developed. Now before standards committees, FDDI II supports circuit-switched services, providing an avenue for the multimedia technologies everyone keeps saying are just around the corner.

CLOSE-UP

What does the future look like for FDDI?

FDDI is the only mature, standard 100Mbps technology currently available. There are literally tens of thousands of installed fiber backbones using FDDI. In spite of this, the protocol hasn't done as well as many had hoped. High costs (of as much as $2,000 per seat) have effectively restricted it to backbone services (and kept it off the desktop). Also, until now there really hasn't been a real case for 100Mbps to the desktop. Now that client/server computing and other bandwidth-intensive technologies are starting to arrive, however, FDDI to the desktop is finding a need, but is also receiving competition from high-speed Ethernet and ATM for 100Mbps dominance. Almost everyone agrees that ATM is the technology of the future. But current implementation costs put it a few years away. When it does arrive, however, watch for a decline in FDDI sales.

Wireless LANs

Cable is expensive—or more correctly, laying it, connecting it, and maintaining it is expensive. And that's in the case of a modern building designed with computers in mind. In some older facilities, cabling simply isn't possible. Enter a technology designed for exactly this purpose: wireless LANs.

There are three options when it comes to going wireless: radio frequency, microwave, and infrared. Each has its own drawbacks and attractions. But it should be noted that none is intended to replace wire (or fiber) entirely; they're complementary technologies.

Radio frequency is perhaps the easiest to work with. However, it's subject to all the same regulations that govern the already overcrowded airwaves. And there are obvious concerns about its security as well. To deal with unwanted eavesdroppers, vendors often employ a spread-spectrum frequency-switching algorithm originally invented for military use; the sending and receiving stations continuously change frequencies in some predetermined fashion, making it difficult to tap in to. It's said that spread-spectrum is more secure than many of the schemes used in conventional wired LANs. Not everyone's buying into that, however.

Most producers of radio-frequency LANs try to stay within the 902–928 MHz range, because no license is required to operate in that band. While operating there, power transmissions are limited by airwave regulators to 1 watt. It's not much, but often it is enough to get through many types of walls. (See Figure 2.11.)

AT&T is a strong proponent of spread-spectrum technology. Employing sophisticated data encryption, its product can safely transmit at speeds in the 2 Mbps range over a distance of 800 feet, reportedly through several types of wall construction.

Microwave can equal or better spread-spectrum in performance. The problem is, microwave needs to be licensed. Not surprisingly, Motorola is an early leader of this style of wireless networking. Microwave operates in the 18GHz region of the spectrum. Motorola's offerings can run at Ethernet speeds or better. They typically have a range of at least 80 feet, and at 1 watt (to keep things—people especially—from getting cooked) can get through most masonry. Compared to spread-spectrum, what microwave gains in speed, it appears to lose in distance.

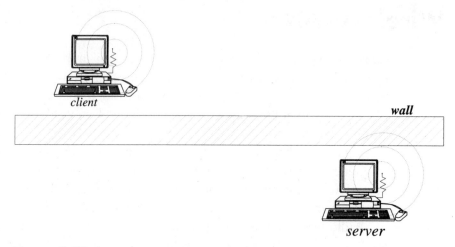

Figure 2.11 Spread-spectrum communications.

The third form of wireless data transmission, infrared, is the most limited. It operates on the same principle as a television remote control and it requires line-of-sight data paths. This means that transmitters and receivers have to be physically lined up to get them communicating. While it's possible to use mirrors to redirect light paths in order to get around corners and other obstructions, a loss of available bandwidth results. The arrangement depicted in Figure 2.12 is sometimes called a "sun-and-moon arrangement." This setup often is used at computer

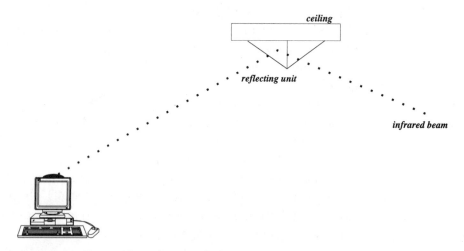

Figure 2.12 An infrared sun-and-moon arrangement.

shows where running cable would be difficult and time-consuming. Since the reflecting surface diffuses the beam, the alignment between sender and receiver doesn't have to be as precise as in a point-to-point scheme. Unlike the other two wireless LAN options, infrared can't penetrate solid walls.

Infrared is surprisingly secure—you'd notice immediately if someone "tapped" into your transmission. A number of vendors use infrared to implement both 4 Mbps and 16 Mbps Token-ring. Infrared is used only to connect the MSAUs, however, not for the entire network. The rest is wire, as usual.

Many predict that wireless will soon reach FDDI speeds (100 Mbps) and even higher with data compression. With the spread of notebook computers and an increasingly mobile workforce, wireless LANs are expected to continue to increase in popularity. The wireless LAN market was between $35 million and $50 million in 1994, and is expected to increase on that by at least 10 percent in 1996.[2] Their costs already rival, and sometimes even better, wired options. Although the technology currently is largely restricted to the health care and manufacturing sectors; it is reaching out to others as well. Watch for wireless LANs to take hold over the next several years.

Wrap-up

Computer networking, and telecommunications in general, is one of the most active slices of the computer business. Client/server, and the newer supporting technologies, such as full-motion video and imaging, are driving the need for speed. The choices are bewildering: fast Ethernet, full-duplexed Token-ring, FDDI, FDDI II, ATM, and so on. Often what looked good just months ago may be gone altogether today. We must choose, and choose well—whenever client/server systems fail, the cause is often traceable back to the network. Client/server is a distributed technology, and reliable, responsive distributed systems require a sound network to deliver them.

With a basic understanding of low-level communication protocols behind us, we move on, in Chapter 3, to talk about higher-level LAN options: the so-called network operating systems (NOS). There we find companies such as Novell and Microsoft standing toe to toe for dominance of this very lucrative piece of the computing market.

Key Terms and Ideas Appearing in This Chapter

ATM:

A high-speed form of packet-switching. ATM uses small (53-byte), fixed-size packets running over optical fiber to reach speeds of 155 Mbps and beyond. ATM is sort of a cross between analog transmission (continuous, wave form) and packetized bursty LAN transmissions. Because of this, it can accommodate both voice and data with the same approach, over the same carrier. We examine ATM in Chapter 4.

bandwidth:

The difference between the highest and lowest frequency that can be transmitted over a line. The higher the bandwidth, the more information can be pumped over the carrying medium.

baseband:

A style of networking popularly used in local area networks (LANs). In baseband networks, only one signal can occupy the communication medium at given moment. Ethernet and Token-ring are the two most widely used examples of baseband network.

broadband:

Another type of LAN. Unlike baseband, a broadband network can accommodate more than one signal at a time. This is accomplished by time or frequency division multiplexing. It requires modulation of the signals at the sending and receiving ends, making broadband more expensive than baseband. Broadband also can be used for backbone transmissions between baseband LANs.

Ethernet:

A contentious networking scheme in which network nodes compete for line access. Following a model known as CSMA/CD (Carrier Sense, Multiple Access with Collision Detection), nodes monitor packets after transmission to ensure their safe arrival. If something goes wrong and a data collision occurs, the transmitting nodes take steps to resend the data. Ethernet is efficient at moderate network loads. Its top speed, as specified by the "Ethernet protocol" (DIX or IEEE 802.3), is 10 Mbps. The Ethernet protocol corresponds to the two lower layers of the OSI model.

FDDI:

An ANSI standard for high-speed fiber optic LANs. According to the FDDI specifications, top-communication speed is 100 Mbps. FDDI is implemented in two ways: as a high-speed alternative to Ethernet or Token-ring LANs, or, more often, as a backbone for connecting such networks. When moving from Ethernet and Token-ring LANs ("802" networks) to an FDDI backbone, a bridging device is required. The bridge either encapsulates the packet (sticks the 802 packet into an FDDI packet) or translates it into an FDDI packet. Translation is a "more open" option; there are no standards in place for data packet encapsulation.

high-speed Ethernet:

Several high-speed Ethernets are emerging. Full-duplexed Ethernet, for example, allows nodes to send and receive data at the same time, effectively doubling capacity. Switched Ethernet uses a star topology wired to a switch in the center. Each participating node has full access to the maximum available bandwidth. Finally, 100 Mbps Ethernet is strongly vying for low-level protocol dominance. There are two contenders, however: Hewlett-Packard's 100VG-AnyLAN and the Fast Ethernet Alliance's 100BASE-T. HP's offering is a completely new networking scheme that can support both traditional Ethernet and Token-ring traffic. The Fast Ethernet Alliance's 100BASE-T, on the other hand, acts like good old Ethernet, only faster. It's currently the industry favorite.

MSAU:

Multistation access unit, a device used in Token-ring networks. The MSAU acts to preserve the ring if any node on the LAN should go off-line by establishing a bypass around that node.

OSI seven-layer model:

The ISO/OSI model for data communication. The ISO examined the process of data communication and splits it up into seven discrete tasks. The bottom layer is the physical line itself. All the other layers are to be implemented in software. Few actual communications protocols follow this seven-layer model exactly.

packet:

The group of bits assembled by the various pieces of software making up the transmitting node's communication protocol stack. Each layer of the stack contributes something to the overall packet. Packets have a set length. If the data to be sent plus header exceed that size, the data must be first re-packaged into pieces small enough to fit. The message is reconstituted on the receiving end.

Token-ring:

A noncontentious style of networking invented by IBM. Token-ring uses a single "token" (an electrical pulse) for all data interchanges. When a node wishes to transmit a message to another on the LAN, it must first capture the token (if it's available). After the data has been received by the target node, the token returns to the sender. Only it can relinquish the token (under normal conditions). Token-ring has been adopted by the IEEE and is known as IEEE 802.5. Token-ring comes in two speeds: 4 Mbps and 16 Mbps. Like Ethernet, it too corresponds to the two bottom layers of the OSI model.

UTP:

Unshielded twisted pair. UTP is the emerging cable of choice in the LAN world. It's inexpensive and easy to work with.

wireless LAN:

Wireless LAN technology is a fast-growing segment of the networking business. There are three styles: infrared, radio-frequency (also sometimes called "spread-spectrum"), and microwave. Infrared is the most limited of the group. It can't penetrate walls. Microwave can get up to Token-ring speeds but requires a license. Spread-spectrum is highly secure and can reach Ethernet speed. As it stays within the "civil band," it doesn't need to be licensed.

Notes

[1] T. Nolle, "Token-ring Networks: Not Quite Dead Yet," *LAN Times*, 12, no. 3, February 1995, 54.

[2] S. MacAskill and M. Le Baron, "Reasons for not Going Wireless Start to Disappear," *Network World*, April 10, 1995, 28.

Chapter 3

Executive Summary

Client/server is a style of computing geared toward end users. It strives to supply them with all the information necessary to do their jobs, regardless of where that information physically resides.

In most implementations, client devices are networked PCs. These machines sport the analysis software used to sift through data in order to support end-user decisions. And most PCs, when running a graphical user interface, such as Microsoft's Windows, can present information in a manner that end users can digest readily. With such strong ties to PCs and LANs, it's understandable that the road to client/server should start with them.

In Chapter 2, we examined the low-level protocols used to string computing devices into a communication network. But we also saw there, that they alone, aren't enough; additional functionality is required to link the network with the applications intending to use it. These additional tasks are performed by higher-level protocols (from the point of view of the seven-layer model).

In the LAN world, these higher-level protocols often are embellished with features that provide the network user with what is essentially a complete operating environment—one that makes better use of available networked resources. Files actually resident on a remote device, for example, appear to the user as though they sat on an extra (local) hard drive. Assuming many of the duties of a full-fledged operating system, these environments have come to be known as network operating systems (NOS).

Novell's NetWare currently dominates the NOS market; seven out of 10 LANs run it. It practically defined the idea of using a centrally networked machine as a file server. But even with its commanding lead over this segment of the business, the momentum is behind a newcomer: Microsoft's Windows NT. A growing number of users feel that it's better equipped to support client/server applications.

CHAPTER

3

Network Operating Systems: First Stop on the Road to Client/Server

The Client/Server Protocol of Choice?

Novell made its reputation, and its money, in the networking business. NetWare, its flagship product, is the industry leader in PC LAN operating software for Intel platforms. Estimates place its share of the market at between 60 and 75 percent. The product's popularity and its level of domination of the LAN market have placed it at the very center of the client/server movement.

Now in its fourth rendition, NetWare goes well beyond file serving. NetWare 4.x is quite different from its predecessors and represents a significant shift away from LAN services toward enterprise-wide computing. But not everyone is ready for that shift. While NetWare 4.x has been available for more than two years, most of Novell's customer base steadfastly holds on to NetWare 3.11 and 12. Version 3 is inexpensive, simple to work with, fast, and meets the immediate needs of most LAN administrators. But thanks to technological shifts, especially the move to client/server, those needs may be changing.

Although NetWare has tremendous market clout, it may be in jeopardy. Rather than accepting version 4.x, many organizations are turning to a relative newcomer to the NOS arena: Microsoft's Windows NT. NT suffers from a dual personality: Both a workstation version and a server version are available. Both share a common core, however, built around a conventional, albeit modern, operating system design. NetWare, on the other hand, really can't be classified as an operating system in the everyday sense. It's more of a stripped-down rendition. Built for speed, NetWare compromises on many of the program management features considered essential to basic operating systems. NT Advanced Server 3.5.x's (that's what it's actually called these days) mix of functionality and features, along with the dependability of a true operating system, is leading many to proclaim it the better foundation for client/server applications.

But it's a little too early to give up on NetWare just yet. While the momentum is behind NT, NetWare's presence and effect on the LAN is just too big to be ignored.

NetWare: File Serving for the Masses

NetWare is more than a stack of communication protocols. It provides everything an organization requires to establish LAN connectivity, including mainframe gateways, links to public data networks, network security, and support for mass storage. It defined the Network Operating System.

NetWare's modular design, pioneered with NetWare 3.x (formerly NetWare 386), allows additional functionality to be "bolted-on" as needed. Called "NetWare Loadable Modules" (NLMs), they provide communication services, database services, and print and file services. (See Figure 3.1.) They can be plugged in to the NetWare kernel without even rebooting the server.

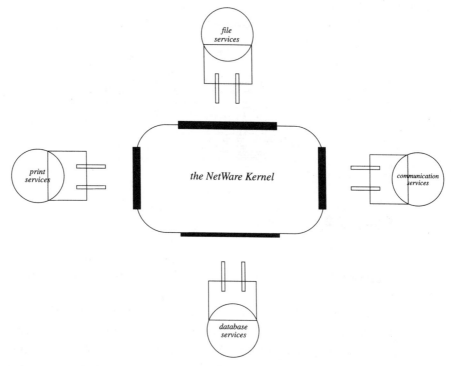

Figure 3.1 NetWare follows a modular design.

NetWare remains best known for its file services, however. It's still considered the best of the NOSs in this respect.[1] File servers extend the notion of a file directory across two networked machines. Software, running in the background (in terminate-and-stay-resident mode) on the desktop client, wraps the operating system—usually DOS—intercepting all commands. (See Figure 3.2.) When a file request is made, the Net-Ware shell determines whether the request is for local or remote files. If the file is local, the request is shunted along to the operating system for it to take care of. If it's remote, the shell issues a read request to the file server. If the file exists, a copy is transmitted to the client. Except for a slightly longer system response, the user is otherwise unaware that the file resides on the server and not on his or her own local hard disk.

Over the years, Novell has introduced several tricks to speed up file server access. One is to keep the location of remote files in server

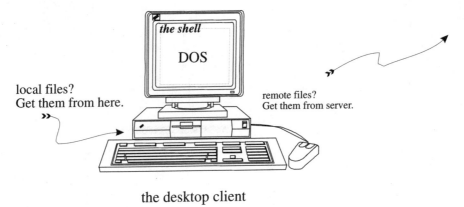

the desktop client

Figure 3.2 File serving.

memory. Known as "directory hashing," it's really just an indexing system.

Another technique, widely used in other facets of the computing business as well, is "caching." Caching is implemented by software resident on the server that tries to anticipate file requests. The logic is simple: If one user found a file interesting, another might do the same (or the same user might want the same file again). If it's kept in server memory, access to it is faster than if it's exclusively retained on disk. An area of server memory is set aside for caching. As blocks of data are read from disk in response to a user file request, they're simultaneously placed in the cache. As they're copied, they're time-stamped. Eventually, when the server runs out of cache memory, files that have been sitting around the longest are bumped out in favor of new ones.

A third method for speeding server-based file access is called "elevator seeking." File servers frequently receive multiple, simultaneous requests. Novell has developed a strategy for performing efficient disk (file) accesses. By considering the current position of the disk drive read heads relative to the data location on the disk, an optimal file-read order is planned out. This maximizes data throughput.

In addition, of course, NetWare has to contain some data communication software somewhere. That somewhere is the NetWare kernel. And like TCP/IP and SNA, briefly discussed in the last chapter, NetWare also follows a stacked (modularized) approach to data communications.

Does file serving qualify as a form of client/server computing?

With all this talk of clients and servers, you might assume that file serving *is* client/server. That's a bit controversial though. For one thing, in its current manifestation, "client/server" generally means client/*data*/server, although when we finally define the term later, we won't necessarily be that restrictive. More important though, client/server has an implied value-added theme—from the client's perspective. To put it another way, the client should do something to the data (if we're talking about data serving) before presenting it to the user. It should contribute in some way. This proviso squeezes file serving out of this category of computing. But as we said, it's controversial—at least for people who care about such things.

The Internetwork Packet Exchange

Within the NetWare kernel sits a stack of (higher-level) communication protocols. These protocols handle file service and access. As shown in Figure 3.3, the first of these protocols, appearing at the OSI network layer, is the Internetwork Packet Exchange (IPX). In many respects, IPX is very much like IP (of TCP/IP fame). It's a connectionless service that delivers packets in a take-what-you-get fashion. That's to say, in networking terminology, it's unreliable. Making sure packets get to where they're going is left to protocols higher up in the stack.

Like all data packets, an IPX datagram is composed of a header and the data to be communicated. The header contains such things as the length of the datagram, who sent it, and where it's going. "Where it's going," of course, means some form of an address. NetWare actually uses three of them: a 32-bit network (or LAN) number, a 48-bit host (or node) number, and a 16-bit socket number. The socket address identifies the actual communicating processes. Protocols higher up in the stack use the services of IPX by stuffing their respective packets into the data portion of the IPX datagram (which is usually up to 546 bytes in length). If a message to be transmitted is longer, first it has to be sliced up into a number of pieces. IPX tends to that too.

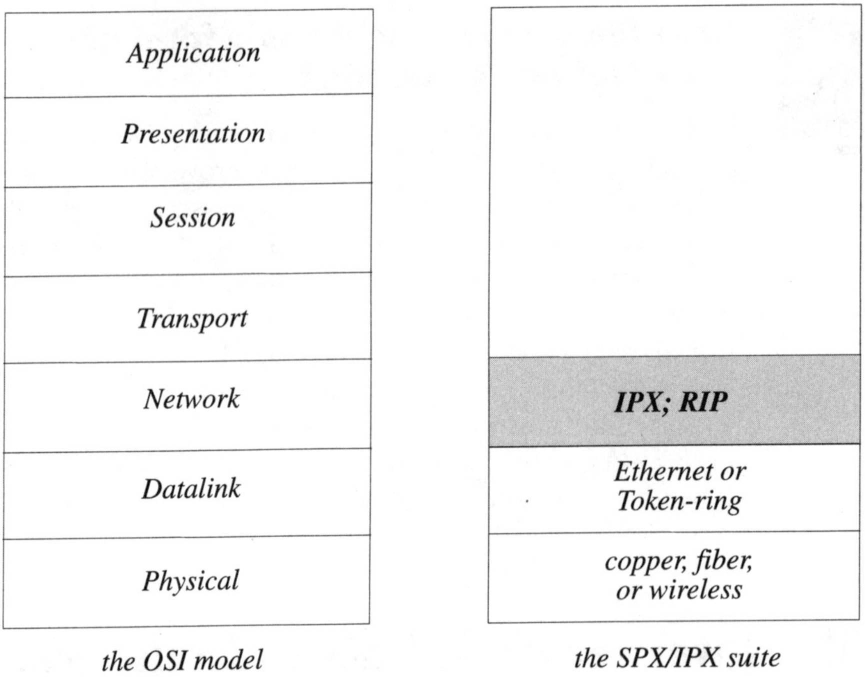

Application	
Presentation	
Session	
Transport	
Network	***IPX; RIP***
Datalink	*Ethernet or Token-ring*
Physical	*copper, fiber, or wireless*

the OSI model	*the SPX/IPX suite*

Figure 3.3 The OSI Model and NetWare's IPX.

IPX then hands its datagrams off to the lower-level protocols—Ethernet or Token-ring. There, the Datalink layer protocol "frames" the datagrams and puts them out onto the transmission medium. This is where we appreciate the benefits of a modular approach to data communications; IPX doesn't care whether Ethernet or Token-ring occupies the lower levels of the protocol stack.

IPX also handles packet routing. One not widely known fact is that all NetWare file servers are also full-fledged IPX routers. Unlike TCP/IP, which we'll talk about in a later chapter, dedicated routers aren't used as much in NetWare networks. When a server/router intercepts a packet, it first decides if the packet's ultimate destination is local or remote (with respect to that server). If it's local, the router just sends the packet along. If it's remote, the router consults its routing table before shipping the packet off to the appropriate server/router.

Maintaining this routing table and planning out routing pathways is the job of another protocol—a service to IPX, in fact, called the "Routing Information Protocol," or RIP for short. RIP keeps the routing

CLOSE-UP

Is NetWare suitable for enterprise-wide networking?

In the past, NetWare suffered from three shortcomings that have restricted its use to local area networks: Its packet routing protocol, RIP, was limited in its ability to plot out efficient transmission routes; it wasn't able to connect disparate computers; and its maximum packet size was considered small for efficient internetwork use. Novell has addressed the first problem with the NetWare Link Services Protocol (NLSP) and the last problem with SPX2, a modification to NetWare's protocol stack that dynamically alters maximum packet size to match network conditions. For the most part, however, NetWare use is still restricted to devices with Intel-manufactured processors. To be a truly enterprise-wide internetworking option, NetWare must be able to cope with whatever computing device happens to exist in an organization. TCP/IP remains the best internetworking option in that it does not suffer from any of these shortcomings.

table current by broadcasting active network numbers every 60 seconds or so, to all network segments with which it has direct contact. RIP is somewhat limited, in that it doesn't account for line speeds when planning routing paths. RIP really is suited only to small LANs, which is one of the many reasons that NetWare has been slow to scale up to the demands of enterprise-wide internetworking. In an attempt to correct this, Novell has introduced the NetWare Link Services Protocol (NLSP). More sophisticated than RIP, NLSP determines optimal packet transmission routes by considering not only distances but related link speeds as well.

The Sequenced Packet Exchange

Moving up the NetWare protocol stack, SPX (Sequenced Packet Exchange) is Novell's transport layer protocol. (See Figure 3.4.) It provides for reliable, connection-oriented service by requiring that all packets sent out be acknowledged at the receiving end. If a confirmation fails

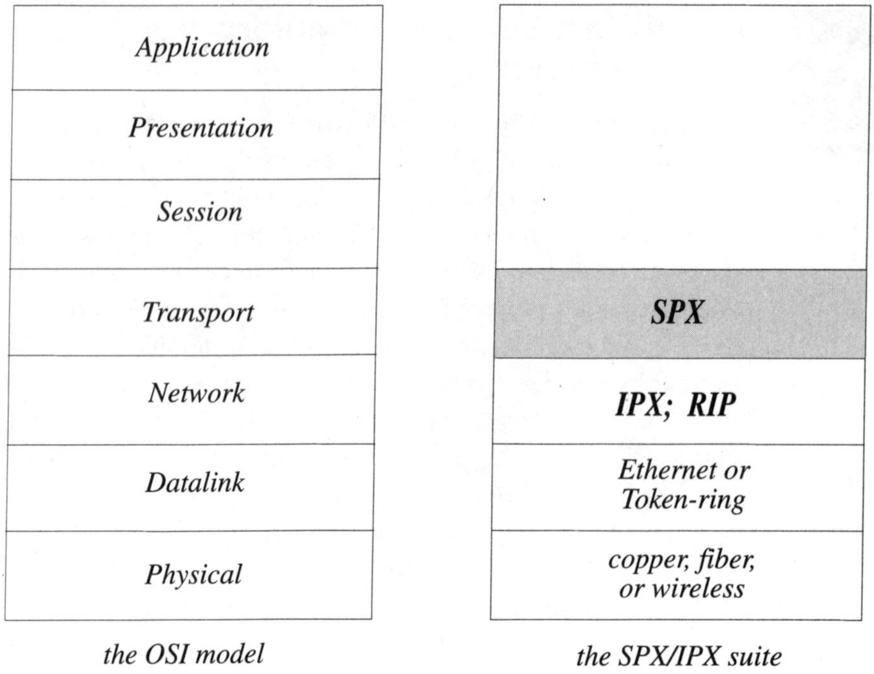

the OSI model	the SPX/IPX suite
Application	
Presentation	
Session	
Transport	**SPX**
Network	**IPX; RIP**
Datalink	*Ethernet or Token-ring*
Physical	*copper, fiber, or wireless*

Figure 3.4 SPX: NetWare's transport layer protocol.

to reach the sending station within a preset period of time, it's assumed to be lost and is retransmitted.

SPX takes its data and its header information, and stuffs it all into the data portion of an IPX packet. Traditionally, this has been restricted to 546 bytes in size. (Recent versions of NetWare have loosened this restriction up somewhat.) But whatever the amount, the SPX header takes up 12 bytes, containing sender and receiver addresses and something called sequence and acknowledgment numbers. SPX uses these bit fields to implement reliable data delivery.

The NetWare Core Protocol

Corresponding to the top three layers of the seven-layer model sits NCP, Novell's NetWare Core Protocol. (See Figure 3.5.) It works closely with the "terminate-and-stay-resident" shell that wraps around each client operating system on the NetWare LAN. The shell filters requests to the

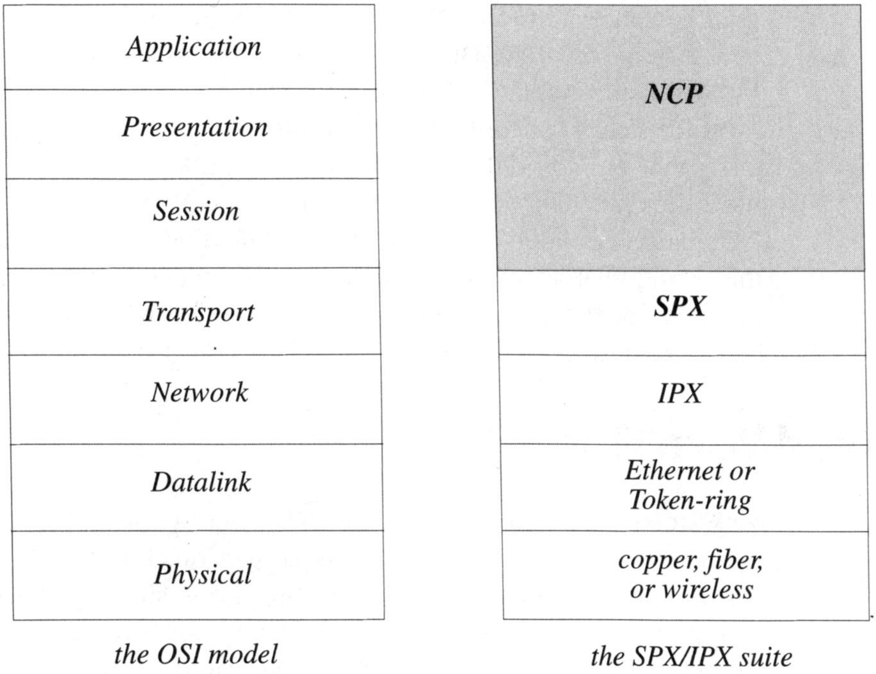

the OSI model		the SPX/IPX suite
Application		NCP
Presentation		
Session		
Transport		SPX
Network		IPX
Datalink		Ethernet or Token-ring
Physical		copper, fiber, or wireless

Figure 3.5 The NetWare Core Protocol.

operating system and the NetWare server. If a request is intended for a networked resource, it passes the request over to NCP. It establishes the connection between the client and the file server. Curiously, NCP actually encapsulates the request and then passes it down the protocol stack directly to IPX—bypassing SPX along the way. NCP takes care of its own session control and reliable delivery service. Just like SPX, it expects an acknowledgment for each packet sent off to the server (or other networked resource).

DOS machines enable IPX (and SPX) through the use of one of two files: IPX.COM or IPXODI.COM. Associated with each is a separate and quite different implementation scheme. IPX.COM must be generated by linking a file supplied by Novell, with another supplied by the manufacturer of the network interface card (NIC) used in the client PC. This can be a frustrating job. There are plenty of variables, and it's difficult to get it right the first time.

The Open Data Link Interface (ODI) is software that allows multiple communication protocol stacks to use a single LAN adapter card. Rather than generate a custom IPX.COM file for each card/machine combination, a single file, IPXODI.COM, can be used instead. ODI was invented by Novell and Apple to allow users to load and access several different protocol stacks concurrently, so that they could access file servers and hosts that employ different protocols. SPX/IPX and TCP/IP could be used simultaneously, for example, if both the NetWare shell and some DOS-based rendition of TCP/IP were installed on the client. Apart from this, using ODI adapters and drivers is also generally easier than their pre-ODI counterparts. This reason alone is often why their use should be considered.

NetWare 4.x

NetWare 4.0 began shipping in July 1993, but by mid-1995, sales were still disappointingly slow for the company. A quick poll of Novell customers may help explain why. NetWare 4.0 is substantially different from its predecessors. Its theme is definitely now one of "information for the enterprise." But many NetWare users simply aren't ready for that. For them, going enterprise-wide is a frightening specter. Yet, version 4 is priced roughly similar to NetWare 3.x, which suggests that Novell has positioned it as an upgrade. And that presents a snag: Migrating from NetWare 3.x to 4.x can be a bit nasty—or at least, it used to be until the arrival of NetWare 4.1 in early 1995. (Nevertheless, the reputation remains.)

Novell's new commitment to enterprise-wide networking is demonstrated in its NetWare Directory Services (NDS). NDS is a distributed database that holds information on every NetWare resource. It's a giant lookup table. With NDS, network administrators are given a "collection point" for internetwork management and control. NetWare version 3.x and below requires administrators to view servers individually, each with its own domain of attached resources that can be managed only locally.

Another interesting feature of NDS is user single logon. Whereas in the past users had to log on to individual servers to access their particular resources, with NetWare 4.x they only need to log on once. If they've been granted sufficient rights to use a particular resource, they just go ahead and use it.

NetWare 4.x continues version 3's theme of integration. Right out of the box, it supports both SPX/IPX and TCP/IP. (See Figure 3.6.) Protocol support for Apple's AppleTalk is also available (for an additional price). Beyond just protocol support, however, the product recognizes the different file structures used in many popular operating systems.

When a file is saved to the NetWare server, NCP does so in the client's native format. It then creates a name for the file in each of the attached client file formats, enabling file interchange.

NetWare 4.x also comes with data compression to extend available server disk space. Novell claims a twofold increase in disk space through file compression. Although decompression is said to be quite fast, not everyone believes that, so users are given the option of flagging off files to prevent them from being compressed. In order to further stretch the availability of valuable disk space, infrequently accessed files

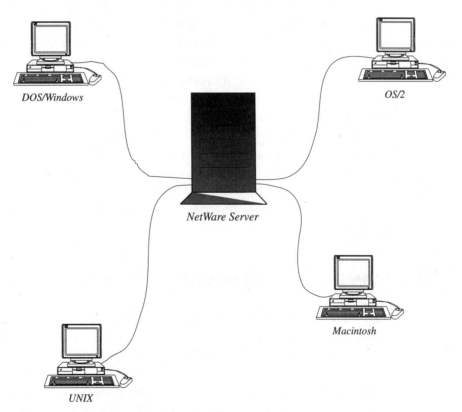

DOS/Windows

OS/2

NetWare Server

Macintosh

UNIX

Figure 3.6 Desktop integration with NetWare 4.x.

can be shipped off automatically to near-line (optical) or off-line (tape) storage. File names still appear in their directories, however, and are dearchived on demand.

In the interest of improving wide-area internetwork performance, a packet burst feature has been introduced. Packet burst is a transmission mode that reduces overhead by allowing packets (frames actually) to be sent before acknowledgments are received from previously sent packets. TCP/IP uses a similar transmission technique. NetWare 4.x also has become more flexible regarding data packet size. IPX packets used to be set to a maximum of 546 bytes. NetWare 4.x determines the maximum packet size that can be handled by the receiving client and scales outgoing packets accordingly. The result is an overall increase in throughput.

NetWare also comes with a number of features for security and business recovery. It has the ability to duplicate hard drive contents. Known as disk mirroring, as the server writes to disk, it mirrors the operation on a second one. This is also known as RAID (Redundant Array of Inexpensive Disks) level 1. If the primary disk fails, attention automatically shifts to the mirrored disk. With server duplexing, users can take this duplication one step further. Here disk write activity is mimicked on a second server—likely a remote one. NetWare 4.x also offers the possibility of retrieving mistakenly deleted files. The system administrator sets the retention period of deleted files.

Overall, NetWare 4.x is a sound offering that goes well beyond previous versions of the NOS. But Microsoft's NT Advanced Server has stolen a lot of NetWare's thunder. Many regard it as a better platform for client/server applications.

Windows NT Advanced Server

Is it a server operating system? Is it a workstation operating system? Stop, it's both. There are actually two renditions of the NT operating system: NT Advanced Server and NT Advanced Workstation (both currently in version 3.5.x).

Windows NT is a full-fledged multitasking, multithreaded operating system. Although there was some confusion as to where it would actually end up, on the desktop or on the server, its market potential seems to be on the server side. There it's directly pitted against both the UNIX operating system (Chapter 6) and NetWare in the NOS arena.

While NetWare is an especially capable platform for file and print serving, to support applications such as database services—of particular relevance to client/server implementations—it has to resort to "bolt-on" software called NetWare Loadable Modules (NLMs). NLMs are popular but are not quite as solid as using a true operating system for application support. Novell wanted UNIXWare (a UNIX variant closely tied to NetWare) to step into that role, but it just hasn't happened. This left the door open for NT, and version 3.5.x was quick to pass through it.

NT Advanced Server features the kind of things LAN administrators want. It's easy to install (some say the easiest of any NOS), it comes with a number of useful network management tools (for adding and deleting users and monitoring server performance), and it scales well. NT comes with support for symmetric multiprocessing, allowing processes to run over as many as 32 separate processors tied to the same high-speed bus. It favors TCP/IP for its high-end communication protocols (but also supports SPX/IPX). Using something called the Dynamic Host Configuration Protocol, the IP addresses of client stations are assigned automatically and managed without human intervention.

Not everyone is prepared to toss out the NetWare investment and adopt NT, however. And that's okay with Microsoft. Add-ons such as their File & Print Services for NetWare lets NetWare clients log on to NT servers and makes NT look like a NetWare 3.x-compatible file server. This offers a gentle migration route to NT if organizations want it. So far, however, most anticipate a hybrid approach, with NetWare handling large-scale file serving and printing and NT taking care of applications.[2]

NT is clearly the better choice for robust application support, but for small applications, and those that aren't "mission-critical," NLM-based support may suffice. It's an option you may want to consider in your move to client/server.

NetWare Loadable Modules

As pointed out earlier, the NetWare core is designed so that additional functionality (modules) can be added as needed—even while the system is running. Novell and a number of third parties produce Net-

Ware Loadable Modules (NLMs) for such things as database services (DBMSs), communications, security and network management. Of the group, database services has spurred a lot of activity in client/server circles.

NLM DBMSs are special versions of database software that run in the 32-bit native mode of the NetWare operating system. They have two big attractions: They're fast and they're cheap. Before they came along, low-end database users were limited to OS/2 offerings or, worse, DOS-based products. When NetWare made its kernel interface specification public, the leading DBMS vendors quickly ported their products to this new platform.

NetWare is designed to be fast. Compared to conventional operating systems, it might best be described as stripped-down. Specifically, NetWare compromises on a number of security features. Because of this, NLM DBMSs run fast—in some cases, as much as twice as fast as comparably sized OS/2 database managers.

But the lack of security features leads to a problem when it comes to fielding data on NLMs—especially mission-critical data. In NetWare 3.x, NLMs operated exclusively in something known as ring 0. Although that is a very speedy place to be, theoretically it was possible for NetWare applications to reach for available resources at the same time, causing the server to crash. It's theoretically possible, since there have been a very few such reported incidents. But even by Novell's own admission, it could happen because NetWare doesn't possess a preemptive scheduler, as most true operating systems do. Without such a scheduler, an application could take over the entire system and not relinquish it until it's done. Noncritical applications could commandeer the network operating system temporarily, locking out more important ones.

Novell has taken steps to reduce the risk. First, it set up an NLM DBMS certification program. For a fee, a DBMS vendor can have its NLM put through its paces in Novell's "Yes it runs with NetWare" program. (Literally, that's what it's called.) If anything quirky turns up, it's flagged by Novell engineers for modification by the DBMS vendor. Currently several hundred vendors have received Novell's seal of approval for their various products.

With NetWare 4.0, administrators also were given the option running NLMs in ring 1, 2, or 3, progressively distanced from the core functionality of the operating system and hence better protected. This is accompanied by a performance impact, however, so in cases where performance is valued over reliability, NLMs can still be run in ring 0.

For many, a big attraction of NLM DBMSs is the possibility of running the database management system and the file server on the same machine. It saves money. Novell and many third parties recommend against it, however. They suggest going with a dedicated database server, no matter what ring you're jumping through.

Database manufacturers were quick to get on the NLM bandwagon. All the big names are included: Oracle, Sybase, Informix. Gupta's SQL-Base has become a popular choice. It requires a minimum of 8 MB of memory plus approximately 10 MB of disk on the server. It's a good, basic DBMS. But let's not sell it short; it comes with a number of very advanced features. Not only that, it's a speedy piece of software as all NLM-based DBMS are. Then there's its price. The cost for an unlimited-person license is around $8,000. Compare this, to say, SyBase's unlimited-seat NLM, which sells for $30,000, and you understand why the industry is taking note. Add a clientcentric tool like PowerSoft's PowerBuilder or Gupta's own SQLWindows, and you're into client/server computing on the cheap.

NetWare 4.x introduces the concept of Virtual Loadable Modules (VLMs). Like NLMs, VLMs provide a special service, but they reside on the client instead of the server. So far they haven't attracted the same level of third-party attention as NLMs have.

With NetWare 3.x, you need a special NLM for TCP/IP routing. NetWare 4.x has built this functionality right into its kernel. Beyond straight support for IP routing, the product also includes a special network driver for encapsulating IPX packets within IP datagrams. This allows NetWare 2.x and 3.x entities to communicate over TCP/IP nets.

NLMs are also available for dial-up communications over analog lines. We'll examine wide area networking in Chapter 4, where we discuss speedier alternatives to dial-up such as Public Data Networks, frame relay, ISDN, and T-1. Novell and various third-party vendors provide communications NLM support for all of those as well.

About the only thing we've left out is mainframe access. In addition to SPX/IPX and TCP/IP, NetWare 4.x has limited support for SNA right in its kernel. It only extends to server management, however; the SNA transport stack present in NetWare 4.x can send alerts to NetView, IBM's network management product. (See Chapter 10.) For anything more, for an additional cost, there's NetWare's Optional Communication Services. Within this category of products is NetWare for SAA. Versions of this gateway software run as an NLM integrated with NetWare 4.x. It supports Token-ring, SDLC (Synchronous Data Link Control), X.25, direct coaxial link to an IBM 3x74 cluster controller, and Ethernet pathways to the mainframe or AS/400 minicomputer. If the host computer is remote, synchronous modem connection to a 37xx front-end processor (FEP) operating at 64 kbps even is possible. NetWare for SAA can run on a file server or on its own dedicated communications server. Version 2.0 of this software from Novell, released in early 1995, improves remote mainframe access.

With the mainframe link in place, 3270 emulation software is all that's required to get Big Red talking to Big Blue. Both Novell (versions for DOS, Windows, and Macintosh available) as well as a number of third parties, such as Wall Data Inc. (Rumba for NetWare) and Attach-mate Corporation (Extra!), offer such software.

Wrap-up

Although both NetWare and NT are proprietary, it's impossible to talk about network operating systems without mentioning them. And, in many cases, it's impossible to build a client/server application without dealing with them. Client/server, very much a grass-roots phenomenon, is a means of improving information-sharing among networked devices, an area in which NetWare and NT rule.

But not all NOSs are created equal. As we've seen, NetWare is best at file and print serving. It's also capable, through the addition of NetWare Loadable Modules, of supporting non-mission-critical applications. NT has laid claim to anything more than that, however. It's now regarded as the best platform for small and medium-size client/server applications.

To break away from its LAN-only confines and to become an enterprise-wide player, Novell recognized that NetWare must support computing platforms other than just Intel. In 1993 the company formulated a plan to develop a Processor Independent version of NetWare (called PIN). This would extend NetWare's reach to include several of the more popular RISC designs in addition to the Intel 80x86 family (as does NT). Existing NetWare customers, however, appeared uninterested, so the project has since been scaled back in favor of a more limited diversification of the NOS to include Macintosh's PowerPC platform only. In response, both Sun Microsystems and Digital decided to go it alone—evidence for Novell's market influence.

Another sore point Novell has sought to remedy is its lack of direct product support. The company has traditionally relied on an array of resellers to sell and support its product. While this may have worked well enough in the past, as NetWare has become more sophisticated, resellers have been increasingly unable to provide adequate support for it.[3] In early 1995, Novell introduced a new direct support program. Following a service and support model similar to WordPerfect's (now a Novell company), customers can opt for Classic, Priority, or Premium service. Premium offers 7/24 support and even provides direct access to Novell engineers if required.

Will it be enough to turn the situation around? While it's unlikely that NetWare will ever be displaced from its top spot, it seems like nothing can stop NT. Over the next few years, watch for it to eat steadily into NetWare sales.

Having talked about local area networks, in Chapter 4 we turn our attention to information exchanges beyond those confines, as we examine the wide area net. As companies become more global, the need to share information over greater distances increases. As we'll see, this has special ramifications for organizations planning to deploy client/server solutions across the great divide.

Key Terms and Ideas Appearing in This Chapter

caching:

A technique used in NetWare to speed file access. Each time a file is called for, it is copied to an area of server memory set aside for file caching. The theory is that if one person wants a file, the chances are good that somebody else might too. First-time access won't benefit (since it comes from disk), but subsequent requests for the same file will be much faster, since it now resides in memory. Files dumped to the cache are time-stamped. They're time-stamped again each time they're reaccessed. When the server runs out of cache memory, files with the "oldest" time stamp are dropped for files accessed for the first time.

directory hashing:

Another technique for improved file access. NetWare keeps records of all files stored in its directories. When a file is requested, rather than sequentially searching the identified directory, NetWare looks up the file's location in its records, goes directly there, and grabs it.

elevator seeking:

Yet another method for faster file access. It's a way of prioritizing file access with respect to the read/write head position of the disk drive. Rather than jump all over the disk, picking up files as they're asked for, NetWare looks at the pending accesses and sorts them relative to their physical distance from the current position of the read/write head. The result is faster overall access and less wear and tear on the disk.

file server:

A file storage device, usually an actual computer, accessible to nodes on a local area (or even wide area) network. More than simply a remote disk drive, a file server contains special software that manages its resident files.

IPX:

Internet Packet Exchange. Novell NetWare's OSI network-layer protocol. Like the IP part of TCP/IP, IPX is an unreliable, connectionless packet delivery protocol. Reliability is left up to SPX, higher up the stack. IPX takes care of such things as forming packets, addressing them, and routing them along their way.

NCP:

NetWare Core Protocols. The NetWare shell, resident on the client, determines whether requests are directed to the server or the client. If they are for the server, the request is passed to NCP. NCP sets up connections between the client and the server.

NDS:

NetWare Directory Services. NDS is a network-wide distributed look-up table that contains information on every networked resource. New to NetWare 4.0, NDS assists in internetwork management and offers users "one logon, one password" functionality.

NetWare:

More than just a stack of communication protocols, NetWare is a highly modular network operating system. At its core does sit communication protocols—IPX, SPX, and NCP—but attachable to it are chunks of code that take care of file and print serving. Other code adds additional functionality as needed. Novell calls these NetWare Loadable Modules (NLMs).

NLM:

NetWare Loadable Module. A piece of software that can be added to the NetWare kernel. NLMs are available for communications (e.g., T-1 support), databases (almost every leading database vendor has one), groupware (e.g., Lotus has an NLM version of its popular Notes application), and a whole bunch of other things. Novell customers can add NLM functionality on an as-needed basis.

NOS:

Network operating system. A NOS is an environment that usually complements a client operating system, endowing it with networking functionality. Usually this extra functionality is just file and print serving. Newer NOSs such as NTAS extend this to application serving as well, however.

ODI:

Open DataLink Interface. ODI is a set of guidelines that, if adhered to, permit multiple protocol stacks to use a single LAN adapter. In the "old days," if you wanted to access a host on TCP/IP and a printer, say, on AppleTalk, you required separate protocol support for each and dedicated network cards as well. Apple and Novell got together to come up with ODI. To work, you need a network card and driver software written to the ODI "standard." In the business, loading up two protocols onto a single LAN adapter is called dual-protocol stacking.

RIP:

Routing Information Protocol. NetWare, TCP/IP, and XNS (a communication protocol stack designed by Xerox) all use RIP. It's a rather simple protocol that aids IPX, in NetWare's case, to come up with the "best" route from sender to receiver. It does this by using the hop count in a router's (NetWare file server's) routing table. Both NetWare and TCP/IP are replacing RIP with newer protocols that also account for the speed of data links between the sender and receiver. (If a 56 kbps line and a 1.5 Mbps line both led to the same collection point in a WAN, for example, these newer protocols can recognize that, and choose the fastest pathway.)

SPX:

Sequenced Packet Exchange. This is NetWare's OSI transport layer protocol. It is responsible for ensuring the delivery of data packets.

VLM:

Virtual Loadable Module. Something new for NetWare 4.0, VLMs are similar in concept to NLMs, except that they reside on and provide the specialized functionality for the client.

Windows NT Advanced Server:

A full-fledged, multitasking, multithreaded operating system from Microsoft. NT actually comes in two renditions: Advanced Server and Advanced Workstation. While sales of the workstation version are doing well, most see the server as the right platform for NT. It features the easiest installation of any network operating system and comes with a number of server management tools. User Manager is used to add and delete end users from the server. Disk Administrator is used for managing disk space, and Performance Manager gauges the performance of server components such as the CPU and disk. It's very scalable, coming with symmetric multiprocessing support for up to 32 processors. The NOS favors the TCP/IP protocol stack but comes with out-of-the-box support for SPX/IPX as well.

Notes

[1] R. Ward, E. Eva, and M. Laitinen, "NOS News is Good News," *InfoWorld*, Dec. 19, 1994, 1.

[2] L. DiDio, "NT Lures NetWare Shops," *ComputerWorld*, Jan. 9, 1995, 1.

[3] C. Gillooly, "At Your Service," *Information Week*, Jan. 30, 1995, 12.

Chapter 4

Executive Summary

The world is getting smaller, or so it seems. Telephone, television, and the Internet communications have had a drastic influence on our lives. And it's had a profound effect on the life of the corporation as well. With substantial global variations in labor costs, just staying in business these days often means moving to where you can afford to get the work done. And often such a move simply wouldn't be possible if it weren't for data communications.

Until quite recently, wide area data communications has always lagged behind local area technologies. Because such wide area data communications are much slower, more expensive, and harder to work with, client/server developers who intend to stretch their applications out to the branch office have faced some valid problems. But a shift is taking place; emerging technologies such as Asynchronous Transfer Mode (ATM) are turning the LAN/WAN relationship upside down. Its base operating speed is more than twice that of Ethernet.

ATM offers more than increased data transfer speeds, however. Soon expected to be reasonably priced for desktop implementations, ATM is not exclusively seen as a wide area alternative; it holds out the welcome possibility of having a single networking fabric that stretches across our entire organizations, one that seamlessly supports voice, video, and data.

CHAPTER

4

WANs: Bridging
the Great Divide

Introduction

Imagine racing across the desert at more than 700 miles per hour and then coming to an instantaneous, near stop. That may sound like a wild idea, but it happens all the time in the communications world whenever Ethernet and Token-Ring data packets move onto wide area networks (WANs) to reach distant information stores. WANs operate at substantially slower speeds than do local area networks, a fact that poses a serious challenge to any communication-intensive client/server applications that involve the branch office. However, some truly amazing things are happening with wide area communications, changes that will affect not only how we communicate remotely but also how we interact with locally networked devices.

63

In Chapter 2 we discussed a number of alternatives for speeding up LANs. With pressure from client/server and new, bandwidth-hungry technologies, a lot of folks are worried that before long, 10 and 16 Mbps just aren't going to cut it. Meanwhile, in WAN circles, 1.5 Mbps is a big thing. And it's always been like that; in comparison to LANs, WANs are slow, expensive, use mysterious technologies, and usually are outside of our direct control—since most involve services supplied by telecomm providers.

In spite of all this, there are plenty of options to choose from—too many perhaps: Integrated Services Digital Network (ISDN), frame relay, switched 56, X.25, T-1, fractional T-1, SMDS, dial-up analog, and more. Selecting the right mix isn't easy; even the experts have different opinions about which technology to support, at least in the short term. In the long term (long being two or three years), everyone, and I mean everyone, agrees that the future belongs to Asynchronous Transfer Mode (ATM).

All of a sudden, every networking technology is regarded as an interim step toward ATM—that's all low-level (from a seven-layer perspective) technologies, LAN and WAN alike. More than just a high-speed data mover, ATM offers the promise that organizations someday will have a single networking "fabric" to support their entire computing infrastructures.

Broadly speaking, there are two types of WANs: circuit-switched and packet-switched. Circuit-switching is an adaptation of the common telephone system. A physical link is established between two communicating parties by a central switching authority and maintained for the duration of the interchange. Modem communication uses analog circuit switching.

Packet-switched networks, a fundamentally digital notion, are a child of the Cold War era. Centrally controlled communication systems are prime targets in any war. Packet-switching spreads switching responsibility across the entire network. Transmissions are broken up into pieces (packets) and, with the help of distributed switching and routing equipment forming a latticework for the net, are allowed to find their own way to their destination. Many routes exist; if one is destroyed by enemy fire, there's just one less for packets to follow. Packet-switched nets are a fast and efficient way to move data over large areas. ATM is a packet-switched technology.

With these definitions behind us, let's take a closer look at these two approaches to bridging the great divide.

Circuit-Switched WANs

Circuit-switched technologies have been around for what seems like forever. They work by establishing a physical connection between two communicating parties that is maintained as long as it's needed. Contrasted with conventional packet-switched technologies, circuit-switching is better suited for the transmission of voice and video. The emergence of things such as desktop videoconferencing has renewed interest in circuit-switching. The explosive growth in Internet access has also promoted circuit-switching, because the most popular way to get onto "the Net" is with a dial-up modem.

Dial-up Analog Lines

Dial-up lines can provide synchronous or asynchronous communication at transmission rates that range from 300 bps to 56 kbps (with data compression). If you've ever had to endure modems operating at 1,200 or 2,400 bps, some of the more recent 14.4 or 28.8 kbps offerings sound like a dream. But let's put this into perspective. Figure 4.1 compares some everyday data transmission rates.

As you can see, compared to LAN speeds, even 28.8 kbps is downright depressing. Why so slow? Dial-up line speed limits are set by noise sources, imperfect line filters, and the random route selections through the public switched telephone network. Make two calls to the same number, and you'll very likely pass through two different physical connections.

Dial-up transmission requires a modem at each end of the line. The sending-side modem converts the digital signal from the computer into an analog (continuous) wave form that can be sent over a standard telephone line. The receiving-side modem changes it back to digital form. When modems first make a connection, they "introduce" themselves through a series of audible tones (more like squawks really). Called handshaking, part of this introduction establishes an appropriate transmission speed that both modems can cope with.

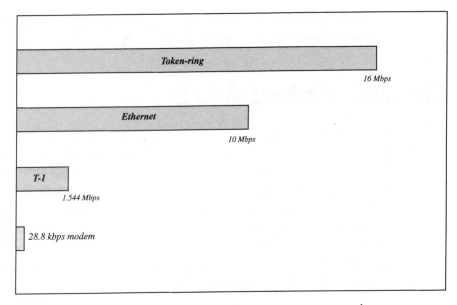

Figure 4.1 A comparison of common data transmission speeds.

The CCITT (Consultative Committee for International Telegraphy and Telephony) is an influential force in data communications. Its "V-series" standards permit modems from different vendors to intercommunicate. There are four or five standards worth knowing about. V.32, for example, is a CCITT standard for modems operating in the 4,800 bps to 9,600 bps range. It's essentially a modulation standard (a way of manipulating the analog signal to pack more information into it). Using something called trellis encoding, V.32 bolsters signal performance,

CLOSE-UP

Synchronous and asynchronous communications

When using a modem for synchronous communication over standard telephone lines, data is transmitted in blocks. Synchronization bits also are tacked on and actually sent ahead of each block. Asynchronous communication, on the other hand, uses a continuous bit stream. Start and stop bits are book-ended around each character to aid in identification. All this extra overhead usually means that async is slower than synchronous communications.

CLOSE-UP

Baud versus bits per second

Transmission rates are sometimes referred to as the "baud rate." The baud rate isn't necessarily equal to the number of bits transmitted per second, however. Baud rate refers to the number of analog signal changes that occur in a transmission during a one-second interval. A signal change can actually encode more than 1 bit. For example, a 3,600 baud modem that uses a 4 bit-per-signal-change code operates at 14,400 bits per second. Stick to bits per second when describing data transmission speeds to avoid confusion.

and speed, over standard telephone lines. To correct for possible transmission errors over these lines, V.32"bis" was created. This standard also raised the transmission rate to 14,400 bps. Moving error correction into hardware further improved transmission speeds. That's what V.42 is all about. V.42bis introduced data compression (using a technique called Lempel-Ziv) to take rates up to a theoretical maximum of 38,400 bps. And it continues; V.34, also known as V.Fast, is the latest member of the V-series family. Under ideal conditions, modems operating with V.34 can transfer information (with heavy compression) at up to 115

CLOSE-UP

Should you purchase a V.34 modem?

V.34 is a very new standard. In fact, it can't even be fairly called a standard yet. It's more of a loose specification among vendors. There's no guarantee that two V.34 modems from two different manufacturers will communicate as they're supposed to. To make matters worse, millions of "V.34" modems were produced even before the CCITT had a draft standard outlined. Deciding whether to purchase a V.34 modem depends on what you intend to use it for. Many phone lines won't accommodate 28,800 bps transfer rates—particularly if they're heavily trafficked. If achieving high data transmission rates is important, you may want to consider some of the digital technologies we discuss later. ISDN, for example, is becoming quite attractive. And if you do a lot of faxing, and intend to purchase a V.34 fax/modem, keep in mind that maximum fax speeds are still limited to 14.4 kbps.

kbps! The first modems to reach the market touting V.34 compatibility operate at 28.8 kbps, however.

Telephone lines continue to improve in quality and modem designers are quite resourceful in squeezing every last drop of bandwidth out of them. While this makes it tough to predict an ultimate speed limit for dial-up data transfer rates, many believe that, with digital technologies dropping in price, we may be seeing the upper limit of dial-up analog communications—one imposed by economics, if not technology.

Dial-up service is really only suitable for ad-hoc remote host access, such as e-mail, for example. Employees in branch offices, or on the road, can call in to a central site and exchange text-based messages and small files as needed within the bandwidth confines of analog lines. You can take this idea further. Software such as XcelleNet's RemoteWare offer a novel approach for linking outlying employees to the home office. A server located at a central site oversees the management of remote (dial-in) client stations. Each time a remote user dials in to send or check for e-mail, the server examines the remote station to see if it's loaded with the proper office productivity tools. If something is missing, or an upgrade is required, it does it automatically overnight. (The user is prompted, during the live linkup, to leave the computer and modem on that evening.) It's a good way of dealing with remote users who aren't overly conversant in "DOS-ese."

Every time an analog dial-up circuit is established, a new path is chosen. This doesn't pose much of a problem when the line is being used for voice communication; even if the line is a bit noisy, we can compensate for what we can't hear clearly with our expectations derived from the context of the conversation. But when data is being sent, line noise is directly proportional to channel capacity; machines aren't nearly as versatile as the human ear in separating noise from useful information.

One solution is to remove some of the unpredictability by setting up a constant circuit in the form of a leased or even private line. Since the pathway then is always the same, it becomes possible to "tune" the line to reduce noise effects. This is called "line conditioning."

But once monthly modem usage or required data transfer rates passes a certain point, it becomes necessary to consider something beyond analog dial-up. Digital pulses are less susceptible to noise, which permits higher data transmission speeds. Telephone companies offer an array of digital-based choices that take up where analog communications leave off. First in line is a long-time favorite called Switched-56.

Switched-56

Telephone companies have been offering switched-56 for quite some time now. It offers transmission speeds up to 1.5 Mbps in 56 kbps increments although it's most often run at its base speed. It's probably the most popular switched digital service in use in North America today. It operates very much as does a standard analog telephone connection: A constant pathway is maintained during the transmission and usage is paid for by the minute.

But unlike analog services, switched-56 is digital. This means it doesn't require a modem at each end of the circuit, but it does need a modemlike device called a Data Service Unit/Channel Service Unit (DSU/CSU). Practically all forms of digital communication do.

Switched-56's reasonable cost and widespread availability have contributed to its popularity. But there's a growing feeling among both telephone companies and their customers that its days are numbered. Emphasis is clearly, and finally, moving toward ISDN, another digital circuit-switched technology.

ISDN

For a while, it looked like ISDN (Integrated Services Digital Network) was never going to arrive. We had been told about its virtues for years, but it never seemed to catch on with the phone companies. Now, just in the last year or two, it's taken off. It's being driven by a rapid increase in telecommuting and by a growing interest in desktop videoconferencing.

ISDN is a circuit-switched service that permits the digital transport of voice, data, and image over the same line. It uses two types of communication channels: "B," or "bearer channels," for voice and/or data, and a "D," or "data channel," for control services. The two B channels can support 64 kbps each and can be combined for a total transmission rate of 128 kbps. The D channel is for the transmission of signal control information and is generally off limits to carrying user information. Telephone companies (telcos) package ISDN in two formats: Basic Rate Interface (BRI) consisting of two 64 kbps B channels and one 16 kbps D channel (for a total of 144 kbps), and the Primary Rate Interface (PRI), which contains 23 B channels and one D channel for a total digital bandwidth of 1.536 Mbps.

ISDN's cost-to-performance ratio is too good for many to pass up. Some report that, in many parts of the country, you can equip both a sender and receiver for about one-fifth of the cost of switched-56.[1] And to become equipped, users require an ISDN "line" and an ISDN CSU/DSU. Typically, this shouldn't cost much more than $1,500 per user. Just as with standard telephone usage, telco customers are charged only for the time they actually use the line.

ISDN's 128 kbps data transmission rate is faster than the raw numbers suggest. This is clearly demonstrated with an ISDN WAN in place at Southern Hills Hospital in Tennessee. Radiologists there are required to be on call each evening. If a patient is in need of their services, a series of images are transmitted to their home PC. In the past, they used a 9600 bps modem over an analog line. The problem was, transmitting a complete set of images could take up to thirty-five minutes—far too long to wait in the case of an emergency. With the help of a network consulting group, the hospital moved to an ISDN solution utilizing a four-to-one data compression. The same set of images can now be transferred in 17 seconds. If you do the math, this works out to a speed increase of 123.5 times the previous arrangement; however, the raw numbers predict a speed increase of only 53.3 times. ISDN's digital underpinnings makes establishing a line connection cleaner and hence, faster, accounting for some of this difference.

While ISDN is certainly coming on strong, it's still not universally available. About 10 percent of the United States remains unserviced. But that's a far cry from the situation just a few years ago. ISDN has finally arrived. The ISDN Primary Rate Interface (PRI) has a top speed of 1.54 Mbps. This corresponds to another long-popular WAN technology known as T-1. Like switched-56, T-1 is an older telco service that's slowly being superseded by emerging telecommunications technologies.

The T-Carrier Facility

Many years ago, Bell engineers came up with something called time-division multiplexing in order to make better use of existing commu-

Is ISDN suitable for remote client/server applications?

The answer depends on a number of things, not the least of which is what you want your client/server application to do. If it's to make use of images, ISDN might be sufficient. For anything more exotic, such as full-motion video perhaps, ISDN is less likely to be suitable. One thing to remember when talking about ISDN, switched-56, or any other WAN technologies is that they're concerned with the bottom of the OSI protocol stack just as Ethernet and Token Ring are. Higher-level protocols "ride" on them. This is important because not all of these higher-level protocols are equally well suited for WAN usage. Novell's SPX/IPX, for example, can seriously tax a 56 or 64 kbps line because of its requirement that the receiving node acknowledge every single packet. TCP/IP, on the other hand, doesn't take error checking that far. That, combined with its consistently larger packet size, makes TCP/IP more amenable to WAN applications. The simple answer is yes, both ISDN and switched-56 can be used for remote WAN-based client/server applications, provided the level of data traffic between the client and the server isn't too great.

nication lines. Multiplexing allows signals from more than one source to be sent over a single physical line. This is done by interweaving a number of signals within the line over time. Devices that do this are called multiplexers (or "muxes," for short). For digital data transmission, multiplexing leads to a WAN alternative called the T-carrier facility.

The first "step" in the T-carrier facility is T-1. Using a four-wire path, T-1 can transmit digital information (voice, video, and data) down the line at a speed of 1.544 Mbps. But T-1 isn't cheap. It's priced on a distance basis. For this reason, some companies, and particularly utilities, often set up and take care of their own T-1 lines.

Like ISDN, T-1 is digitally based. So it too requires a CSU/DSU resident on the customer's premises. (See Figure 4.2.) The CSU/DSU accepts digital information from the T-1 mux before handing it over to the network interface to be put out onto the line.

At 1.544 Mbps, T-1 is a significant improvement over BRI ISDN, but it's still significantly slower than Ethernet and Token Ring. While it

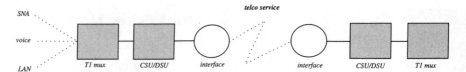

Figure 4.2 T-Carrier configuration.

could possibly accommodate a few remote stations as part of a client/ server application, more speed is called for to cope with tomorrow's higher-bandwidth needs.

Higher up in the T-carrier facility is T-3. Equivalent to 28 T-1s, T-3 is capable of transmitting data at 44.736 Mbps. It's one of the few in-service WAN options that's faster than LAN rates. Telcos have been eager to attract customers to this newer technology and have priced it accordingly. But therein lies a problem. T-3 needs more time to mature. Currently the market is besieged with proprietary vendor solutions. If it does get the chance to stabilize, T-3 would certainly be adequate for most WAN-based client/server applications. (It can even be multiplexed to reach transmission speeds of 560 Mbps.)

As always, cost must be balanced against need. And today, when many customers weigh their leased-line options, they often find something in between switched-56 and T-1 is more appropriate. For just this situation, the telcos introduced fractional T-1. Fractional T-1 lines are configured in 64 kbps increments up to a maximum of 1.544 Mbps. (That is 24 steps, which sometimes are referred to as T-0 lines.) While setup costs are not much different from that of full T-1 (a mux and a CSU/DSU are still needed), monthly leasing costs are invariably cheaper. Furthermore, once FT-1 is in place, customers can, in theory at least, add additional FT-1 lines as their needs increase. It's an idea known as bandwidth-on-demand.

Circuit-switching may be the most popular form of WAN technology, but these days all the action is in packet-switching. Here's where we find frame relay, SMDS, and ATM.

Packet-Switched WANs

Circuit-switched WANs operate in a point-to-point fashion. If an organization has to connect a handful of distributed LANs, point-to-point connections may be fine. But when faced with more than that, the costs, and the headaches, add up fast. In Figure 4.3, five sites are connected with 10 point-to-point lines.

Six sites would need 15 lines. And so it goes. Before too long, things become unwieldy. Packet switching doesn't run into this problem. It doesn't establish dedicated pathways between sender and receiver but instead breaks up transmissions at the sending end and then allows these data packets to find their own way through a wide area network of packet routing and switching equipment. To the sender, this network is cloudlike; the details of how packets get to their destination aren't relevant—all that matters is that they get there in a timely manner. Many wide area "clouds" are services provided by Public Data Networks (PDNs).

X.25

PDNs are packet-switched service providers that can be thought of as data-only versions of the phone company. There are a number of them out there. AT&T's Accunet, Sprintnet, Datapac, Tymnet, and even companies such as CompuServe are some common service providers.

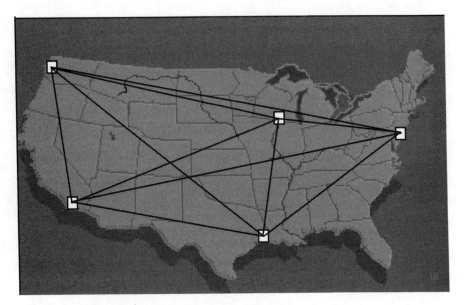

Figure 4.3 Point-to-point lines between five sites.

Accessing these networks today almost universally involves use of the X.25 CCITT protocol. The protocols actually used inside the PDN cloud are at the discretion of the service provider.

When using PDNs, even X.25 access tends to be user-transparent; generally, customers gain entry into the network by analog or digital dial-up connection to a service provider's modem. That modem and associated server take care of the X.25 connection. In comparison to circuit-switched point-to-point connections, only a single dial-up link from each site is needed to connect into a packet-switched cloud. (See Figure 4.4.)

The X.25 PDN interface corresponds to the first three layers of the OSI seven-layer model. The physical layer stipulates the media for the connection. The data link layer transfers and checks the data. The network layer routes it.

X.25 is known for its reliability. Networks using this protocol check packets for errors at every hop along the way. All this checking is a bit of overkill, but X.25 was designed at a time when data transmission was more art than science. Its designers assumed error-prone analog (telephone) lines as the principal carrier. It has been estimated that as

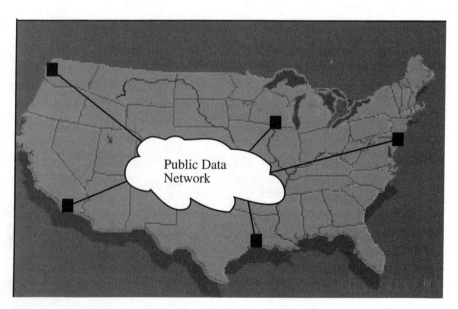

Figure 4.4 A PDN cloud connecting the same five sites.

much as two-thirds of X.25's possible bandwidth is dedicated to error checking. This limits the top speed of any networks using this protocol to about 56 kbps.

X.25 is really suitable only for e-mail, terminal traffic, and small file transfers. But it's still widely used (especially in Europe); in many parts of the world, it's the only WAN data transmission option. In North America, however, it's being rapidly replaced by a follow-on technology known as frame relay.

Frame Relay

What if you check for X.25 errors only at the end points of the transmission, instead of at each step in between? This leads to an enhancement to X.25 called frame relay. Dropping all that checking increases throughput to T-1 speed. As with X.25, frame relay officially deals only with the interface to the PDN.

Frame relay is offered by the telcos as an alternative to private, leased lines. In fact, even though it's packet-switched, it's set up so that it appears as if it were a dedicated channel technology. Service customers identify communication end points and estimate the amount of bandwidth required between them. This leads to the creation of Permanent Virtual Circuits, or PVCs. With committed information rate of zero, customers pay only for what they use.

Frame relay is generally available in 56 kbps increments up to T-1 (or slightly better) speed. A number of vendors support a version that operates up to T-3 speeds, even though the original CCITT specification only goes as high as T-1. The WAN alternative receives a lot of attention from router manufacturers, which is a good indicator of the health of what is essentially a router-to-router, point-to-point networking technology.

SMDS

The Switched Megabit Data Service (SMDS) is an emerging WAN alternative that uses the public telephone system. Packets are "dropped" into it and allowed to find their own way to their destinations. It debuted at T-1 speed but today ranges from 56 kbps to 43 Mbps.

Whereas frame-relay emulates leased lines, SMDS emulates a LAN. It can support most of the better-known, higher-order communication protocols. To link up a LAN to an SMDS-based WAN requires a router and an SMDS-compatible CSU/DSU. This is easier than with frame relay, where customers must also identify PVCs.

SMDS uses a fixed-length data frame similar to that used in Asynchronous Transfer Mode. It isn't suited for the transfer of real-time video, however. But using a similar data frame structure means that when ATM finally arrives, SMDS users can migrate their WANs to it readily if they elect to. In fact, both frame relay and SMDS will be directly supportable by ATM.

SMDS is being somewhat upstaged by frame relay, largely because of a lack of widespread and consistent support for it by regional telephone companies. None of the long-distance carriers has made a true commitment to SMDS yet—a definite drawback for a WAN technology. Frame relay, on the other hand, currently is offered by all long-distance carriers as well as a number of WAN service providers.

ATM

ISDN, switched-56, high-speed Ethernet, SMDS, frame relay: What do all these wide area networking technologies have in common? They're all seen as an interim step toward Asynchronous Transfer Mode, better known as ATM. More than just a high-speed WAN alternative, ATM promises three things: to provide a single "pipe" for the transfer of voice, video, and data; to introduce a common base networking fabric for both LANs and WANs; and to supply sufficient bandwidth to take data communications well into the next century. It will radically alter the face of computing.

ATM data transfer rates range from 25 Mbps at the low end to literally gigabits per second at the high end. How is this possible? ATM uses fixed-length data frames (called cells). Fifty-three bytes in length, five bytes are dedicated to header information, leaving a 48 byte payload. An ATM network consists of a latticework of high-speed data switches. These switches establish a virtual channel between the sender and the receiver. Because the cells are of constant length, they can be switched in hardware. This, combined with minimal error checking and flow control, results in an exceptionally high-speed data transfer.

Interest in ATM has brought together a large number of vendors (more than 400 at last count) in order to shepherd through a series of operational standards. The forum is striving to agree on transmission standards for rates of 25, 51.8, 155, and 622 Mbps. The ATM forum recently has drafted a standard for running ATM over unshielded twisted pair cable at 51.8 Mbps, for example.

ATM makes no distinction between data, voice, and even video. That's rather surprising; the three have little in common. Data, such as the type coming from LANs, tends to be bursty in nature. Video and voice are continuous. ATM compromises between the two. (See Figure 4.5.) Its small and constant packet size make switch latency, the amount

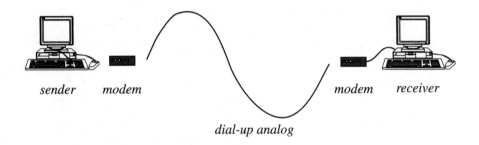

sender   *modem*   *modem*   *receiver*

dial-up analog

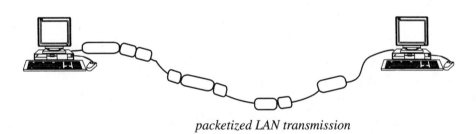

packetized LAN transmission

switch

ATM Transmission

Figure 4.5 ATM simultaneously supports continuous and packetized transmissions.

The road to ATM

There is considerable controversy over which currently available WAN alternative is best positioned for migration to ATM. SMDS and ATM use the same cell size, but ATM and frame relay both emulate connection-oriented leased lines. Numerous press releases from the ATM forum and others indicate eventual ATM support for both SMDS and frame relay. Some suggest, for example, that frame relay could feed LAN traffic into a carrier's ATM service, whenever one is established. The SMDS Interest Group has constructed a plan to provide SMDS services over ATM networks. So it then comes down to a head-to-head comparison of frame relay and SMDS against a backdrop of an organization's current needs. Frame relay is better suited to situations in which there are few communicating sites with well-understood information flows between them. SMDS is more flexible and scalable than frame relay. But some people have expressed concern about SMDS security, as it uses the public telephone system. Features such as source code validation to enhance security are being added, however. This lets users validate who's sending the information. It's also not offered consistently across the country yet.

of time a packet spends in the switch, consistent. With a high enough transmission speed, the incoming feed appears smooth and continuous.

There are already tens of ATM products available. Before long, that number will certainly stretch into the hundreds. And although its cost is still somewhat high, it's already being adopted by some companies. Bear Stearns, an international investment banking firm, for example, has elected to install an ATM network in order to collapse three existing networks supporting data, voice, and video. It is the first Wall Street firm to standardize on the new technology, but it certainly won't be the last.

SONET

SONET is an ANSI standard for the high-speed, optical transmission of data, voice, and video. It works hand-in-hand with many of the technologies we've already looked at but is an especially potent partner for ATM. Acting as a backbone carrier, SONET can transport ATM cells within its own data frames.

SONET transforms digital transmissions into high-speed optical ones. Using it is sort of like switching from a side road to a multilane superhighway. It offers enormous bandwidth; initial implementations start in at 51.84 Mbps and range up to 2.488 Gbps. Bandwidths in the tens of gigabits are the eventual target. In late 1994, the Advanced Research Projects Agency funded a project to develop a means of running ATM over SONET at speeds up to 10 Gbps.

SONET is like FDDI in some ways. It too is designed for dependability as well as speed. Some versions, such as Sprint's, employ a ringed architecture, allowing the network to "self-heal" in the event of a line break. Sprint claims its SONET backbone can do this in as little as 60 milliseconds. AT&T also is working on a nationwide SONET backbone service.

Wrap-up

These days there's a lot of talk about the "information superhighway." Many of the technologies we've just talked about will take that idea from hype to reality. At SONET's 2.45 Gbps data rate, for example, a 500-page novel could be transmitted over significant distances in as little as a few seconds. With capabilities like that, it's easy to understand all the buzz surrounding SONET and ATM.

But ATM is a few years away—at least from the desktop. What do we do in the meantime? Since there's little doubt that eventually we're going to need the bandwidth levels afforded by ATM, whatever we elect to install today should make that migration as cheap and as easy as possible. And keep in mind that we're not necessarily just talking about WANs in this respect. ATM will soon be in a position to be considered as a viable alternative to Ethernet and Token Ring.

For the time being, at least, WANs and client/server can be a tough mix. A 128 kbps ISDN link between a client and a server might be adequate, provided that the link is dedicated and not shared by a LANs-worth of users. Even then, once you account for protocol overhead (for whatever higher-order protocol stack you use), there's not much useful bandwidth left over. Opting for something that's only marginally satisfactory will almost certainly lead to trouble later. At the same time, you don't want to overestimate and end up paying for something you don't fully use. Bandwidth-on-demand services are a way of coping with this uncertainty. It's difficult enough to estimate accurately data traffic on LAN-based client/server applications. The inclusion of a WAN link just makes it that much more difficult. There are numerous accounts of LAN-based client/server applications experiencing substantial performance degradation after being scaled up to an enterprise-wide scope.[2]

Concerns around WANs as part of a client/server implementation is more than just a matter of bandwidth, however. Client/server is severely challenged when it comes to system management and security. Of course, the situation doesn't improve any when one or more of the clients sit at the distant end of a patchwork communications channel. Management tools are arriving, but there aren't many to choose from today.

Client/server and the idea of enterprise-wide access do, however, go hand-in-hand. Client/server is, after all, sort of a "technology by the people, for the people," kind of thing. As organizations become more horizontal, artificial barriers to corporate information will need to be breached. Doing so may not be that easy today, but relief is on the way. We just have to position ourselves now to take full advantage of it when it arrives.

In the next chapter we return to high-level communication protocols—ones specifically designed for internetworking applications. Able to run over WANs and LANs alike, the hands-down choice here is TCP/IP, the Internet protocol.

Key Terms and Ideas Appearing in This Chapter

ATM:

A high-speed form of packet-switching. ATM uses small (53 byte), fixed-size packets running over optical fiber to reach speeds of 155 Mbps and beyond. ATM is sort of a cross between analog transmission (continuous waveform) and packetized, bursty LAN transmissions. Because of this, it can accommodate both voice and data with the same approach, over the same carrier.

CCITT:

Comité Consultatif Internationale de Télégraphie et Téléphonie—a European organization that recommends international communication standards. It's most notably known for its V series (V.34, V.42) and X series (X.25, X.500) standards.

frame relay:

A streamlined successor to X.25. Frame relay is also a CCITT standard. It's a popular packet-switching WAN option that starts in at 2 Mbps but will soon reach T-3 speeds (44 Mbps). Frame relay is now seen as the next logical step toward ATM.

ISDN:

Integrated Services Digital Network. ISDN is designed to permit the simultaneous transfer of voice, data, and image over the same network. It uses two separate channels: B (bearer) channels for data and voice that run at up to 64 kbps, and a D channel that carries control information. ISDN has been talked about for a long time and is only now arriving.

packet-switching:

A method of digital communication in which data are broken up into "chunks" and are routed to their destinations over a number of different communication channels.

SMDS:

Switched Multimegabit Data Service. SMDS is a packet-switched service strongly supported by the telephone companies. It has a lot in common with ATM in that it too is a cell switching service. Cells are fixed-length data frames. SMDS came to market later than frame relay, and there are indications within the industry that it's in for a rough ride.

SONET:

Synchronous Optical Network. More of a standard than a tangible technology, SONET is intended to aid in very high speed (international) optical communications. Sprint and AT&T currently are leading the charge toward SONET.

T-1/T-3:

Both T-1 and T-3 are part of the T-carrier facility. If you're wondering what ever happened to T-2, well, it exists—as part of T-3 services. T-1 is a digital multiplexed technology that's usually leased from telephone companies. It operates at 1.544 Mbps. In Europe, the T-1 equivalent is called E-1; it "runs" at a slightly higher speed (2.048 Mbps). T-3 is a newer technology but essentially takes up where T-1 leaves off. Its speed is approximately 44 Mbps. T-1 and now T-3 have a reputation for being expensive WAN options. This is why many telcos came up with fractional T-1, or FT-1. FT-1 lets you step up to full T-1 capability in 64 kbps increments. There's little or no mention of FT-3 yet.

V series:

A set of modem standards created by the CCITT. The series covers modem speeds, signal modulations, and data compression. Within the series are V.32, a modulation standard for modems in the 4800-to-9600 bps range; V.42bis, a data compression standard for transmission speeds up to 38,000 bps; and now V.34, an emerging standard for modem communications at speeds that may someday reach 115 kbps.

X.25:

Another set of recommendations by the CCITT. X.25 defines the connection between a terminal and a packet-switching network. X.25 is known for two things: It's dependable, and it's slow. Both of these are related, of course; X.25 expends a great deal of available bandwidth checking for transmission errors. It is generally expected that frame relay will succeed X.25. (It's a CCITT standard too, by the way.)

Notes

[1] A. Censor, "Pumping Up Your Phone Lines," *PC Today*, Jan. 1995, 49.

[2] C. Loosley, "Performance Design: Going for the Gold," *Database Programming & Design*, Nov. 1994, 26.

Chapter 5

Executive Summary

When it comes to a high-end networking option to run on top of basic WAN and LAN technologies—something to take care of packet routing and error checking—TCP/IP, the networking underbelly of the Internet, the world's largest network of networks, is a natural. It runs on just about every type of computer, over just about every type of low-end protocol suite, and over practically every fundamental networking technology. And what's more, it's nonproprietary. Nobody owns it.

TCP/IP resulted from government research into wide area information sharing. This research evolved into the current-day Internet, which is massive. It connects tens of thousands of LANs and millions of users into an internetwork (network of networks) that offers global e-mail and information on practically every subject known to humans. Over the years it has served as a live test bed for TCP/IP, as the protocol stack was reviewed and enhanced.

Using TCP/IP doesn't mean necessarily having to deal with the Internet. The protocol stack is quite commonly used in organizations that have no link to the "Net" whatsoever. Often these organizations turn to TCP/IP when fielding their first client/server applications. There's several reasons for this. The application might employ a UNIX-based server. There's a long-standing relationship between UNIX and the protocol stack. Windows NT, which is challenging UNIX for the role of server operating system, also comes with intrinsic TCP/IP support.

Another reason to invoke TCP/IP in client/server applications is to act as an intermediary protocol. Often client/server applications bridge mainframes and LAN workgroups. Placing a "server" in between the two offers a number of distinct advantages, one of which is that it can simply act as a translator between these two very different computing environments. With the mainframe "speaking" IBM's SNA, and the LAN probably based on NetWare, TCP/IP becomes a neutral protocol wedged between the two.

Finally, with the explosive growth of the Internet, more and more organizations are "getting connected." By definition, this means dealing with TCP/IP.

CHAPTER 5

The Internet Protocol: TCP/IP

Introduction

Underlying WAN technologies such as SMDS and ATM are only part of the enterprise-wide solution. Something more is needed. As with Ethernet and Token-ring, WANs need higher-order protocols to take care of routing and error checking and to interface with applications. This is the function of the so-called internetworking protocols.

TCP/IP, the best-known of these, is a suite of protocols originally developed for the Internet. It's available for literally hundreds of different computing devices, from PCs to supercomputers. Even IBM offers a version of it for its mainframes.

TCP/IP runs "on top" of everything from Ethernet to ATM. This makes it an attractive mediator when moving from one networking technology to another. It's the perfect common denominator protocol set. With heterogeneity being a characteristic of most client/server implementations, TCP/IP has become a obvious choice for tying everything together.

The problem is, many of those systems to be brought under the client/server banner already have a complete networking infrastructure in place. SPX/IPX is the dominant LAN-based protocol set, and IBM's Systems Network Architecture (SNA) has an even tighter grip on the mainframe end of things.

Supporters of these traditionally distinct environments are understandably unwilling to drop protocols they've worked with for years to jump onto the TCP/IP bandwagon. To muddy the waters even more, both Novell and IBM have made significant improvements to their protocol suites to better position them for an internetworking role. But with slow market acceptance of NetWare version 4.x, the struggle for internetworking dominance has largely been left to TCP/IP and SNA.

By some accounts, there are as many as 50,000 SNA networks out there.[1] Numbers like that have made it a de facto standard: an evolving one, as it turns out. Recognizing the shortcomings of hierarchical computing, IBM began an overhaul of SNA back in the late 1980s. Now called APPN, Advanced Peer-to-Peer Networking, it is the most sophisticated enterprise-wide networking framework yet devised, many believe. Like TCP/IP, APPN deals with the upper layers of the OSI model. But while APPN is being taken more seriously than NetWare as an internetworking alternative, it isn't doing that well either. Sales have been slow and it has yet to extend across even IBM's own product line.

The biggest strike against SPX/IPX and SNA is that they're owned by computer companies. They're proprietary. Third parties must pay a fee, often a very steep one, to Novell or IBM to have any dealings with their respective protocol suites. TCP/IP, on the other hand, resides in the public domain. Most of its code is free.

Although it's often billed as a race, the idea of "internetworking dominance" is a bit of a contradiction in terms. Internetworking doesn't involve a conversion of the masses; rather it's an exercise in adapting to what's already there. No matter how popular TCP/IP becomes as an go-between protocol, it will never completely displace either SNA or SPX/IPX in their respective environments. Client/server implementators seeking access to corporate data and to the LAN-based office productivity tools used to make sense out of it will in all likelihood have to deal with multiple protocol sets.

TCP/IP has its own traditional following as well—and usage is steadily increasing. As the basis for the Internet, it is possibly the most widely used of all the networking protocols. Their relationship is so close that it's difficult to discuss TCP/IP without also talking about the Net.

The Net

Back in 1969, the U.S. Defense Department's Advanced Research Projects Agency (ARPA) funded an experiment in information sharing. It was interested in fault-resilient communication networks able to link together the vast number of different computers used by the military. You can't easily stop a communication line from taking a hit during battle, so having more than one line seemed to be the answer. If a pathway was out of commission, "the network" would know about it and route data over an alternate route. Having many different pathways between computers also allows for the possibility of enhanced security. Rather than send a message down an available line—a line that could be tapped by the enemy—why not instead transmit pieces of the entire message down a number of different paths (and reassemble everything at the receiving end)? That way, if any line were tapped, and the intruder managed to capture the transmission, only a small bit of the whole thing would be lost. As we discussed in Chapter 4, this type of data transmission is called packet switching.

The initial ARPA experiment, ARPANET, was quite advanced for its time. It interconnected four different sites across the country, allowing them to communicate at a speed of 56 kbps. To manage the network—to monitor available routes, to bust the data up into packets, to reassemble them at the receiving end, and to ensure packets got where they were going—a suite of high-end communication protocols, called TCP/IP, was developed.

ARPA made TCP/IP available to the public at low cost. It even commissioned Bolt Beranek and Newman Inc. to develop a version of TCP/IP for the UNIX operating system—a favorite of the educational and research types who pioneered the ARPANET. Eventually TCP/IP became a part of the UNIX "package," and the two have been closely tied ever since.

Within just a few years of startup, ARPANET embraced at least 50 military and research institutions. By that time other packet-switched wide area networks were around: USENET (User's Network), CSNET (Computer Science Network), BITNET (Because It's Time Network), MILNET (a declassified version of ARPANET), and a couple of others. All ultimately were to become a part of "the Internet," or "the Net" for short.

Physically speaking, the Net is a huge network of networks. It's estimated that it connects more than 6,000 computing networks, with somewhere on the order of 300,000 to half a million computers attached to them.[2] It spans every continent. Every day approximately 20 million people access the Internet for electronic mail, file transfers, research, remote computer access, and, of course, games. Even the president and vice president have Internet addresses.

But the Net is more than a physical thing. There are several virtual aspects to it as well—which is what usually confuses most people new to the Net. Being a massive information source, virtual "spaces" have come into being that are really just different ways of looking at, and getting to, all this stuff. Gopherspace and the World Wide Web (WWW) are the two best-known virtual spaces. Thousands of Gopher servers attached to the Net define Gopherspace. The information contained on these servers is cross-indexed, allowing users to move from one server to another in search of information. The WWW is similar, except that the links between Web servers are hypertext-based. Selected terms in each Web document appear highlighted, or in a different color. Selecting these terms with a mouse takes the Net user (sometimes called an "internaut") to another Web site, possibly on a different machine, that contains information associated with the highlighted term. From there, the user might select another highlighted term to move to yet another document, and so on. This is where the analogy of Internet surfing comes from.

In 1991 the Internet was opened up to business. Before that, it was restricted to noncommercial use only. This is expected to drive up Net activity exponentially over the next couple of years. In fact, it's become a cause for concern. The Internet is running out of available addresses.[3] Averting address exhaustion (predicted to occur sometime before the end of this decade) requires a change to the basic Internet communication protocol, TCP/IP. Such a change is currently under consideration.

Amazingly, no one actually owns the Internet. It's entirely run by groups of volunteers. One such group, based at Stanford University, accepts and manages Requests for Comments (RFCs) from members of the Internet user community. These RFCs often deal with suggested enhancements to the Internet and its operating protocols. They're available for anyone to review and comment upon. In this way, the Internet serves as a live, daily proving ground for the TCP/IP protocol suite.

TCP/IP from the Ground Up

Figure 5.1 contains a layer-by-layer comparison of the OSI model and TCP/IP. TCP/IP can operate over any transmission medium specified by the DataLink layer protocols. This includes copper, fiber, and even wireless. At the DataLink layer, TCP/IP is content to use Ethernet, Token

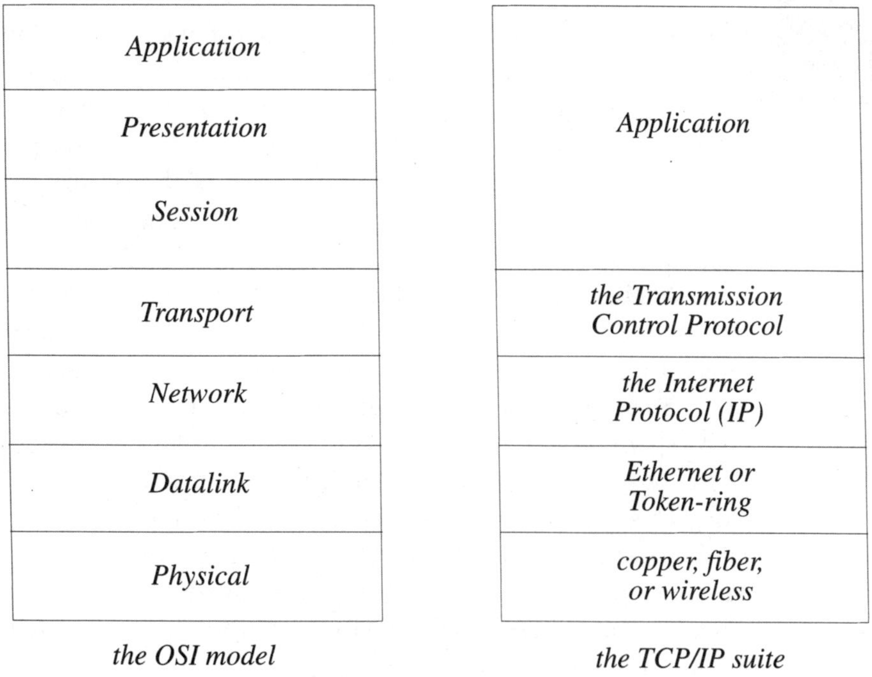

the OSI model	the TCP/IP suite
Application	*Application*
Presentation	
Session	
Transport	*the Transmission Control Protocol*
Network	*the Internet Protocol (IP)*
Datalink	*Ethernet or Token-ring*
Physical	*copper, fiber, or wireless*

Figure 5.1 The OSI model and the TCP/IP protocol stack.

Ring FDDI, and a host of wide area networking technologies. It's so often partnered with Ethernet, however, that sometimes it seems odd to see one without the other.

As you'll recall from Chapter 2, Ethernet follows a branching bus topology that doesn't contain any loops. (Although, as more sites install cheaper, unshielded twisted pair, a physical star network often is preferred. It's still a virtual bus though.) Ethernet features a data transmission scheme known as Carrier Sense Multiple Access—with Collision Detection (CSMA/CD).

Every single Ethernet transceiver has a unique (factory-stamped) 48-bit address. When a message is sent, both the sender's and receiver's address are attached to the data before it's put out onto the network. This, of course, isn't done in some random fashion—certain rules (protocols) are observed in building Ethernet messages. The maximum allowable size of an Ethernet transmission is 1,536 octets. (An octet is eight bits.) This isn't really very large, so before most messages can be sent, they

CLOSE-UP

Multiprotocol routers

Multiprotocol routers are the top dogs of the information-moving business. These devices deliver data frames to networks running different protocols and select the fastest or cheapest way to do it. Many can route data from one physical network type to another: Ethernet copper to FDDI fiber, that kind of thing. At a high level, routers fall into three categories: high level (all the bells and whistles) mid, and low level.

Low-level routers are the least capable, but they're also the cheapest. The problem is, unless you have a very small internetwork, you're going to need at least a few of the more expensive high-level types as well. They're the "smartest." Being also the most expensive, they're used sparingly.

Changes are coming to the router business. With the rise in popularity of switches, networks are shifting from the "party-line" model of the past. As we saw in Chapter 2, Ethernet switching is rapidly becoming a preferred technique of inexpensively increasing bandwidth. There are also pressures from ATM to consider packet switching over packet routing.

must first be broken into chunks of 1,536 octets or smaller. Ethernet people call these chunks of information "frames." At the receiving end, the frames are reassembled into the original (complete) message.

A TCP/IP internetwork often is built out of Ethernet cable segments, repeaters for segment extension, bridges for connecting Ethernets, routers for converting and transferring data packets, and gateways for protocol conversion. Routers form the framework for the TCP/IP internetwork. Frames are shunted along from router to router until they reach one at the periphery of the destination node. (Routers can be likened to windows onto a LAN.) If the sending node and the destination node are on the same TCP/IP LAN, it's easy. And thanks to the "Internet Protocol Address," it's not a big problem even if they're not.

The Internet Protocol

Assume for a moment that we have an internetwork composed of both Ethernets and Token-rings. Although both are packet-switched, they don't use the same addressing scheme; Token-ring cards don't carry unique Ethernet addresses and vice-versa. So how do we transmit data frames over our internetwork and make sure they get to the intended destination? Answer: by establishing a neutral, intermediate data packet and addressing scheme. This is the essence of internetworking.

Although the distinction is not rigorously observed in the business, we should distinguish between frames and packets. Frames are the bit groupings that actually traverse the network. The is the job of Ethernet, Token-ring, or FDDI. Packets are a higher-layer concept. They are enveloped by the frame. The idea is illustrated in Figure 5.2.

As the frame is converted from an Ethernet format to a Token-ring one, the TCP/IP packet is preserved.

Figure 5.2 The TCP/IP packet is preserved through the gateway.

The neutral addressing scheme is known as the IP address and is a part of the Internet Protocol (that's what IP stands for), corresponding to the network layer of the OSI model. This layer, you may recall, deals with packet routing between known entities on the network. IP addresses identify machines on the network regardless of their native networking persuasion.

Actually, IP addressing goes beyond this somewhat. It contains an address not only for a particular machine, but also for the network that the machine resides on. It is supposed to be an internetworking protocol, after all.

The IP is said to be an unreliable, connectionless packet delivery system. When you hear this for the first time, this statement doesn't inspire a lot of confidence. Actually, it's nothing to be worried about. It's simply a statement of fact. IP doesn't guarantee the delivery of packets. As far as it's concerned, that's someone (well, some*thing*, really) else's job. Connectionless means that the data packets aren't connected—how about that? We've talked about this kind of thing before. Both Ethernet and Token Ring, for example, place limits on the amount of data that can be stuffed into a frame. If a message is larger than that limit, it has to be broken up into pieces before it's sent. And those frames can be sent, and even arrive, in any order. Each one has enough identifying information to reconstruct the original message on the receiving end. The same thing happens with the higher-level data packets. This may seem a little redundant at first, but it permits TCP/IP to run over a number of different lower-level protocols.

IP Addressing

TCP/IP networks and internetworks follow an addressing scheme that was laid out originally by the people who manage and operate the Internet. If you use TCP/IP and never intend to link up to the Internet, you don't need to worry about applying for an Internet address. You can use anything you want. But you still have to follow the basic addressing format, however.

IP addresses are 32 bits long. And of this 32 bits, a number of distinct four octet combinations are possible. The particular one used reflects the type of internetwork an organization intends to deploy.

One combination describes an internetwork with only a few networks and many host machines; another, just the opposite. These different options are referred to by class name: A to E. Only the first three seem to be used, though. Using "N" for network, and "H" for host, the class addresses can be written like this:

Class A: N.H.H.H.
Class B: N.N.H.H.
Class C: N.N.N.H.

As shown here, IP uses a "dot notation." Each class is identified by a leading flag bit, or bits; class A is denoted by a leading 0; B by two leading bits: 1 and 0; and class C, by three leading bits: 1,1,0. These class-indicator bits actually become part of the (internetwork) address. Invoking a bit of binary arithmetic, we can compute the lowest class B address to be:

1 0 0 0 0 0 0 0.0.H.H., or, 128.0.H.H. in decimal form

Being in the middle of the three commonly used IP address classes, class B tends to be a favorite. Through a similar approach, the largest possible class B internetwork address is:

1 0 1 1 1 1 1 1.1 1 1 1 1 1 1 1.H.H.

in binary, or 191.256.H.H. in decimal. If an organization intends to connect to the Internet, it must apply to the Internet authorities for the N.N. portion of the address (assuming it is using a class B addressing scheme). This leaves the host portion, which is left up to the Internet applicant. But if connection is not planned, the organization can do what it wants. The problem is that it's becoming common—especially these days—for someone later to get the idea of connecting to the Internet. Then changing all the addresses around can be a headache.

While there are two octets are available for the host address, by convention, most use the first byte to address a subnetwork (LAN), leaving eight bits to identify any of 256 possible hosts on that LAN.

To get a clearer understanding of how all this works in practice, let's consider an example. Subnets 20 and 21 (two LANs) are linked to an internetwork backbone. (See Figure 5.3.) The backbone (which itself is actually treated as a LAN) is identified as subnet 2. A router stands between each LAN and the backbone. As internetwork entities, routers possess two addresses: one for the port to the LAN side and another for the port to the backbone. All nodes on a TCP/IP net can perform some degree of routing. They can all get packets moving, at least. To do anything beyond that requires a full-fledged router. As we saw earlier, routers come in various flavors. The LAN router that interfaces LAN 20 and the backbone, for example, might not be particularly sophisticated—limited functionality might be sufficient here. But no matter what type of router you use, they all need information on what to do with frames when they get them. For this, they turn to their routing tables. Returning to our example, let's assume that host 136.28.20.11 wants to send data to host 136.28.21.2. The routing table on the LAN 20 router, the first stop on the way, would look something like this:

136.28.2.0	136.28.2.60	1
136.28.21.0	136.28.2.60	2
0.0.0.0	136.28.2.61	1
136.28.20.0	136.28.20.33	1

The first line tells the router that to get to the backbone (136.28.2.0), packets should be routed through IP address 136.28.2.60 (the router port facing the backbone). The number "1" following that address is the "hop count"—the number of routers that need to be traversed to get to this destination. It's used in determining optimal routing paths. The next entry in the table tells the router what to do with packets destined for LAN 21. To get to that destination, they have to pass two routers. The third line supports the notion of an internetwork router hierarchy. Top-of-the-line routers are expensive—they should be used prudently. Our little internetwork has only one, which serves as the default. Any packets that the low-end, LAN 20 router doesn't know what to do with are sent there. That's what the zeros mean—anything unknown goes to port 136.28.2.61. That device will figure out what to do with it. The last line tells the router how to handle any packets destined for LAN 20. Routing is a two-way street.

Back to our example, the LAN 20 router intercepts frames addressed to LAN 21. Accessing its router table, it will "see" that to get to there,

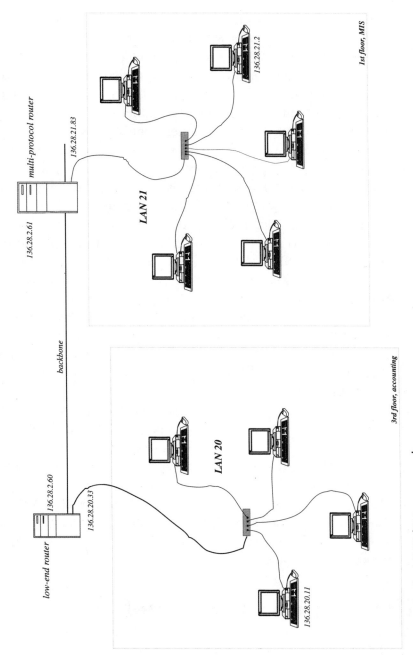

multi-protocol router

136.28.2.61

136.28.21.83

LAN 21

136.28.21.2

1st floor, MIS

backbone

low-end router

136.28.2.60

136.28.20.33

LAN 20

136.28.20.11

3rd floor, accounting

Figure 5.3 A TCP/IP internetwork.

they should be sent to IP address 136.28.2.61. That router's table will contain information about what to do next.

Routers, especially the high-end (multiprotocol) kind, spend a lot of their free time talking to each other: the status of the internetwork, who's where, that kind of stuff. This is how they keep their tables up-to-date. This is the responsibility of another protocol also sitting at the network layer called ICMP (Internet Control Message Protocol). ICMP messages also are issued when network problems, such as unreachable ports or network congestion, occur. This is all accompanied by a performance hit, but this interchange is necessary, especially in situations where network topologies are highly changeable.

The task of routing itself is performed by a subprotocol of IP. There are actually two possibilities here. The older, and still more widely used, is called RIP, the Routing Information Protocol. It was assumed in our example. RIP just uses the hop count to compute the best route from A to B. It's pretty simple. The newer routing algorithm being used in TCP/IP is the Open Shortest Path First (OSPF). OSPF also can account for the speed of certain data links. A 56 kbps data link is substantially slower than, say, an Ethernet one. If the two represent alternative pathways to an end point, clearly, you'd prefer to use the Ethernet link, if it is available.

As we've discussed, IP addresses and the data to be sent to the destination node are assembled into packets. Then they're stuffed into Ethernet (Token-ring, or whatever) frames for actual transmission across the network. Because there are two addresses, an Ethernet address and an IP address, some way of relating the two is required. That's handled by a special service to the Internet Protocol called ARP: Address Resolution Protocol. (See Figure 5.4.) When a transmitting host needs a physical address, ARP broadcasts: "What's the Ethernet address corresponding to IP address X.X.X.X?"

Addressing on the Internet

Rather than use a cryptic numbering scheme, aliases can be substituted for TCP/IP addresses to make them a bit easier to use and remember. Still following a dot notation, the address has two parts: a user name and a domain name. The two are separated by an "@" sign. The domain

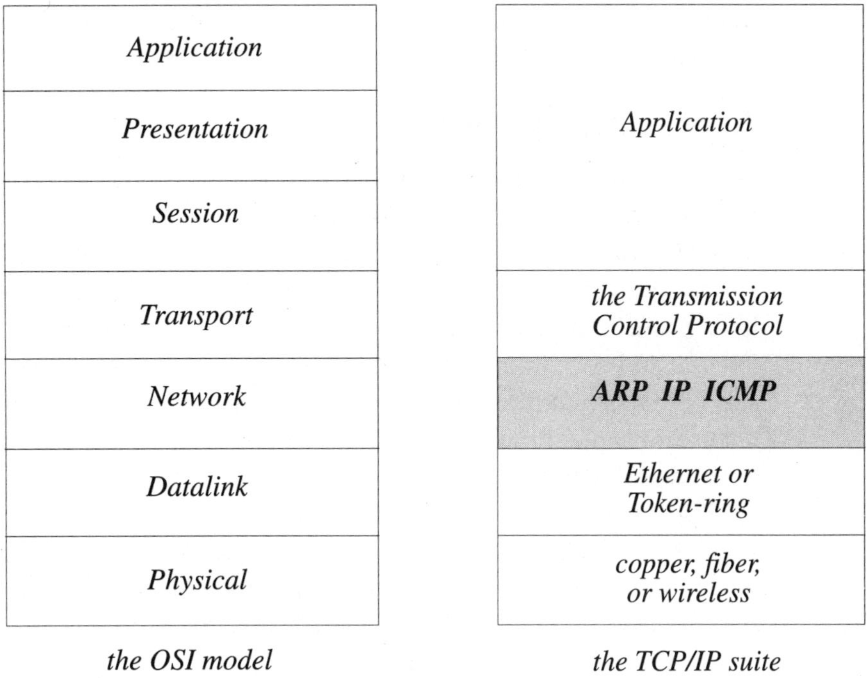

Application	*Application*
Presentation	
Session	
Transport	*the Transmission Control Protocol*
Network	**ARP IP ICMP**
Datalink	*Ethernet or Token-ring*
Physical	*copper, fiber, or wireless*
the OSI model	*the TCP/IP suite*

Figure 5.4 The TCP/IP network layer.

name includes such things as the computer name and the type of institution that houses it. The institution type is signified by the last few letters of the alias. A few of the common ones are:

COM	commercial organization
EDU	educational institution
GOV	government agency (nonmilitary)
MIL	military government site
xx	two-letter country codes

There can be sublevels within the domain name as well. They commonly include the name of the organization and departments within it. For example,

Aperson@blinky.mis.somecompany.com

"Aperson" is the user name. They have an account on a computer called blinky in the MIS department of "somecompany": a commercial organization. You'll often see colorful computer names like this on the

Internet. But remember, this is just an alias. The actual IP address would be something like 132.12.86.9.

Accessing the Net

There are three ways to connect to the Internet: directly link to an Internet host computer, dial in to an Internet host computer, or dial in to an Internet access service provider (an ISP). Universities and large corporations doing a lot of business on the Net often opt for a direct link. These links are permanent and, if open to the public, become an integral and contributing part of the Internet itself. Connections like this can be expensive though. They require medium- to high-speed WAN links, and someone must be assigned to administer Internet traffic and to oversee security practices.

For less-frequent, and hence cheaper, access, there are dial-in services. Depending on how these operate, the dialing device either will be a full Internet peer or not. This is important; if the device is not a full Internet peer, only a subset of possible Internet services are available.

Running TCP/IP is generally a requisite for full Internet peer status. A remote device, supporting either SLIP (the Serial Line Interface Protocol) or PPP (the Point-to-Point Protocol) and running TCP/IP, can dial into an Internet-connected host—either a private one or one belonging to an Internet service provider—for direct access. Additionally, if the accessing device is running Microsoft Windows, an Application Programming Interface (API) generically referred to as a Winsock is necessary. Microsoft's Windows 95 will contain a Winsock. (See Chapter 8 for more on Windows 95.) It manages the interface between Windows and TCP/IP.

SLIP is an older protocol designed to allow remote devices to use TCP/IP over serial lines. Although it's widely implemented, it's currently being replaced with PPP. PPP was created through the Internet Request for Comments process—the open "cyberforum" in which members of the Internet community submit technical suggestions and review those of others. PPP is more versatile than SLIP. It can, for example, work with other OSI network-layer protocols such as IPX. It also has better facilities for error control.

Indirect Internet dial-up services are very popular. There are all kinds of them. CompuServe, Prodigy, and America Online all provide limited Internet services. (Actually, at last look, CompuServe provided quite extensive Internet services. It now offers access to the World Wide Web, for example. But to do this, a more direct form of link is required: Clients need to run TCP/IP, the networking language of the Net.) Since the accessing device generally doesn't need to run the TCP/IP protocol stack, indirect dial-up Internet access is the easiest connection option and creates less worry about security too. With dial-on-demand Internet access (and that includes PPP and SLIP connections), there's no permanently addressed Internet node for intruders to hack into. That threat's borne by the ISP.

The Transmission Control Protocol

IP takes care of packet routing. It's left up to the Transmission Control Protocol (TCP), another protocol higher up in the stack, to make sure packets actually get to where they're going.

When a packet reaches its target application, TCP, on the receiver end, issues an acknowledgment saying it was received. If the sender fails to receive an acknowledgment, it knows something went wrong so it retransmits the unacknowledged frame. But how long should TCP wait, on the receiving end, before declaring a frame to be lost? The protocol uses a statistical technique to estimate what a reasonable round-trip send/acknowledge time should be. But there's a little more to it than this.

Following a send-and-wait-to-get-acknowledgment approach would not work well for internetworking over large distances. This very behavior often is pointed to as a shortcoming of NetWare's SPX/IPX, you may recall. Instead, TCP doesn't actually wait for an acknowledgment before sending the next frame. It fires it off immediately. Then the next. As TCP can send and receive at the same time, when the first acknowledgment finally comes in, TCP on the sender side computes a "data send window" (the number of frames that can be sent before an acknowledgment should be received). When acknowledgments start taking longer than this period, TCP assumes network congestion and reduces the window to compensate.

To get something, often you must give up something. So it is in networking as well. TCP provides this level of reliability at the expense of network overhead. All that acknowledging uses up some of the available bandwidth. When combined with all the checking that lower-level protocols such as Ethernet and Token Ring do, and the overhead can become a bit of a concern.

Not all applications may require this same degree of care. Some designers may be willing to compromise somewhat in return for enhanced performance. For these applications, the User Defined Protocol (UDP) exists. (See Figure 5.5.) UDP is a peer protocol to TCP and is designed to exchange small pieces of data quickly and, alas, unreliably. For it to work, the applications using this alternative transport protocol somehow must contend with data transmission issues. In some respects, UDP provides little beyond the basic IP services that it stands upon.

This brings us to the application layer of the TCP/IP protocol stack.

The Application Layer

The upper three layers of the OSI model are represented by several application-specific protocols in the TCP/IP stack. Five main ones are a part of most TCP/IP installations: the Simple Mail Transfer Protocol (SMTP), the File Transfer Protocol (FTP), Telnet, the Simple Network Management Protocol (SNMP) and the Network File System (NFS). (See Figure 5.6.)

SMTP is a bare-bones e-mail utility. Concerned only with the transmission of messages between two hosts, it uses TCP for reliable store and forward data transfer. If a delivery fails, transmission time is recorded, and, after some suitable wait period, the system tries again. SMTP comes with a language that contains only 14 commands (HELLO, MAIL, QUIT...), and it doesn't even have an editor. But in spite of all this, it's one of the most popular e-mail services around; it's used by hundreds of thousands of people every day on the Internet. Also it often serves as a foundation for other, more sophisticated e-mail offerings.

FTP is another popular application-level protocol. It allows users to transfer files from a remote host regardless of that host's hardware design or even operating system. It can be used interactively, provided the user has a password on the remote device, or in a batch style by programs, as per its original design. When used interactively, the user

the OSI model
Application
Presentation
Session
Transport
Network
Datalink
Physical

the TCP/IP suite
Application
TCP UDP
ARP IP ICMP
Ethernet or Token-ring
copper, fiber, or wireless

the OSI model   *the TCP/IP suite*

Figure 5.5 The TCP/IP transport layer.

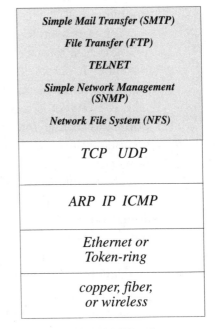

the OSI model
Application
Presentation
Session
Transport
Network
Datalink
Physical

the TCP/IP suite
Simple Mail Transfer (SMTP) / *File Transfer (FTP)* / *TELNET* / *Simple Network Management (SNMP)* / *Network File System (NFS)*
TCP UDP
ARP IP ICMP
Ethernet or Token-ring
copper, fiber, or wireless

the OSI model   *the TCP/IP suite*

Figure 5.6 The TCP/IP application layers.

101

logs on to the remote system and then traverses the file hierarchy on the remote host with basic UNIX-like commands—even if the remote OS isn't UNIX. The user then identifies the files for transfer, and FTP handles all file format conversion. A growing number of graphical tools, for good or bad, buffer the user from raw FTP. CompuServe, for example, offers members a pseudographical FTP facility for Internet access. The File Transfer Protocol is one of the more complex protocols within the TCP/IP family. It uses two TCP connections: one to pass commands and another to pass data.

FTP often is used to transfer files over the Internet. Housed on servers scattered across the Net are literally terabytes of information (text, executables, and graphics for practically every machine type)—much of it free. To get it, you use a special incarnation of FTP called "anonymous FTP." These special server areas don't require a dedicated user account and password. Using "anonymous" as the account name and "guest" as the password, users can access these devices, locate files, and download them to their computers (using FTP). Internet interfaces provided by many Internet service providers automate logon to remote anonymous FTP sites.

Telnet is a protocol for virtual terminal operation. It allows a user to log onto a remote host and proceed as if seated in front of that very machine. It passes keystrokes from one machine to another. It's not exactly a terminal emulator, however; Telnet is a bit more than that. Like FTP, Telnet is receiving increased attention because of the rise in popularity of the Internet. Internet users commonly telnet to remote computers in order to take advantage of that device's extra compute power.

The Simple Network Management Protocol, SNMP, is used to manage remote devices on an internetwork. Unlike the previously mentioned protocols, it uses the UDP, not TCP. SNMP traps performance statistics of hosts, routers, and other networked entities, which can be reviewed by the internetwork administrator. SNMP has been embraced by many host and router vendors as the de facto network management protocol—for both UNIX and non-UNIX operating systems alike.

Hundreds of network products currently support SNMP. NetWare, AppleTalk, and DECnet networks all now include SNMP support. Surprisingly, the protocol itself is free. Originally developed at the University of Tennessee, it's been placed in the public domain. Vendor-neutrality and its basic simplicity have made SNMP *the* internetwork management protocol.

The Network File System (NFS), another of TCP/IP's application-layer protocols, was introduced by Sun Microsystems in 1985. It's used to create a distributed file system that is both machine and operating system independent. Like SNMP, it too uses UDP instead of TCP for its operation.

Once exclusively a denizen of the UNIX operating system, NFS is now available on more than 100 different platforms. Like a NetWare file server, it makes files of remote computers appear as if they are attached to the user's own local machine. The user wouldn't know where the files physically resided.

Internet Applications

Beyond these basic applications, common to most TCP/IP installations, several additional ones were designed specifically to help users find their way around the Internet. Most run in a client/server fashion. For example, "Archie" (a name adapted from the word "archive") is a huge indexing and file-finding facility that runs on a series of servers distributed around the Net.

Archie actually can be run in three different ways. (See Figure 5.7.) Most commonly, a traditional (remote) client/server arrangement is followed, with the Archie client residing on the desktop device and the Archie server geographically remote. Alternatively, users can telnet directly to a known Archie server and run the service locally, although this still constitutes a client/server application. Finally, Archie even can be accessed over e-mail. This isn't widely done, however.

Archie is used in one of two ways. If you know the file name you're looking for but don't know where it's located you can query an Archie server to find it for you. Alternatively, if you don't know the file name you're after, you can ask Archie to review its database to look for any that contain a specific sequence of letters in their names. Archie keeps information on both files and directories in its database, so a search for the string "startrek", for example, will return both files and directories with that "word" in their names. You could then FTP to any of the listed sites to browse and download files. Many ISP Archie clients combine

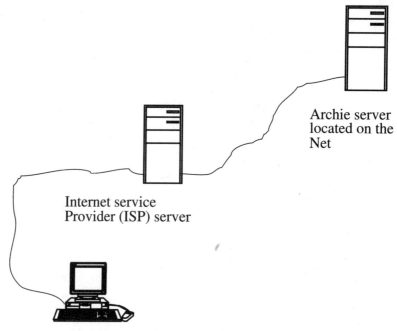

Archie server
located on the
Net

Internet service
Provider (ISP) server

1. desktop Archie client
2. telnet to Archie server
3. e-mail access to Archie server

Figure 5.7 Three ways to access an Archie server.

Archie with FTP so that users can directly download any files that Archie
returns after a search.

Although Archie is of great help in locating files, it doesn't know
anything about the content of the files themselves. Searches are strictly
performed on file and directory names. If a particular file you're interested in hasn't been given a name indicative of its contents, Archie
can't help you. Also, Archie limits its database listings to files stored in
anonymous FTP sites. If a particular file isn't located in that area of a
server, you're out of luck.

Archie is very popular. And since Archie servers limit the number of
clients that can access them simultaneously, during peak hours (7 A.M.
to 7 P.M.) the program either will be very slow or you'll be denied access
altogether. To get around this, you can direct your Archie query to an
server located elsewhere on the Net that's in a time zone outside of these
core hours. Table 5.1 lists several of the more popular ones. Overall,

Table 5.1 Some Popular Archie Servers

Server Alias	Server IP Address	Country
archie.sura.net	128.167.254.179	U.S.A. (Maryland)
archie.rutgers.ed	128.6.18.15	U.S.A. (New Jersey)
archie.doc.ic.ac.uk	146.169.11.3	United Kingdom (England)
archie.au	139.130.4.6	Australia
archie.unl.edu	129.93.1.14	U.S.A. (Nebraska)

approximately 15 publicly available Archie servers are on the Net. Each is responsible for interrogating the contents of anonymous FTP sites on its own specific list of servers and maintaining its own database. In spite of this, the information listed in the different databases is more or less the same, although there are some differences.

Another useful Internet tool—one that also adheres to the client/server model—is WAIS: Wide Area Information Server. WAIS is a textual information hunter. With it, users can perform full text searches on reams of textual information held in numerous databases on the Net.

To use WAIS, a user issues a keyword search that the WAIS client passes along to a WAIS server. If successful, it returns a hit list of matches, scored out of 1,000, from most relevant to least. Some refer to WAIS as a "tunable fishing net." A user selects a WAIS server and then performs a keyword search to see what that dredges up. If too much information (or too little) surfaces, a different search term is tried.

The biggest problem in using WAIS is finding the right WAIS server to access. There are hundreds of them—each associated with different data stores. And there's really no way to know what's on them beforehand. Some Internet interface software simplifies things by providing users with menus to guide the search. Users who wanted to learn more about WAIS, for example, might start with Technology, drill down to Computers, and zero in on a WAIS server containing information on Internet services (called Internet Services).

Archie and WAIS are the workhorses for seasoned internauts sifting the Net for research materials. But two other applications—Gopher and the World Wide Web—fire the imagination of the general public. Both are really just ways of structuring and indexing information, however. Gopherspace is a massive cross-indexed, traversable list of lists of information (executables, text, graphics, sound) scattered around the Net.

As users move from topic to topic, they move from server to server around the world.

Gopherspace consists of thousands of Gopher servers. Each contains (menus of) information relevant to local interests in addition to information of a more generic nature. Some are information-oriented, others focus on services. Most contain links to other Gopher servers. Figure 5.8 shows the menu contents of the popular panda Gopher server at the University of Iowa.

When users start up a Gopher client on their system, it points to the menu list on the client's default Gopher server. From there, the users can move to other Gopher servers as they literally "surf" the Net. If, on the other hand, you are looking for specific information, moving from Gopher server to Gopher server isn't very efficient. For this, there's another Internet application called Veronica, an acronym for—are you ready for this?—Very Easy Rodent-Oriented Net-wide Index to Computerized Archives. Is it possible that they started with the acronym first and worked backward?

Veronica can perform keyword searches of the menus of most Gopher servers in Gopherspace. A search returns a list of relevant Gopher sites, to which users can move directly, in order to take a firsthand look at the information.

First Archie, now Veronica. All we need is Jughead. Well, he's immortalized on the Net too; Jughead (Jonzy's Universal Gopher Hierarchy Excavation and Display) is a localized version of Veronica that performs a keyword search of local Gopherspace.

Gopher sites have become so popular that a few years back, someone decided to package a group of the favorites into something known as the Gopher Jewels. The Gopher Jewels is an alphabetized list of Gopher sites containing topics that range from Agriculture to Travel information. Many Internet front ends have direct entries for the Gopher Jewels.

Gopher introduced the world to the notion of Internet surfing, but the World Wide Web (WWW) really got the ball rolling. The WWW is a virtual space of thousands of WWW servers scattered across the Net. These servers contain all sorts of information, from text to video. Unlike Gopher, the Web organizes information through hyperlinks instead of menus. A hyperlink is a physical association between electronic documents. Just like in MS Windows Help, selected terms of a hyper-

panda.uiowa.edu (128.255.40.201)

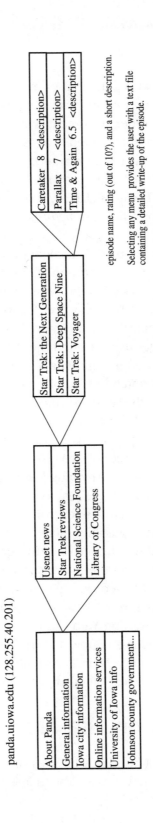

| About Panda |
| General information |
| Iowa city information |
| Online information services |
| University of Iowa info |
| Johnson county government… |

| Usenet news |
| Star Trek reviews |
| National Science Foundation |
| Library of Congress |

| Star Trek: the Next Generation |
| Star Trek: Deep Space Nine |
| Star Trek: Voyager |

Caretaker	8	<description>
Parallax	7	<description>
Time & Again	6.5	<description>

episode name, rating (out of 10?), and a short description.

Selecting any menu provides the user with a text file containing a detailed write-up of the episode.

(not all menu entries shown)

Figure 5.8 The University of Iowa's "Panda" Gopher menus.

107

text document appear highlighted or in a different color (or otherwise marked). Selecting these terms with a mouse or other pointing device takes the user to another document, which itself may have hypertext links to other documents (called "pages" in Web-speak). Linked documents may very well reside on another Web server geographically distant from each other. Web servers, or sites, are identified by their Universal Resource Locators (URLs), Web-specific addresslike designations that take the form http://*something*. (http stands for the Hypertext Transfer Protocol.)

Like most Internet navigational applications, the WWW is also client/server based. To get around it, users require client software, generically referred to as a Web browser. Lynx is one of the most widely used of these. But it's a text-only Web browser. Many hypertext-based applications are graphical in nature, and the Web is no exception. While Lynx will certainly get users around the Web, to really take advantage of all the Web has to offer, you need a graphical brower.

There are three contending graphical Web browsers: Cello, the first of this breed; Mosaic, the standard; and Netscape, the emerging favorite. Netscape has captured top honors by streamlining Web usage. While graphics and sound clips can make using the Web more interesting, it also makes it slow—especially if you're accessing the Net via an ISP over a 14,400 bps modem. (Anything less than that, forget it.) Netscape allows Web users to read the text content of Web pages while the graphics and additional stuff is en route to the client. Text traverses the Net a lot faster than graphics (simply because it's a lot smaller), so waving the text on through, ahead of the graphics, means users don't have to wait as long to get the information they're after. Netscape also caches the last few accessed Web pages in local memory. So as users navigate the Web, they don't have to wait as long after backtracking out a tangentially interesting Web site.

The Web is attracting people to the Net like never before. And where's there people, there's the possibility of selling something. Businesses are falling over each other to get onto the Web.

Doing Business on the Net

The list of businesses fielding Web sites has taken a virtual 90 degree upswing in the last few years. You name them, they've got a site.

Big and small, the list of represented companies (currently in the tens of thousands) is astounding. In fact, small companies find getting on the Net especially beneficial; big companies can afford television and national radio campaigns, but on the Net, everyone's equal. For a small investment (as little as $100!), companies (or just average citizens, for that matter) can put up a WWW "home page."

Most commercial Web sites are informative only, but a growing number are actually conducting business transactions right over the Net. This is where companies such as First Virtual Holdings (800.570.0003) come in. Their First Virtual Internet Payment System provides a secure, on-line environment. It does this by not (that's not) using the Net for

CLOSE-UP

Should your organization be on the Net?

It's intoxicating: navigating about the Internet in search of amusing tidbits of information. One moment you're at a Web site in Australia, then you effortlessly slip onto another in Japan. It's certainly entertaining, but is it good for business? To put this another way, should your organization be on the Net? And if so, to what degree? E-mail is the most-used application on the Net. It's a useful tool for interacting with people outside of the range of your own organization's communication services. But clearly, this isn't something everyone in your organization needs. What about a Web home page? This is useful, from an advertising perspective, but it's still early in the game to use the Net for business transactions (although some are doing so). While you can set up your own Internet server for a relatively small fee ($10,000 or so—not including the cost of the device itself), Web sites can be indirectly procured from an Internet "cybermall." Not only will these agencies rent you space on their Web servers, but many will even design and create your home pages for you (for an additional fee, of course) as well. As for research needs, in many cases data stores on the Internet are helpful, but a lot of what's on the Net can be best described as junk. Often even a lot of the relevant stuff is dated. When you add all this up, it makes a strong argument for an indirect (dial-on-demand) Internet link for a chosen few—especially when you weigh in security threats that come with a permanent, on-site Internet address.

actual credit card exchanges. Instead, transacting parities are registered with First Virtual by telephone ($2 fee for buyers, $10 for sellers). When buyers register over the phone, their credit card is recorded and kept in a database that's not directly tied to the Net in any way. To buy a product on-line, a customer fires a message off to First Virtual, where it performs authorizations behind the scenes, taking a 2 percent slice of the purchase price of the product in the process.[4]

In addition, a consortium of companies is proposing a revision to the Hypertext Transfer Protocol (http) that will allow for the inclusion of various cryptographic schemes. Known as S-HTTP, the Mosaic 2.0 Web browser is already incorporating this feature. Encryption, while secure, requires management, however. Both the sender and receiver have to possess and use the same algorithm and be able to get at each other's keys. It can be kind of messy. We'll take a closer look at data encryption in Chapter 10.

In spite of these efforts, many feel that the Net isn't ready to support financial transactions—and won't be for several years to come. It's going to take more than the effort of just a couple of companies to make the Internet a secure place to conduct business.

Internet Security

In its "as-is" form, the Internet is not a secure environment. Practically every large organization with a direct Internet link has been broken into at one time or another. Some downplay this by suggesting that companies with a large Internet exposure simply have a higher probability of getting hit. Perhaps, but what's alarming security managers these days is the nature of the attacks. A few years ago, most hackers were largely joyriders who broke into commercial systems just for the fun of it. Now, it appears, hackers are becoming more professional—they're in it for the money. As an indication of just how serious this has become, there are reports that foreign intelligence agencies have turned their talents to corporate espionage and Net hacking in order to gain competitive advantage for companies that employ their citizens.

The threats are many, but one of the latest is something called "IP spoofing." In 1995 hackers got into Stanford University by forging the IP source addresses of data packets. Changing the IP address in most systems that use TCP/IP is actually quite easy. Changing it to one that's internal to an organization and therefore known, and trusted, can give no cause for alarm to ill-configured Internet "firewalls" charged with keeping undesirable traffic on the other side of the fence. This is exactly what happened in Stanford's case. Once inside, hackers were able to commandeer the computing center for several hours.

Firewalls are a hot topic these days. (Sorry about that.) Usually they're routers that can filter IP addresses, discarding any deemed undesirable. (See Figure 5.9.) Spoofing has forced organizations to revisit their definition for desirability; now trusted (internally sourced) packets don't qualify if they come from the outside. There's a growing concern that routers alone aren't sufficient to protect adequately against hackers. Full-blown, computer-assisted routers can not only filter packets but log activity and trip alarms as well. Routers alone can be programmed to allow for the two-way flow of traffic or customized to block all inbound access. We'll revisit firewalls in Chapter 10, when discussing client/server security.

Before we conclude this chapter, we should spend a little time talking about IBM's contender for internetworking dominance: APPN. Many believe that APPN is technically superior to TCP/IP. Whether true or not, it's kind of beside the point these days, with customers snapping up TCP/IP-related products like never before. But the subject is particularly relevant to those of you with existing SNA implementations, since APPN undoubtedly will make at least some presence felt there. And if a mainframe is destined to be a part of any of your client/server systems,

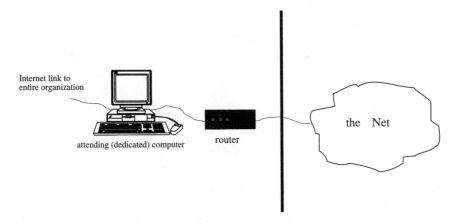

Figure 5.9 A firewall.

you'll need to become familiar with at least the basics of mainframe communications, no matter which internetworking protocol is chosen. But first, a bit of background.

Classical SNA

When IBM introduced SNA back in 1974, it reduced its growing inventory of mainframe access methods to just one: VTAM (Virtual Telecommunications Access Method). VTAM is software that makes a mainframe a mainframe. But SNA did more than that.

SNA also "filtered" mainframe communications through a front-end processor (often referred to as a "FEP"). In the pre-SNA era, such devices existed, but they were limited in what they could do. The newer, more capable FEPs represented a step toward distributed computing. These gatekeepers to the mainframe handle tasks such as error recovery, through the introduction of a software package known as the Network Control Program (NCP). This frees up the mainframe for other, more pressing matters. Early FEPs carried easy-to-remember (not) monikers such as "3704" and "3705". The latest device in this line is the 37XX Communications Controller. Figure 5.10 depicts SNA in its traditional form.

The System 370 (308X, 3090) and now, the newer System 390 (ES/9000) flaunt their mainframeness via the VTAM program. In front of them usually sit 37XX communications controllers, the heir to the 370X line. Connected to the 37XX are two peripheral devices, or "nodes": a 3770 and a 3274 (or 3174). The 3770 is SNA's device for Remote Job Entry (RJE). RJE is used for unattended mainframe batch processing. The 3770 does such things as data compression to reduce line charges associated with a batch upload or download. The 3274 is a "cluster controller." It's a connection point for as many as 32 printers or interactive terminals, such as the IBM 3278 (old "green screen" terminal). PCs also can be connected to a 3274 controller using coaxial cable and 3278 emulation software like IRMA; one such micro/mainframe interface is marketed by Digital Communications Associates. The latest device in the 3274 line is the 3174. (For some reason, the designation goes backward for the newer controllers.) It sometimes goes by the rather grand title of Enterprise Controller.

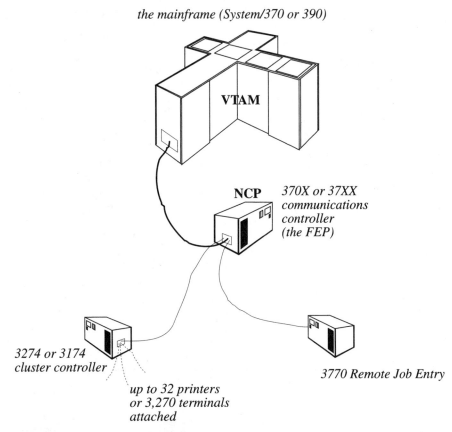

the mainframe (System/370 or 390)

VTAM

NCP 370X or 37XX
communications
controller
(the FEP)

3274 or 3174
cluster controller

up to 32 printers
or 3,270 terminals
attached

3770 Remote Job Entry

Figure 5.10 A typical SNA implementation.

In most organizations, PCs are locally networked. So rather than
have each also directly linked to a cluster controller to provide mainframe access, a PC gateway is commonly used. (See Figure 5.11.) This
device is able to imitate a 3274 cluster controller and often supports
synchronous modem communication to a remote mainframe as well.

To make this work, each of the nodes on the LAN needs to be
equipped with 3270 emulation software too. The gateway PC, outfitted
with special host-session management software, can usually juggle up to
64 concurrent sessions. Token-Ring LANs also can be directly attached
to the FEP, providing yet another avenue for LAN-to-mainframe access.
No matter how it's done though, the end-user stations end up emulating
3270 (or 3770) terminals in order to communicate with the mainframe.
In this arrangement, the desktop station has two distinct identities. On

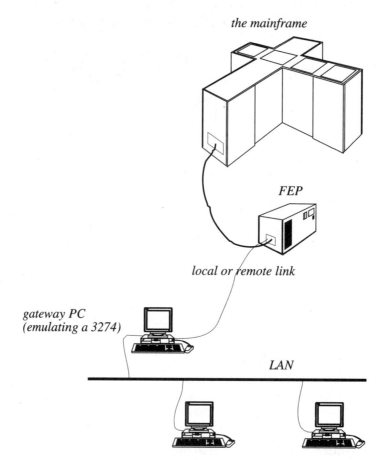

Figure 5.11 LAN-to-mainframe access.

one hand, it's used to create and send e-mail, compose documents, analyze financial data, write computer code, and all the other things we do with our networked PCs. In its other state, as part of an SNA network, it's simply a display screen and a keyboard.

The New SNA

Raw 3270 emulation leaves a lot to be desired. This is one of the reasons IBM began evolving SNA back in the mid-1980s. Even a quick glance of Figure 5.12 suggests that, if this is SNA, something is definitely different. A disclaimer accompanying this new version of SNA could

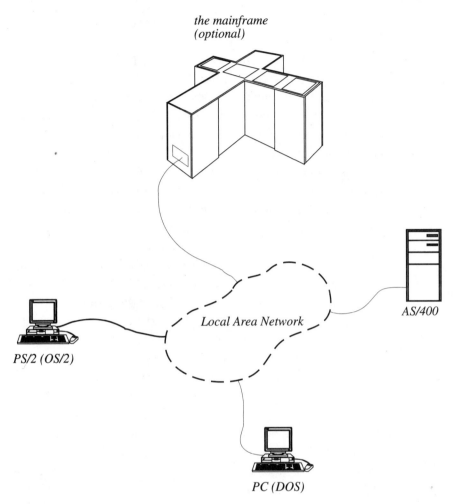

Figure 5.12 APPN: The new SNA.

read "mainframe not required." This new SNA is called APPN: Advanced Peer to Peer Networking.

In many respects, it's hard to imagine APPN as being a follow-on to the hierarchical SNA we've known in the past. They have little in common. In classical, or hierarchical, SNA, all network resources have predefined, static addresses. In contrast, APPN is geared to a dynamic network topology; the addresses of available resources are dynamically modified as the network changes. But the biggest change is the delegation of network routing responsibilities to specific nodes (known as Network nodes) on the PTP (peer-to-peer) backbone. There is no longer a single "brain."

As with any network, nodes on an APPN net often will be added, moved, or taken away. Unlike hierarchical SNA, APPN doesn't have to be manually reconfigured whenever such changes occur. APPN networking software dynamically reconfigures itself and then propagates the changes throughout the network. APPN also can locate network users dynamically.

Let's assume that a new APPN network node is added to the backbone. The physical link used to add it to the network could be IBM's proprietary SDLC (Synchronous Data Link Control), a Token-ring LAN, or even an FDDI connection. Once the link to the new node is activated, it establishes communication session (using an IBM application programming interface called LU 6.2) with its neighbor to introduce itself. They exchange network topology tables—that's how APPN nodes keeps track of where things are. After that, only topology changes (rather than entire tables) are exchanged, according to a routing scheme sometimes referred to as APPN+. Broadcasting the modifications, instead of the whole table, makes more sense; it reduces unnecessary network overhead.

How does it actually all work? In Figure 5.13, Logical Unit (LU) A—LUs are sort of like windows onto the APPN network; each application requiring network access needs one—seeks access to the network user represented by LU Z. This could be an actual person (using e-mail), a program, or a device. The whole process starts with LU A sending out a session ACTIVATE request to its port on the backbone: (APPN) Network Node 1 in this case. Software resident in NN1 searches its local directory for LU Z. It could be that the target LU sits on NN1 or is somehow otherwise attached to it. It's not. So NN1 next searches its cache directory. This contains the locations of the most recently accessed LUs by NN1 or any of its dependents. If it's a rarely accessed LU or a first-time request, no entry will exist for LU Z. Let's assume this is the case. NN1 then commences an undirected search through the network. It begins by sending out search requests to all of its adjacent APPN network nodes (forming the network backbone). When NN3 and NN4 receive the request, they search their local directory, but to no avail. They return a negative response, but they take up the cause.

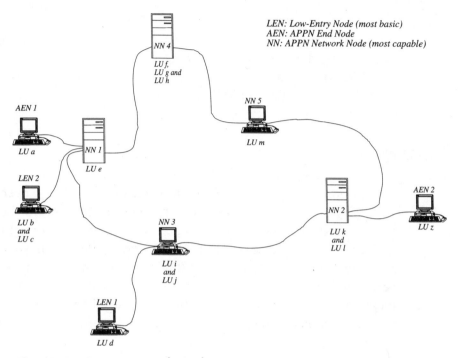

Figure 5.13 Locating nodes with APPN.

They, in turn, pass the request to their adjacent neighbor(s): NN5 and NN2. NN2 recognizes LU Z as a locally supported LU on an APPN end node (end nodes don't possess routing abilities of their own) attached to it. A "found it" response is backpropagated to NN1. Knowing the location of NN2, NN1 computes the optimal path to get to that node (clearly, NN1–NN3–NN2) and gives this information to LU A. It's added to the SNA BIND request that LU A will use to establish the session with LU Z.

System 390-class mainframes, AS/400s, and PCs running OS/2 are all capable of assuming the role of APPN network node. These nodes establish the APPN backbone and can be likened to high-end routers in a TCP/IP network.

Although APPN is a sophisticated internetworking option, it looks like it is just too late. Most of its components became available only in 1995. Two years earlier, when Forrester Research interviewed a group of 50 IS managers about their plans for SNA, 64 percent reported that they expected SNA (and APPN) usage to drop.[5] This doesn't appear to have changed. Undeterred, IBM plods boldly onward. But just to be on the safe side, the company also is developing a number of schemes for shipping SNA traffic over TCP/IP internets.

Wrap-up

Organizations turn to TCP/IP for four reasons: (1) They need inter-network support for an array of disparate networks and devices; (2) they're tired of dealing with a gaggle of different network protocols and want to standardize on one across the enterprise; (3) they introduce UNIX/RISC servers into their infrastructures—often as part of a client/server implementation—and inherit the protocol by default; and/or (4) they want closer connections to the Internet. With all this going for it, TCP/IP is increasingly becoming a part of many of our computing vocabularies.

Nowhere in this list is there any mention of technical prowess. In fact, many contend that TCP/IP is technically inferior to protocols such as IBM's APPN which was built from the ground up to handle mission-critical, enterprise-wide internetworking needs. But, as mentioned, it may be too late for APPN. While there's a huge SNA installed base and doubtless many will adopt APPN, it's now questionable whether its reach will ever extend much beyond that.

The UNIX operating system used to be the exclusive plaything of scientists and engineers. These days, however, it's riding the client/server wave right into businesses across the country. And TCP/IP, its entrenched networking facility, is coming right along with it. Some assume that UNIX's newfound favor is attributable to its unparalleled openness. Not so. With more than 30 different, and incompatible, flavors of the operating system kicking around, it can hardly be called "open." Instead, increased interest in UNIX is probably more attributable to the long-standing relationship between it and the powerful RISC processor line than anything else. RISC-based devices often are the preferred choice for the role of server. We'll take a closer look at both UNIX and RISC processing in Chapter 6.

Key Terms and Ideas Appearing in This Chapter

access method:

Software used to get at network resources. VTAM consolidated a growing number of access methods into one when SNA was introduced in 1974.

APPC:

A marketing term for LU6.2. APPC (Advanced Program to Program Communication) is intended to assist programs running on different computers to communicate directly and exchange data. It is used by many generic IBM transaction services.

APPN:

Advanced Peer to Peer Networking, the new SNA. Unlike hierarchical SNA, APPN doesn't require a mainframe—but mainframes aren't excluded either. Although APPN is still SNA (a radical extension of it), the term often is used on its own.

Archie:

A file/directory locator designed to complement FTP. Archie works in a client/server fashion to track down files and directories in anonymous FTP sites on the Net. It knows nothing about the contents of these things, however. It searches based on a user-provided sequence that's part of the actual file name or directory.

AS/400:

IBM's mid-range computing platform. It runs the OS/400 operating system and comes with a built-in relational database engine known as SQL/400.

firewall:

A device (often a router) that's used to filter Internet traffic. For the sake of security, if you have a direct link to the Internet that's open to the public, you should have a firewall standing between you and the Net. Firewalls can selectively shut out almost any type of traffic.

frame:

Datalink frames are groups of bits containing data and tombstone information. While the terms "frame" and "packet" sometimes are used interchangeably, TCP/IP definitely distinguishes between the two. Using Ethernet, Token-Ring, and FDDI at the Datalink and physical layers, a frame is the actual bit grouping that is transmitted across the medium.

FTP:

File Transfer Protocol. Another of the upper-layer TCP/IP protocols. FTP is used to transfer files between hosts, regardless of platform type or resident operating system.

Gopher:

Gopher servers scattered about the Net form what's often referred to as Gopherspace. Gopher servers contain all kinds of information and they're all linked; you can logically move from one server to another in the pursuit of information. Gopher, the application, runs in a client/ server fashion to help people get around Gopherspace.

IAB:

The Internet Advisory Board, a volunteer organization that manages the Internet. The IAB recently came under fire for suggesting that IP be dumped in favor of the Connectionless Network Protocol (CLNP). One of the reasons it did so was to avert Internet address exhaustion, now predicted to occur sometime before the year 2000.

The Internet:

A massive, global internetwork spanning every continent. The Internet may have as many as 750,000 computers directly attached to it. It's used every day by tens of millions of people. E-mail is the most popular application, but the Internet is an important information resource as well. It contains databases on practically every imaginable subject. The Internet is the offspring of ARPANET. Funded by the U.S. Defense

Department, ARPANET was a test bed for battle-tolerant communication networks. TCP/IP was the communication protocol designed to run it. Its use continues today in the Internet and in thousands of private communication LANs and WANs.

Internet address:

Initially defined by the ARPANET and now used on the Internet and every TCP/IP network as well, Internet addresses are 32 bits long. They come in five classes, of which only the first three, Classes A, B, and C, are commonly used. Class A have the following form: N.H.H.H (where N represents network and H represents host). Class A favors an internetwork with few networks containing many hosts. Class B is of the form: N.N.H.H. It's the most popular. On the Internet, Class B addresses are in danger of being exhausted within the next few years. To cope with this, a revised form of IP has been proposed. Known as IPng, it is designed to create more address space. Class C is applicable to internetworks with many networks each containing few hosts and takes the form: N.N.N.H. On the Internet, aliases are used in place of decimal or binary addresses.

IP:

Internet Protocol. Corresponding to the Network layer in the OSI model, IP takes care of packet creation and routing. It is a connectionless, unreliable packet delivery system.

IP Spoofing:

The modification of the address portion of IP packets in order to fool firewalls into believing they originate from a trusted source.

LU6.2:

A special Logical Unit designed for program-to-program communication. An API is necessary in order to use LU6.2.

NFS:

Network File System. An upper-layer TCP/IP protocol. It makes remotely stored files appear to reside locally. It was invented by SUN Microsystems in 1985.

packet:

IP packets are sort of like vendor-neutral Datalink frames. This is what makes TCP/IP a true internetworking protocol stack. The packet acts as a mediator among Ethernet, Token Ring, and FDDI LANs. To do this, an independent addressing scheme was required—the IP address.

SMTP:

Simple Mail Transfer Protocol. One of five upper-layer TCP/IP protocols. SMTP is a basic e-mail facility that's used on the Internet. It also serves as the basis for more sophisticated packages.

SNA nodes:

Often, but not always, the actual devices composing an SNA/APPN network. There are four types: Type 5 (mainframe), Type 4 (communications controller), Type 2.0 (a hierarchical SNA node), and Type 2.1 (peer-to-peer peripheral node). Within the Type 2.1 grouping, there is further division; the most capable node of this type is the APPN network node. These nodes define the backbone of an APPN net-handling dynamic routing and route selection. Next in peer-to-peer capability, is the APPN end node. It possesses local (it independently recognizes local LUs) directory and routing functionality. Last in this hierarchy is the Low Entry Networking (LEN) node. LEN nodes exclusively function as end users in an APPN network. They have no dynamic routing capability. They can communicate only with physically adjacent nodes.

SNMP:

Simple Network Management Protocol. An upper-layer TCP/IP protocol. SNMP is fast becoming the de facto internetwork management environment.

TCP:

The Transmission Control Protocol. TCP sits at the transport-layer level of the OSI protocol. It ensures reliable delivery of packets. TCP creates a packet containing the data to be sent plus address information. It hands this off to IP, which envelops all this into an IP packet. Upon reaching its intended destination, the packet is disassembled.

Telnet:

An upper-layer TCP/IP protocol. Telnet is used for remote host logon.

UDP:

User Datagram Protocol. A low-overhead alternative to TCP that offers little beyond basic IP services.

Veronica:

A keyword search application designed to complement Gopherspace searches.

WAIS:

Wide Area Information Server. Another Internet application, used to search databases attached to the Net.

World Wide Web:

Like Gopherspace, the WWW is a virtual space created by thousands of Web servers. These servers all contain information that's associated by hypertext links. Once onto the Web, users can move from Web site to Web site by selecting these links with a mouse or other pointing device.

Notes

[1] S. Randesi and D. Czubek, *SNA IBM's System Network Architecture*, (Van Nostrand Reinhold, 1992).
[2] M. Gibbs and R. Smith, *Navigating the Internet*, (SAMS Publishing, 1993).
[3] P. Kirvan, "Missing in Action: Internet Address," *Communication News*, April 1995, v32, 50.
[4] C. Levin, "Can You Trust Digital Bucks?" *PC Magazine*, Dec. 20, 1994, 32.
[5] C. Krivda, "A Different Perspective," *Internetwork*, 5, no. 11 (Nov. 1994), 25.

Chapter 6

Executive Summary

For many, "UNIX" equals "open." It's easy to understand why; this operating system has inspired many of the efforts to bring order to the computing business. But this has occurred because of the fractious state of the UNIX market, not because of any unprecedented degree of openness associated with the operating system itself. Today there are at least 30 different versions of UNIX in circulation built around three or four common cores. The existing open systems movement has largely been an attempt to consolidate them and to bring some uniformity to UNIX.

Nevertheless, UNIX has many features of interest to client/server developers. In its 25-year history, the operating system has evolved to embrace multitasking, multithreading, and symmetric multiprocessing. Its stability and scalability make it one of the leading choices for the role of server in client/server implementations.

We often hear that UNIX is fast. On the contrary, it's not a particularly fast operating system at all. Its perceived speed has more to do with the type of computers it traditionally runs on. Originating in the engineering and scientific communities, the operating system was used for computationally intensive applications on hardware suited to the job. As workstations became their preferred computational platform, UNIX began its long-standing relationship with the RISC (Reduced Instruction Set Computing) processor. RISC chips generally are faster than CISC (Complex Instruction Set Computing) designs. The gap has narrowed in recent years, however, as CISC (Intel primarily) designers have incorporated RISC design features into their chips.

Until the arrival of Microsoft's Windows NT, few other operating systems were as suited to the server role as UNIX. And although it's still the favorite in the majority of client/server applications, many now see a time when NT will overtake it. But it's somewhat of a domestic struggle: NT designers drew heavily upon UNIX in their work. To many, NT is the new UNIX.

CHAPTER

6

UNIX: On the Way to Open

Introduction

A lot of things can go wrong in client/server computing. Therefore, it's important to select a server that can roll with the punches. It should be a proven product, one that can cope with numerous, concurrent requests, be unflappable in the face of system glitches, be easily shoehorned into the existing infrastructure, and scale well as client/server demands increase.

But a "server" (in client/server terms) isn't one thing, it's three: the hardware, the operating system, and the database engine that runs on top of it. And they aren't independent; certain database engines work only with certain operating systems, and certain operating systems run only on certain microprocessors. Ideally, operating systems and microprocessor types would be transparent to client/server system designers. But this isn't so; it's that old open systems thing again.

Ironically, there's more commonality across high-end database engines than there is among operating systems and CPUs. Because of vigorous competition, Oracle's database engine isn't drastically different from Sybase's product, and Sybase's engine has a lot in common with Informix's.

While there are a handful of contenders for the role of server operating system (OS), the market gravitates towards two in particular: UNIX and Microsoft's Windows NT. There are indications that NT will someday wrestle the lead away from UNIX, but for the moment, it's still out in front. NetWare is also a strong player in the server market, but because it really isn't a full-blown operating system, and because it doesn't do a particularly good job of supporting applications, it's fallen behind.

UNIX has a lot going for it. It's stable. It can perform a large number of tasks at the same time. It can accommodate multiple, simultaneous users. It's available from just about everybody. It's closely associated with some very high-speed hardware; it runs on everything from PCs to supercomputers and, it's the preferred operating system in Internet circles.

But it's not without its downside. While it's true that it's available from just about everybody, just about every company has added its own unique twist to the base operating system. As a result, there is no single UNIX. Although it's difficult to keep up, there's at least 30 different versions in use today. They might all look similar, but under the covers, they're different enough to make porting from one to another painful.

Having been around for such a long time, UNIX has inspired many OS designs that came after it. DOS's hierarchical file structure, for example, is something right out of UNIX. In fact, when you see UNIX for the first time, you'll note many things that are vaguely familiar about it.

UNIX: Under the Hood

There are three basic components to the UNIX operating system: the kernel, a file system, and a shell. (See Figure 6.1.) A part of the kernel called the "scheduler" implements time sharing. This is how UNIX juggles multiple tasks and even multiple users. When a number of users want to run their respective programs, copies of each are written to the

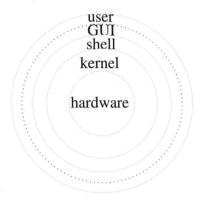

Figure 6.1 The UNIX operating system.

computer's memory. In UNIX terminology, they're now referred to as "processes." The actual programs remain stored on disk. On a uniprocessor device, the scheduler submits each process, in turn, to the CPU for a small period of time, thereby creating the illusion of simultaneous execution.

The scheduler is a sophisticated piece of software. It monitors how long a process runs, within its allotted time slice, before it stops to perform an I/O (disk write or read) operation. If it's steadily running and performing very little I/O activity, it's branded a "CPU hog" and its priority is lowered. On the other hand, if a process is "I/O bound," its priority is raised since it hasn't had a chance to use very much of its allotted CPU time. Of course, the scheduler is a UNIX process too. It and all other system processes are given a high enough priority to make sure everything keeps running as it should.

The scheduler can track several hundred simultaneous processes. But when the number of active ones exceeds the available memory capacity of the machine, processes start getting "swapped out" of memory. This is the job of the ever-so-aptly named "swapper"—another component of the kernel. Swapping simply means copying everything associated with a process from main memory to the hard disk at the moment that process loses control of the CPU. Swapping is done on an as-needed basis, according to how long a particular process has been resident in memory and how much memory is available.

Standing between the kernel and the user is another system program known as the shell. The shell is a programmable command interpreter.

Given the history of UNIX, it should come as no surprise to hear that there are more than one shell kicking around. The three most popular are the C shell, the Bourne shell, and the Korn shell. The C shell is the standard for a version of UNIX developed at the University of California at Berkeley and was subsequently adopted by a number of UNIX vendors. The Bourne shell is an AT&T standard. It's now used by most licensees of its core operating system. (Actually, Novell owns the core now.) The Korn shell is sort of a cross between the two.

Any UNIX command that can be executed from the command line can be included in a shell "script." To this can be added variable substitution and a variety of common programming declaratives such as "if statements" and "while loops." Scripts provide a means for automating program submission in a manner similar to mainframe JCL, for those of you who can recall that.

The final component of the UNIX OS is the file system. UNIX deals with files in a familiar, hierarchical manner. (See Figure 6.2.) Ironically, the top of the hierarchy is called the root. Every UNIX file system has a structure similar to that shown in the figure. Within it there are a number of typically "dedicated" directories. For example, system administration files are usually kept in the /dev, /etc, and /export directories. A user's personal directories are normally kept under /home/*some-user-name*. Pathnames are used to move around the hierarchy, just as in DOS. (In fact, this is where Microsoft got the idea.) To move to Bob's directory, for example, you'd use the command "cd/home/Bob". (Again, as in DOS, "cd" simply means change directory.)

UNIX is harsh, as operating systems go. All its commands are terse and succinct. And there's no handholding. That shouldn't come as a surprise, I suppose; the operating system originally was designed by engineers for engineers. It wasn't pretty, but it worked. But if the operating system was ever to gain a substantial following outside of technical spheres, it would have to don a newer, friendlier face. This time around, UNIX borrowed from Microsoft.

X Windows

In the late 1980s, two graphical user interfaces (GUIs) for UNIX came to the fore. One was Open Look from UNIX International (a now defunct group of UNIX vendors aligned behind AT&T's vision for the OS). The

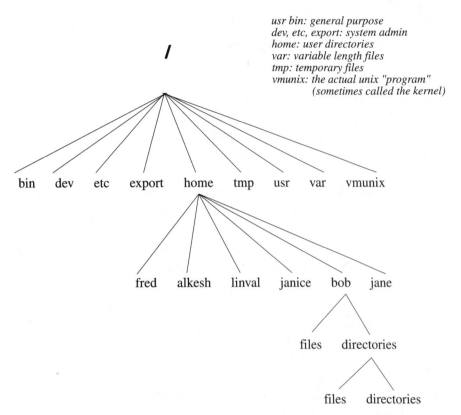

usr bin: general purpose
dev, etc, export: system admin
home: user directories
var: variable length files
tmp: temporary files
vmunix: the actual unix "program"
*   (sometimes called the kernel)*

Figure 6.2 UNIX's hierarchical file structure was a model for DOS.

other was Motif from the Open Software Foundation. Both GUIs were constructed using MIT's X Windows System, and both were inspired by Microsoft's Windows.

It's easier to describe what X isn't. First of all, contrary to popular belief, it's not the UNIX world's version of Microsoft Windows. That's what Motif and Open Look are all about. Windows, too, could have been built from X. But X is more than just a tool kit. It "understands" how to work with networks. Running on top of either TCP/IP or DECnet, X is capable of transmitting graphic information between networked devices. Its close ties to TCP/IP is one reason X is often associated with UNIX (which itself, of course, is closely linked to the protocol stack), but it can run on any computer with enough horsepower to drive X and that can use TCP/IP (or DECnet).

At its heart, X has more than 300 basic commands. They deal with things such as watching for mouse clicks and movements (known as events in object-oriented programming lingo). Others exist for drawing curves and other graphics.

It's interesting to note that X is fundamentally "client/server" in its design. But it has its own unique spin on exactly what that means.

The "X way" of looking at things starts with the desktop. It's seen as providing a presentation service to an application program running on a networked host. So the desktop is the server, and the networked host is the client—an interpretation opposite from what we're accustomed to. It brings up a relevant point though. Strictly speaking, it's the *software* running on these respective platforms that makes them server and client, not the platforms themselves. Defined in software, "client/server" is an abstract notion. The terms are so overused in this business, however, that it's sometimes easy to forget that.

Being defined in software, it's completely possible—especially with a multitasking operating system such as UNIX—for both the X server and the X client to reside on the same physical device. A standalone UNIX platform running Motif or Open Look does precisely that, in fact. Even though X was designed to accommodate networked devices, this is the most common way that it's used.

A GUI may make UNIX more approachable, but it demands some pretty serious hardware to support it. This is precisely why scientific types did without one for so long; with compute-intensive applications to tackle, they needed every ounce of CPU power they could squeeze out of their computers. But in the business world, presentation and computation are on a more equal footing. By the time the Intel 80386 arrived on the scene in the mid-1980s—the first mainstream microprocessor (barely) capable of running UNIX and a GUI—Microsoft's Windows had the desktop market already sewn up. And so it is today. The next best hope for UNIX was the server.

The UNIX Vendors: A Who's Who

UNIX has had a tumultuous history. Although it was developed by AT&T back in the late 1960s, the company failed to recognize its value, and did little to market the product. Instead, AT&T licensed the core off to such vendors as IBM, Digital, Hewlett-Packard (HP), the Santa Cruz Operation (SCO) and Sun Microsystems to do with what they wished. About all they couldn't do was use the name "UNIX." That was the sole property of AT&T. That's why we have a slew of product names with the letter "x" embedded in them somewhere: AIX (IBM), Ultrix (Digital), HP-UX (Hewlett-Packard), Xenix (SCO), and so on. With no real guiding force, the market, and the product, fragmented into what we have today.

But it may not be as bad as it first appears. Sure, there are incompatibilities between many of these "unixes," but there are really only four fundamentally different versions of the OS in circulation: those based on AT&T's (now X/Open's, by way of Novell—who bought the UNIX core from AT&T in 1992) System 5, Release 3; those based on System 5, Release 4; those based on the University of California at Berkeley's "Berkeley Software Distribution" (BSD); and those based on the Open Software Foundation's OSF/1. HP, Sun, IBM, and Novell have generally stuck with System 5, Release 4 (with a few smatterings of BSD tossed in). Porting between any of their products shouldn't be too overwhelming. SCO held with the earlier release of System 5. Digital went with OSF/1; NeXT, these days a software-only company, also built upon the same foundation as used in OSF/1.

IBM, HP, and Digital have aimed their operating systems exclusively at the server and high-end engineering workstation. They run only on high-speed RISC-based platforms, a traditional favorite for the OS. Sun, SCO, Novell, and NeXT, on the other hand, are also hoping for a slice of the desktop (and small departmental server) market. Each has versions of the OS tooled for the Intel CPU. Sun, the UNIX market leader, has both.

When people talk about the "speed and power of UNIX," they often confuse the operating system with the platform that it runs on. To be sure, UNIX is a highly capable operating system, but there's nothing intrinsically speedy about it. Because of its predominantly technical origins, UNIX has been closely associated with high-performance hardware and, in particular, with a special design of CPU known as "RISC." RISC plus UNIX is a powerful contender for the choice of server.

Why Is UNIX so RISC-y?

There has been a long-standing association between RISC (Reduced Instruction Set Computing) processors and the UNIX operating system. This has more to do with what people were using UNIX for than with the operating system itself. In fact, as we've just seen, UNIX is CPU independent.

As mentioned, UNIX had its origins in the engineering and scientific world. It met its users' needs at the time. Of course, the operating system itself wasn't foremost on their minds—they needed computers to do something. And that something was most often pretty compute-intensive. RISC designs have, over the years, proven to be the better CPU architecture for that kind of work.

The RISC vs. CISC (Intel-like) debate has raged for more than a decade. Processors adhering to the RISC philosophy of CPU design have small instruction sets that feature basic, commonly used commands. Many of these are optimized right in hardware. Because of this, RISC instructions often execute within one machine cycle. CISC (Complex Instruction Set Computer), on the other hand, contains larger instruction sets in which the individual instructions have been "macroized" to handle common tasks. These instructions usually require several CPU cycles to complete.

But the differences are more than just in instruction size. RISC and CISC differ in how, and when, they move operands to memory. CISC processors commonly specify several memory interchanges per single instruction. Every one invokes a microprogrammed unit. This tends to be slower than dealing exclusively with on-chip memory registers—the RISC philosophy. Loading and storing the data in the RISC registers is handled by separate instructions dedicated to this task.

Instruction size, memory interchange philosophies—does all this stuff really make a difference? It must, because RISC chips *are* faster. But on closer analysis, we find that RISC's speed advantage is also attributable to some rather ingenious innovations in chip design—innovations CISC designers are now adopting to realize some significant improvements in processor speed.

Practically all RISC and newer CISC chips employ pipelines in their design. This implementation of microparallelism is a proven approach for reducing the number of machine cycles per instruction. Pipelining breaks instructions down into basic components and executes each independently—provided no relationship exists between them. When one does, the pipeline stalls. It's the compiler's job to identify such dependencies and move to minimize them, without corrupting the original program logic.

Pipelines have proven so popular that some have taken the idea a bit further. The MIPS R4000, for example, introduced superpipelining. In superpipelining, instructions are reduced to even more basic components and then passed through less granular pipelines. It's a great idea, but it places even more onus on the compiler.

Another often-used design feature is the so-called superscalar architecture. Superscalar chips contain dedicated integer and floating-point units, both often sporting their own pipelines. IBM's RS/6000, Digital's Alpha, and Intel's Pentium all share this characteristic.

The performance gap between CISC and RISC has eroded with Intel's latest designs—designs that for the most part borrow heavily from their reduced instruction set counterparts. Not only that, many RISC chip makers are discovering that having the fastest chips doesn't always mean having the fastest systems. So the choice between RISC and CISC isn't always clear.

Even if it were, there's still the question of whose RISC chip to use. Unlike the CISC market, where Intel holds practically all the cards, there isn't any clear leader among RISC designers. Digital's Alpha and IBM and Apple's PowerPC are both receiving a lot of press, but in a slice of the computer business as tempestuous as chip design, that may not mean much a few months down the road.

Digital's Alpha

The *Guinness Book of World Records* calls the Alpha the world's fastest computer chip, and it's the industry's first across-the-board 64 bit microprocessor. The latest version of this RISC chip, the 300MHz DECchip 21164, is clocked at a SPECint rating (an average of six C-language integer programs providing a measure of processor speed, memory bandwidth, and compiler effectiveness) of 330. (See Table 6.1.) Its SPECfp

Table 6.1 Some Alpha Specs

	21064	21064A	21164
ship date	now	now	now
transistors	1.7 million	2.8 million	9.3 million
MHz range	150–200	200–275	250–300
Instruct/cycle	2	2	2
SPECint92	80–140	140–180	220–350
SPECfp92	110–200	200–250	400–525

rating (an average of nine double-precision FORTRAN floating-point programs, three single-precision FORTRAN programs, and two single-precision C programs) is an eyebrow-raising 500. And Digital is promising some even faster stuff, in the form of the 21264, a 1,000 SPECmark CPU.

But, as RISC chip makers learned, Digital is discovering that having the fastest chip doesn't necessarily result in the fastest system. With slow peripheral support, Alpha platforms often perform more poorly than expected.[1]

While Digital struggles to shake the bugs out of its machines, its 21164 remains the fastest RISC chip on the market. Quite an accomplishment for a company that seemed unable to come up with a successful RISC design of its own just a few years ago.

Why is Alpha so fast? In the late 1980s, Digital was in trouble. Big trouble. Its VAX line was faltering, and profits were drying up. To many, the company just wasn't in the game any more. While IBM, Sun, and HP were off playing microprocessor leap-frog, Digital watched from the sidelines. But it knew that if it was going to survive, it was going to have to pull out all of the stops. To come up with Alpha, the company used every trick in the book and then added a few chapters of its own.

The 21164 is a full 64-bit design capable of issuing several instructions at the same time. It's designed for multiprocessing—companies such as Cray Research have adopted Alpha for their latest generation of supercomputers. One of the hard lessons that Digital learned toward the end of the 1980s was that the day of the proprietary solution was over. For Alpha to be successful, it had to bridge the past as well as the future. And it had to be operating system independent. To some extent, it is. Alpha runs VMS, OSF/1, and Microsoft's Windows NT. Digital is looking to NT eventually to take over most of its existing VMS base.

Alpha's flat 64 bit addressing provides an address space 4 billion times larger than current 32 bit designs. All integers, floating-point numbers, and character strings are represented as 64 bit sequences. Do you need that much memory? Maybe not today. But as multimedia and other memory-hungry applications become more prevalent, 64 bits may not only become desirable, they may become mandatory—especially on the server.

Alpha supports multiple operating systems through the use of something called PALcode (Privileged Architecture Library code). PALcode adds five additional instructions to Alpha's RISC repertoire. They're used to tune the chip for the particular operating system that's running on it.

Digital's RISC chip is designed to encourage, not simply accommodate, multiple instruction issue. It uses a deeply pipelined, dual instruction-issue design. To minimize pipeline stall, the chip provides a series of "bypass paths" that funnel results of the various pipeline stages to subsequent instructions where they're needed, before they reach the end of the pipe.

Even though Alpha can support Windows NT, it cannot by itself run Windows 3.x applications. To do that, the chip must turn to software emulation. The leading Windows emulator for Alpha is Insignia's Soft-Windows for UNIX. It comes with a fully licensed copies of Microsoft Windows 3.1 and DOS 6.x. But how fast is it? According to a Byte test, if you're interested in MS Windows 3.x applications, you can't beat Intel CISC.[2] Testing several RISC designs for Windows spreadsheet, word processing, and database performance, the mean workstation emulation was found to be less than 20% that of a 80486DX2/66MHz PC.

Another RISC design seeking to establish a beachhead is IBM/Motorola/Apple's PowerPC. While IBM struggles to adapt OS/2 to this new chip, more than 1 million Power Macs have been sold already. Marking the biggest technological change in the company's history, the PowerPC has virtually breathed new life into Apple.

CLOSE-UP

How do Alpha-based devices stack up for the role of server?

As noted earlier, having the fastest chip is no guarantee of also having the fastest system. And there's more to consider than raw speed when shopping for a server anyway. In May 1994 *PC Magazine* evaluated a number of servers and rated the DEC 3000 Model 800S Deskside Server second after the Compaq Proliant 2000 5/66 in terms of price/performance.[3] The Proliant uses a multiprocessor design composed of two Pentium processors, while the Model 800S uses a single Alpha 21064 chip.

The PowerPC

As CISC chips have gotten more complicated, and as RISC designers continued to perfect their craft, RISC has surpassed CISC in terms of price/performance. At about $450 each, the PowerPC 601, the first result of a joint venture among IBM, Motorola, and Apple, is about half the price of the Intel Pentium. And it's faster. The 601 has demonstrated that it's approximately 1.5 times faster than first-generation Pentium for numeric sorts and twice as fast when it comes to floating point calculations.

The MPC601, as it's also called, is also 50 percent smaller than the Pentium. This translates into reduced chip production costs. It also consumes less power—slightly more than half as much as the Pentium. So it runs cooler. Implementation costs will be less. Both of these factors will find their way into eventual platform prices.

The MPC60x (several renditions of the chip are available now) supports a number of different operating systems: AIX (IBM's version of UNIX) and OS/2, Solaris (Sun's operating system), Apple System 7, and NT.

All these operating systems (running in native mode, no less) means that users can select the interface they're most comfortable and stick with it. But there's one very important operating system that's noticeably absent from the list. If the PowerPC is ever going to make inroads into Intel's territory, it has to support DOS/Windows. Right now, like Digital's Alpha, the 60x relies on Insignia's SoftWindows Windows emulator for that. IBM has been working on a number of options to improve upon this, however. In the end, though, it may simply rely on increasing RISC processor speed to deliver better Windows 3.x performance. The new 604 is claimed to emulate a low-end Pentium, for example.

PowerPC is modeled after IBM's POWER chip—the RISC design used in its RS/6000 line. In fact, IBM's first commercial use of the PowerPC was in an RS/6000—the PowerStation 250T. Like POWER, PowerPC follows a superscalar architecture that defines three separate execution units. Unlike POWER, however, PowerPC is a single-chip design.

With both Apple and IBM backing the PowerPC, you can bet that Intel's not taking the arrival of this new chip lightly. But will the PowerPC or the Alpha spell an end of Intel domination? It's not likely, at least

PowerPC-based platforms in the server role

PowerPC-based machines haven't been real players in the server market, but that's about to change. The MPC620, due out in 1996, is expected to be powerful enough to be considered a server-capable chip. There is a SMP (Symmetric Multiprocessor) MPC601-based server on the market, but many people view it as just a place marker for the 620.

for the foreseeable future. Intel's got history on its side. Not only that, the company keeps on redefining the performance levels of CISC-based design.

Intel's Pentium

The Pentium is Intel's follow-on to its enormously popular 80386 and 80486 lines. This time, the company packed more than 3 million transistors onto a single chip—more than 10 times that of the original 80386. The result is a rather large chip—2.16 inches square—with 273 pins. It is also dramatically faster than anything else Intel has ever fielded. The Pentium's entry-level SPECint92 rating is a highly respectable 64.5, while its SPECfp92 is 56.9. These numbers put Pentium smack dab in RISC territory and put it way ahead of its forerunner, the 80486.

While both Pentium and the 486 employ pipelining in their designs, Pentium has gone it one better, by adding a second pipeline for integer calculations. If two simultaneously fetched integer instructions are simple enough that they don't require additional microcode and are independent of each other, they're executed in parallel.

Pentium includes an overhauled floating-point unit. Its designers introduced dedicated circuitry for multiplication, addition, and division—a first for any Intel design. The result is a speed-up of 3.5 times over the 486 for floating-point calculations. Floating-point operations are also pipelined. It features eight distinct stages, three more than on the integer side.

The chip's data bus also has been expanded to 64 bits; each memory access scoops up twice as much data as on a 486. Pentium's address bus remains 32 bits wide, however. This isn't anything to scoff at, mind you; the chip still can access more than 4 GB of stored data, although some are claiming that this eventually might prove a limitation for server duty.

While Pentium defines the edge of the envelope of the 80 × 86 family, it's not a leading-edge chip. Rival (and one-time Intel clone) ×86-compatible chip makers AMD, Cyrix, and NexGen are today either fielding superior designs or soon will be. And so is Intel. In late 1995, the company plans to launch the P6, successor to Pentium.

The P6

Facing greater competition from rival chip makers, Intel's engineers have been forced to become ever-more shrewd in their designs. They've also been forced to turn them out with ever-increasing frequency. The P6 is scheduled to come out just two years after the debut of Pentium.

Adhering to a 14-stage superpipelined design, the P6's 5.5 million transistors are expected to produce a chip that's at least 30 percent faster than the fastest Pentium. This would place its SPECint rating at about 200.

At first glance, the most unusual thing about the chip is that it's not one chip, it's two. The second chip is a closely coupled secondary cache. If the P6 can't locate a needed instruction in its onboard cache (the primary chip), it next looks to the secondary one. If it still can't find the instruction, then it must turn to main memory. Since cache memory accesses are considerably faster than those from main memory, the P6's data-crunching units should be kept churning.

The P6 is a RISC chip in CISC's clothing. Admitting that smaller, RISC-like instructions can be processed more easily, a decoder unit actually converts the CISC instructions into something Intel calls "micro-ops." These are then fed into P6's superpipelines.

Intel's decision to use superpipelining seems a bit odd at first; many manufacturers have given up on the idea. Superpipelines are great in theory, but when the pipeline stalls, as they often do, there's a recovery penalty. To reduce the occurrence of this, the P6 employs dynamic execution.

In-order CPUs can stall while waiting for dependent instructions to complete. Using dynamic execution, the P6 looks multiple steps ahead (20 to 30) into the program in an attempt to predict which instructions are likely to be executed next (taking branches in the logic flow into account). It then analyzes these instructions and constructs an optimized schedule of execution composed of those apparently free from dependency. This schedule is implemented in what's said to be a speculative fashion, with the results being stored temporarily in a buffer. Once the true logic flow is confirmed and all dependencies are resolved, the results are actually committed.

While the P6 represents a significant improvement over the Pentium, it may not be enough to keep the competition at bay. Both AMD (with its K5) and Cyrix (with its M1) will begin shipping almost as soon as the P6 hits the streets. Both are expected to offer similar performance levels. And it doesn't end there. Intel also is directly threatened by pure RISC-based designs such as Alpha (still the fastest, even with the P6, by the way) and PowerPC as well. The reason is Windows NT.

Windows NT: The New UNIX?

Windows NT runs on both Intel CISC and RISC designs from Digital, IBM, and MIPS. Therefore, for the first time, CISC and RISC designs compete head-to-head against each other. Intel's chips have a heap of history going for them though. They're binary compatible with all previous 80×86 designs. This means that they can run DOS, OS/2, and Windows 3.x applications. Currently RISC-based systems have to resort to software emulation to do the same. This can be less than impressive—much less. But the ability to support Windows 3.x applications may not be much of an advantage to Intel in the server market. As more native applications are developed for NT (there are more than 1,000 now), the operating system will begin to stand on its own.

Windows NT is the biggest thing Microsoft's ever done. It's a scalable, multithreaded, multitasking operating system that runs DOS, Windows 16-bit applications, 32-bit applications, and OS/2 applications. Best of all, though, it looks a lot like Microsoft Windows 3.x.

Like good old UNIX, NT comes with out-of-the-box support for TCP/IP, and is, or soon will be, portable among 80386, 80486, and selected RISC processors such as the PowerPC and Digital's Alpha. According to Microsoft chairman Bill Gates: "It's a better UNIX than UNIX."[4]

NT's arrival was a bit anticlimactic, to say the least. In the months leading up to its arrival, NT mania was running wild. As it neared production, more than 40,000 people snapped up developer's kits. Organizations around the world delayed OS purchases and waited with bated breath to see if NT would deliver. But it was delayed, and it was delayed, and it was delayed, and then . . . it arrived quietly. People sometimes still ask if it's available yet. It is. But the operating system fell short of its prerelease hype. Microsoft predicted sales of 1 million units in its first year. In reality, it sold roughly only half of that amount.

Few are surprised at NT's less-than-stellar performance in its first year. It is a new operating system, after all. Most people expected that the company would need at least a year to shake out the bugs.

And now, more than 12 months later, we have a new NT: version 3.5.x. It's a slimmed-down, faster version of the original that requires less memory and comes with improved TCP/IP (minus NFS, however) and IPX support. Reviews of Daytona, as it used to be (unofficially) known, are glowing. It's a server operating system from Microsoft finally worthy of serious consideration.

As we saw in Chapter 3, NT 3.5.x comes with a gateway service that allows networked Windows for Workgroups and DOS clients to access NetWare file and print facilities. But just in case, it also contains a migration toolset that allows users to do away with NetWare altogether, if they so desire.

Windows NT suffers from a bit of an identity crisis: Is it a desktop OS, or is it designed for the server? As it turns out, it's both. There are two official versions: NT Server 3.5.x and NT Workstation 3.5.x. The latter has been trimmed and outfitted for high-end desktop use.

But it's pretty clear now that NT's real opportunity lies on the server. Even by mid-1994, the OS had already managed to grab about 3 percent of NetWare's business.[5] And things have picked up considerably since then; version 3.5.x will almost certainly improve upon that. Being a full-blown operating system, there's less danger of spurious applications commandeering the server than there is with NetWare (especially pre-NetWare 4.x). A lot of folks figure that NT will possibly overtake UNIX, in terms of raw unit sales, by 1996.

Microsoft is promising a completely new version of NT around about that same time. Code-named Cairo, it is an object-oriented operating system similar to NeXTstep. Originally slated for late 1995, the delay has given Microsoft cause to consider an interim solution: a version of NT 3.5.x called Indy that sports a Windows 95-like interface (which is also object-oriented).

As it is the property of a single organization, NT isn't burdened with much of the baggage that surrounds UNIX. Industry watchers are probably correct in their predictions that it will someday overtake UNIX. If it ever does, it will owe much to the avant gardist and ever-irascible operating system that preceded it.

But in some respects, UNIX is more than just an operating system. The 25-year struggle to reconcile diverging versions of the operating system largely defined the open systems movement. The work of the Open Software Foundation, the Common Open Software Environment, and X/Open Company Ltd. grew directly out these efforts. But before they came along, there was POSIX.

POSIX: In Pursuit of Openness

POSIX stands for Portable Operating System Interface eXtensions. It is a collection of more than two dozen IEEE standards aimed at making computing more open. (See Table 6.2.) Of primary interest to application developers and system integrators, POSIX addresses portability, but also deals with common development tools and interoperability too.

Table 6.2 The POSIX Standards Group

POSIX.1	system interface
POSIX.2	shell and tools
POSIX.3	testing and validation
POSIX.4	real-time systems
POSIX.5	Ada language bindings
POSIX.6	security extensions
POSIX.7	system administration
POSIX.8	networking
POSIX.9	FORTRAN language bindings
POSIX.10	supercomputing
POSIX.11	transaction processing

POSIX got its start in UNIX camps back in the 1980s. It was seen as a way of reconciling the many different flavors of the operating system. Today, however, it applies to both UNIX and non-UNIX operating systems alike—NT, MVS, VMS, and OS/400 either support, or soon will support, some degree of POSIX compliance.

Applications written to the POSIX interface standard can, in theory, be recompiled and run on any POSIX-compliant operating system. That certainly sounds open. The problem is that vendors are playing a bit of a shell game; many claim POSIX compliance, or POSIX conformity, but neither term necessarily means strict adherence to the standards. Furthermore, not all operating systems support all available POSIX standards. Digital's VMS, for example, is one of the few that supports POSIX.1 (system interface), POSIX.2 (shell and tools), and POSIX.4 (real-time). Most others include only POSIX.1 or POSIX.2. While that's good for VMS users, that venerable old operating system is on the way out, to be replaced eventually by NT.

IBM even has announced that MVS OpenEdition, its mainframe operating system, will support POSIX. This will open the door for improved data and application sharing between MVS mainframes and other POSIX-compatible hosts, which will have ramifications in the move toward client/server. As holders of the corporate information, mainframes often are an important element in the client/server equation.

You don't hear as much about POSIX as you used to. Some say that it's in need of an overhaul. Others say it's dead. To many, though, it remains one of our real and best hopes for system and application openness.

Less abstract than POSIX is the work of organizations such as X/Open and the Open Software Foundation (OSF). The OSF began as a protest action. Outraged by increases in licensing fees for the UNIX core levied by AT&T, companies including IBM, HP, Digital, and others, banded together with the goal of creating an entirely new version of UNIX. Known as OSF/1, it stands upon a kernel constructed by researchers at Carnegie Mellon University.

OSF/1 wasn't exactly a ringing success. To date, only Digital actually uses it. But another of the OSF's projects did strike a chord: one that rang in the ears of UNIX and non-UNIX vendors alike. They call it the Distributed Computing Environment (DCE).

The Distributed Computing Environment

DCE is a set of services for the creation and implementation of distributed applications. (See Figure 6.3.) It permits applications to run piecewise simultaneously, on an array of different hosts, featuring a variety of different operating systems and designs. And what's more, it does it in a manner that's completely transparent to the user.

UNIX was the "reference environment" for DCE although it's not limited to the OS. But, admittedly, there is a strong connection between the two. This is just another of the many reasons why people often equate UNIX with "openness."

DCE relies on something called multithreading. Multithreading is the process of breaking applications up into small, executable fragments, that can be executed at the same time, on an array of microprocessors. NT, OS/2 SMP and the OSF's OSF/1 are all multithreaded operating

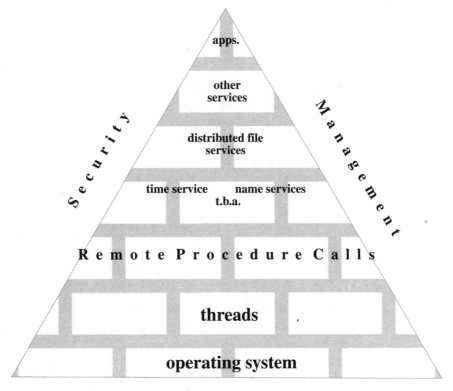

Figure 6.3 The components of DCE.

systems. But DCE is supposed to be operating system independent. So, for those "thread-barren" operating systems, DCE comes with an add-on package that gives it multithreading capability.

Multithreading goes hand-in-hand with the remote procedure call (RPC). A remote procedure call is exactly as its name describes: an extension of the familiar local procedure, or subroutine, call but now across networked hosts.

There are two facets to DCE's RPC implementation strategy. A Remote Procedure Call tool takes care of all the low-level communications stuff; it "binds" to the identified server—whatever it might be (as long as it's DCE compliant). Once a programmer has written the "main" (the calling program) and the remote procedures that support it, the whole thing is then passed through an RPC compiler a couple of times: once to generate the client source code (main) and a second time to create the server routines.

Many of DCE's services rely on RPCs. One is a naming service that's responsible for keeping track of where things are. That's actually a tough job; not only does the service have to know about users and equipment, but it also has to monitor the whereabouts of remotely running procedures. DCE follows a two-level naming service: one level for local system objects in a geographically linked region called a cell and another for everything outside. The thinking is that, generally, locally networked devices probably will have greater interaction with each other.

Another important DCE service takes care of time synchronization. To tie together an enterprise-wide network that probably contains heterogeneous computing devices, it's necessary to have a common time datum, for general system management as well as for security purposes. Many authentication routines, for example, compare file dates and times in deciding when users can access networked services.

Security is one of the most exciting aspects of DCE. Enormous security risks accompany a move to a distributed form of computing such as client/server. Back in the late 1980s, researchers at MIT began studying the problem. They came up with an authentication scheme they called Kerberos, named after the mythical three-headed dog that guarded the gates to Hades. Kerberos is a key component in DCE's security strategy.

As shown in Figure 6.4, the security scheme relies on the arbitration of a trusted third party: the Kerberos server. When a client wants access to an application server on the network, it must first be authenticated by Kerberos. This is a two-step process: first the Kerberos server confirms the user's USERID. This identification number belongs to a person the server theoretically should recognize. To verify the person's identity, the Kerberos server fires back an encrypted "ticket" that can be decrypted only with the user's registered password. Once decrypted, the client station next asks the Kerberos server to grant it access to a specific application server on the network. If the client was able to decrypt the first ticket, it's granted a second one—one that can be decrypted only by the application server. This second ticket is sent, along with the client query, to that server. If it all works, the client receives its requested service.

The tickets contain quite a bit of information, including a time stamp. (Here's where DCE's time service comes in.) Tickets are valid only for a limited period of time (usually eight to 24 hours). And while they're valid, they can be used only to obtain services from the specified server. If the client needs a different service, it must poll Kerberos for another time-stamped ticket.

But Kerberos is only an authentication service. Authorization—adjudicating over who can do what—must still be performed at the

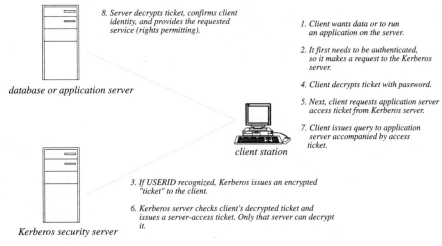

8. Server decrypts ticket, confirms client identity, and provides the requested service (rights permitting).

database or application server

1. Client wants data or to run an application on the server.

2. It first needs to be authenticated, so it makes a request to the Kerberos server.

4. Client decrypts ticket with password.

5. Next, client requests application server access ticket from Kerberos server.

7. Client issues query to application server accompanied by access ticket.

client station

3. If USERID recognized, Kerberos issues an encrypted "ticket" to the client.

6. Kerberos server checks client's decrypted ticket and issues a server-access ticket. Only that server can decrypt it.

Kerberos security server

Figure 6.4 Kerberos in action.

application server level. If a client wants access to data stored on a particular server, Kerberos only helps in the identification of the user. The database engine decides if that person has the required access rights.

Kerberos is just taking hold. Although there are approximately 1,300 organizations piloting Kerberos security, only a small number of them are putting it into practice.[6] One reason for this is the all-or-nothing approach that Kerberos places upon its users: If it's going to be implemented, it has to be implemented everywhere. (Otherwise, what's the use?) But widespread industry support for Kerberos isn't quite here yet. Costs are also a concern, but as Kerberos gains momentum, they're beginning to fall. Several companies, such as OCSG (Open Computing Security Group), offer standalone versions of Kerberos.

Another feature of DCE, also relevant to client/server computing, is its Distributed File System (DFS). DFS is designed to provide transparent access to any file sitting on any server or client attached to the network (access rights permitting). Although at first it sounds similar to TCP/IP's NFS, DFS actually is modeled after a product from a company (and OSF sponsor) called Transarc. To use DFS, each node on the network needs to be outfitted with DFS software. This software takes care of such things as file caching, to improve retrieval performance of frequently accessed files.

As organizations continue their trek toward client/server, demand for DCE, or something like it, will rise. As we'll see later in Chapter 10, security is one of the most troublesome aspects of the client/server model. Vendors are responding. IBM, for example, has added DCE support to its AIX operating system.

Wrap-up

Like it or hate it, UNIX has had a profound influence upon computing. Many of the things that it evolved to do have now become respectable, and even coveted, outside of engineering circles. Multitasking, multithreading, symmetric multiprocessing, client/server: Much of this was pioneered by "UNIX heads" in the quest for ever more CPU power long before the terms became popularized.

But, through no conscious design, UNIX also has become the rallying call for the open systems movement. The IEEE, X/Open Company, OSF, and many others have struggled for years to bring some order to the fractious UNIX market and, in doing so, have brought a much-needed discipline to computing as a whole. There's no doubt that emerging operating systems, such as NT, have benefited from it.

Today UNIX is a capable operating system that has earned the right to be a part of many client/server implementations. Its stability and its scalability in particular have made it a wise choice. In fact, until the arrival of NT, no other operating system could match it.

With a basic understanding of operating systems and networking technologies behind us, we're finally ready to move on to a discussion of client/server. In Chapter 7 we'll wade through some of its definitions and take a look at several organizations that have implemented it successfully.

Key Terms and Ideas Appearing in This Chapter

Alpha:

The Alpha DECchip line is a RISC design that's claimed to be the world's fastest chip. It is Digital's first RISC chip; earlier platforms used chips from MIPS. While Alpha may be fast, platform designers haven't been as successful in getting information on, and off, of it. In actual tests, it usually trails Pentium-powered machines. Digital's working on the problem.

BSD:

Berkeley Software Distribution. The version of UNIX developed at the University of California at Berkeley. It was especially popular on university campuses. BSD x was the first to bundle the TCP/IP suite of protocols right into the OS.

CISC:

Complex Instruction Set Computing. Intel's 80 × 86 line is the archetype for CISC designs and, of that group, the Pentium is the state of the art. CISC designs use more detailed instruction sets—covering practically every imaginable requirement—than do RISC chips. If it were just a matter of instruction size, though, it wouldn't be at all clear why RISC generally is faster than CISC. RISC designers have introduced a number of technical innovations into chip design—many of which are now being adopted by CISC designers as well. Although these innovations lend themselves more easily to the simpler style of instruction set used in RISC, CISC chips such as the Pentium also have made considerable gains in speed because of them. When it comes to integer calculations, for example, the latest generation of Pentiums are as fast, or faster, than many RISC chip out there.

COSE:

Common Open System Environment. An informal grouping of approximately 70 UNIX vendors aimed at bringing greater harmony to the OS as a whole. Really, however, it was seen as a response to the introduction of Microsoft's Windows NT—a possible UNIX killer. The COSE effort has been largely adopted by the revised OSF.

DCE:

The Distributed Computing Environment. DCE is a set of operating system–independent services for the development and use of distributed applications. Designed and developed by the Open Software Foundation (OSF), DCE contains Distributed File Services, Naming Services, a time service, system management services, and security services, the latter of which is based on MIT's Kerberos authentication system.

Kerberos:

Kerberos is a user-authentication system, designed and developed at MIT. It uses a "ticket" system to establish user identities. The whole idea behind Kerberos is first to have users prove who they are and then to limit them to specific services on the network. If a user wishes to access a data server, for example, his or her Kerberos ticket is valid only for that server, and no other. Access to another server would require the acquisition of another ticket. Kerberos has nothing to do with authorization. It doesn't check to see if a user does indeed have the right to access that data server—that's left to that server. Kerberos is part of the OSF's DCE.

Motif:

The graphical user interface designed and marketed by the OSF. It was inspired by Microsoft Windows (which Apple, in turn, says was modeled after the Mac). Motif is now the dominant UNIX GUI.

multithreading:

The simultaneous execution of different parts of the same application, often on different CPUs. OSF/1 is a multithreaded operating system.

Open look:

The graphical user interface acknowledged by AT&T, Sun Microsystems, and supporters of the now-defunct UNIX International. Sun, by the way, called its rendition of the GUI Open Windows. The company now has adopted the OSF's Motif as the standard GUI as part of the COSE movement.

OSF:

The Open Software Foundation. Formed in 1988, the OSF was a protest action against AT&T and Sun in response to what the rest of the UNIX industry saw as an disturbingly close relationship between the two. The protesters also weren't too pleased with revisions to licensing fees levied by AT&T for the System V core. The OSF has produced a graphical user interface, called Motif, now an industry standard; a new operating system, OSF/1; and the Distributed Computing Environment. In March 1994 the OSF unveiled a new business model that included one-time archrival Sun Microsystems. The OSF countergroup, known as UNIX International (headed by AT&T and Sun), folded soon after OSF's move. The new sponsors of the OSF are: AT&T, Bull Worldwide Information Systems, DEC, Fujitsu, Hewlett-Packard, IBM, International Computers Ltd., NEC, Novell, Olivetti, Siemens Nixdorf, Silicon Graphics, Sony, Sun Microsystems, and Transarc.

P6:

A chip that is the successor to the Pentium. With more than 5 million onboard transistors, and some very aggressive designing, it can outpace the fastest Pentium by about 30 percent. It's expected to become available (for both workstations and servers) towards the end of 1995.

Pentium:

The latest in the hugely successful Intel 80×86 family of microprocessors. (The Pentium is the 80586.) Already in its second generation, the Pentium is a sophisticated CISC design able to keep pace with many RISC chips.

POSIX:

Portable Operating System Interface eXtensions. POSIX is a family of standards, proposed by the IEEE, to enhance application portability across platforms. POSIX strives to do this by defining the interface between applications and the operating system. POSIX was originally based on UNIX, but is no longer only restricted to that OS alone.

PowerPC:

A new RISC chip collectively designed by Motorola, Apple, and IBM. Its first commercial use was in an IBM RS/6000 250T. Shortly after, it debuted in Apple's new line of PowerMacs.

RISC:

Reduced Instruction Set Computing. DEC's Alpha and IBM/Motorola/Apple's PowerPC are the leading examples of RISC design. RISC chips do two things CISC (Intel 80×86-like) don't: They work with a smaller instruction set of chip-recognizable commands, and they tend to do most data manipulations right on the chip. Without having to worry as much about history as Intel has had to, with its 80×86 line, RISC designers generally have had a freer hand in their designs. This had led to some revolutionary chips.

RPC:

Remote Procedure Call. RPCs are just an extension to the standard, local, library, or subroutine call. The difference now is, that, as the name implies, the routines being called don't have to sit on the same host. RPCs often are used for remote data access. They are the most interesting when used in conjunction with a multithreaded operating system. Then the main body of the application can issue a number of RPCs and continue to work on something useful while it waits for the responses to return. This is parallel programming.

SPECmark:

Another one of those performance measures popularly bandied about in computer articles. This one makes a bit more sense than some, however. It's an average execution rating for a group of standard programs. There's a SPECfp (floating point) rating and a SPECint (integer) rating.

X:

A network-aware set of display-handling routines for UNIX. X was designed at MIT. Motif is built from X.

Notes

[1] J. Montgomery, "DEC Alpha," *PC Computing*, Feb. 1994, v7, 124.

[2] S. Apiki, "Windows on RISC," *Byte*, April 1994, 109.

[3] M. Jonikas, "DEC 3000 Model 800S AXP Deskside Server," *PC Magazine*, May 31, 1994.

[4] M. Bolzern, "Debunking the Myths about UNIX," *Data Based Advisor*, July 1994, v12, 42.

[5] E. Kay, "Is NT Finally Hitting Stride?" *InformationWeek*, May 30, 1994, 114.

[6] B. Violino, and P. Klein, "A Dogged Security Model," *Information Week*, March 7, 1994, 42.

Chapter 7

Executive Summary

Few other topics generate more interest in computing than client/server. But what is it? Ask three experts, and you'll probably get three answers, maybe more. That's because there is no widely agreed upon definition for client/server.

Client/server has two distinct characters: a technical one and a philosophical one. On the technical side, client/server is seen as a computing model. Part of a spectrum of computing models, it offers the opportunity to put application functionality on the hardware/software combination best suited to the task. The client/server model also offers advantages when it comes to system scalability.

The philosophical side of client/server deals with systems integration. Corporations often hold their data on the mainframe. PCs, now practically ubiquitous, are unsurpassed in their ability to present information to their users. It just makes sense to combine these two environments into a seamless whole. This is client/server by default.

Client/server is our first step toward distributed computing. The challenges that come with trying to link together traditionally disparate computing models make it an expensive and risky undertaking. Client/server solutions often are several times more expensive than comparably sized mainframe systems.

But client/server isn't intended as a replacement for mainframe computing. Contrary to the claims of downsizing advocates, mainframes will remain an essential component to many organization's information technology (IT) infrastructures for some time to come.

CHAPTER 7

Client/Server Computing: Information for the People

Client/Server Is . . .

Client/server is everywhere. Everyone's talking about it. And while they all know that it's a good thing, by their own admission, most of them are hard-pressed to put a definition to it. That's probably because there isn't one; there are several.

Technically speaking, client/server is a model of computing, just as the hierarchical mainframe is a model of computing. Models are abstract notions though. We prefer to think in terms of something more tangible: a PC "client" requesting data from a RISC-based "server" sitting down the hall at the end of a switched Ethernet connection running TCP/IP, that kind of thing. But because the client/server relationship is implemented in software, it's not always that distinct. A computer running a multitasking operating system, such as UNIX or NT, could quite possibly have a "client" and a "server" residing on the same physical device.

But quite apart from the technical definition, there's also a philosophical aspect to client/server. In the late 1980s, we found ourselves with networked PCs, armed to the teeth with office productivity tools. Just one thing was missing: access to the corporate data, which often was safely locked up on the mainframe. Without a painless way to get at it, it might as well have been on another planet. Under a banner of "information for the people," client/server proponents seek to tear down those barriers.

Rather than just break through the walls of the glass house, there are some people who think we should get rid of the mainframe and its style of computing altogether. They're the downsizers. They ask, "Now that we have client/server, why do we need mainframes?" This view is not only misguided, it can be downright dangerous.

Client/server and mainframe computing aren't in contention. Both have their place. Nothing's better at processing information or keeping data more secure than a mainframe. Client/server excels at collaborative computing. While it's by no means unusual (or unreasonable) for both to be a part of an organization's IT infrastructure, we invariably draw comparisons between them. And when we do, we make some rather surprising discoveries.

Mainframes are expensive. Their software is expensive. Their hardware is expensive. They need trained operators to attend to them constantly. They need air-conditioned facilities to run in. Client/server, on the other hand, uses cheap PCs and not terribly expensive RISC- or CISC-based servers. But as it turns out, most people now contend that client/server solutions are much more expensive than we thought—often even much more costly than traditional mainframe implementations.[1]

Client/server is simply more complicated than the types of solutions we've known in the past. Therefore, training is a big part of client/server's hidden cost. Developers, project leaders, designers, administrators, and even end users need to be educated and, in many cases, completely reskilled. Client/server's added complexity is further borne out by the alarming percentage of development projects ending in failure. (Some say as many as 50 percent.) And of those that do make it through development, few actually end up saving money.[2] Maintenance and ongoing technical support—a particularly demanding facet of client/server—usually eat heavily into any savings.

If client/server is so expensive, and so risky, what's the draw? Well, information for the people is a powerful concept. Organizations run on decisions. Giving workers the information they need—when they need it—in a manner that they can readily use should help them to make faster and better decisions. This is a large part of the motivation behind client/server computing.

There's even a third view of client/server. Some see it as a "pass-through" on our way to fully distributed computing. While client/server itself is a form of distributed computing, its extent is limited. In the client/server model, clients are always clients, and servers are always servers. A more flexible, and possibly more efficient, scheme would allow those roles to change as the circumstances dictated. This more distributed style of computing is known as peer-to-peer. Peer-to-peer computing is, realistically, several years away; most of us simply aren't ready for it. But even when it does arrive, there's no reason to assume that client/server will go away. It will always have a place, just as mainframe computing will.

Models of Computing

Client/server is a computing model. So is standalone. So is monolithic mainframe. So is file serving. They're all part of a spectrum of possible computing models illustrated in Figure 7.1.

As we move from left to right, things become progressively more complicated. The relationship between the various members of each model also becomes more democratic. Finally, in the peer-to-peer model, at the far right, all members are equal; mainframes are no more important than any other device on the network. But the figure doesn't tell the whole picture; computing models aren't just a matter of hardware alone. Software is what bestows their identities.

The client/server model is said to have a one-to-many relationship; usually, a number of clients request the services of a single server. And what might those services be? A server might dispatch, accept,

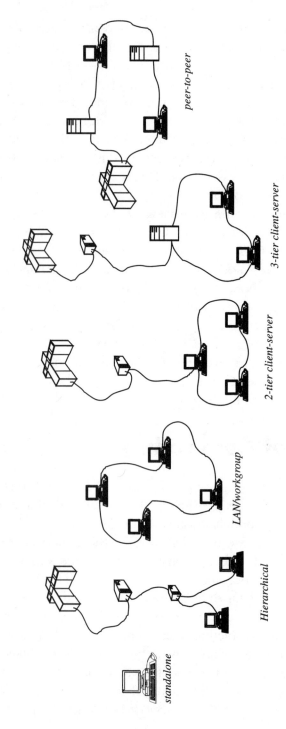

Figure 7.1 Models of computing.

standalone

Hierarchical

LAN/workgroup

2-tier client-server

3-tier client-server

peer-to-peer

156

and manage faxes on behalf of its clients. Alternatively, a server might perform information searches, as we saw during our discussion of the Internet. If it was running on a particularly capable machine, a server might perform computationally demanding calculations for its clients. Or, as in the popular usage of the term "client/server," a server might hold departmental or corporate data and provide database query and management capabilities to its clients.

To truly qualify as "client/server," there's an implicit requirement that both the client and the server add value to the information they process. Therefore, file serving is *not* client/server. A file server—a separate device and a separate software "entity" to be sure—doesn't do anything other than serve up data and applications requested by the desktop. It's like a big, remote hard disk. A data server, on the other hand, responds to a query from the client for certain information, locates it in its database, possibly performs a calculation upon it (if the client so desires), and presents it to the client. Or the client might take the raw data and present it to the user in a special way. It might even perform some calculations of its own, before it does. All along the way, value is added to the raw information.

Certain attributes of a client/server application best belong on the client or the server. We can regard an application as being made up of a presentation component, a computation component, and a data component. Deciding what goes where is called partitioning. Presentation, for example, is almost always best relegated to the client. Data and computation can be associated with the client, the server, or both. (See Figure 7.2.)

Designating a server for data and a separate server for computation within the same client/server implementation doesn't contravene the one-to-many relationship. In fact, data and computation even can be distributed across multiple servers and still uphold the model. In fact, often this is how the mainframe participates in a client/server solution.

Mainframes often are the holders of the corporate data. But in many client/server systems, a mid-range device (unfortunately usually called the server) stands between the mainframe and the clients. This is the so-called three-tier client/server model, and when exclusively working with data, is sometimes also referred to as "data warehousing." In this

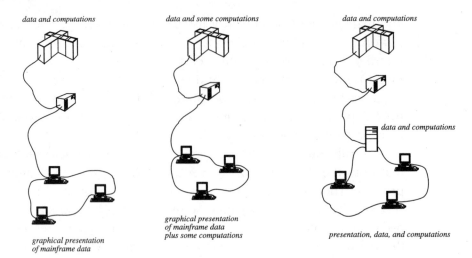

Figure 7.2 Some possibilities for the placement of data, computations, and presentation.

arrangement, working data is kept on the server with a master copy on the mainframe.

When the mainframe is factored in, and when data and computation are allowed to exist on any or all devices, the number of permutations becomes considerable. Here client/server possibilities vary in their degree of distributedness. On the far right of the spectrum, once data and computation are free to move, and once the roles of clients and servers can change, we transition into peer-to-peer computing.

Peer-to-peer computing exhibits a many-to-many relationship. What's a server in one instance can be a client the next, and every client or server can interact with every other client or server. Given that we're still coming to terms with client/server, however, peer-to-peer computing is, realistically, several years away.

What's Good about Client/Server

What can client/server actually do for us? We've seen that it's loaded with risk, so whatever it is, it had better be pretty good. Benefits of client/server come from both its technical side and its philosophical side. The argument for the technical benefits goes something like this: If we can separate presentation, computation, and data, each area can be taken care of or performed on a hardware/software combination best suited for the task. This should produce a higher-quality end product and result in a solution that's more adaptable to change.

Consider the typical client/server system. Presentation and computation are the responsibility of the desktop station. Departmental, or even corporate, data resides in a database on a dedicated server. If system response time begins to suffer because of additional user demands or swelling data volumes, the database and its engine can be migrated to a more powerful server without affecting the user side of the application whatsoever.

Instead of one database server, there could just as easily be two. Mirror images of each other, if the primary server fails, client queries could be shunted automatically to the secondary server located at another location. To the client, nothing's different.

Network traffic also can be kept in better check with the client/server model. If an end user needs to review a derived value instead of raw data, the computation can be performed on the server, with only the result sent over the network to the client.

Then there are the benefits that come out of the philosophical side of client/server. Initially, at least, these have more to do with system integration than client/server, however. The general thread of logic often takes this form: If workers can access information seamlessly whenever they need it, they should be able to make faster, and better, decisions. But to maximize benefit, the information should be provided in an easily understood, and quickly digested format: something that personal computers are especially adept at. The information itself usually resides in a central store, on a mainframe or departmental minicomputer. Linking high-presentation-value PCs to these machines backs us into a client/server style solution.

Finally, there's the "let's make better use of what we've got" argument. PCs are a lot more powerful than they used to be. Moving presentation and some measure of computation off of existing mainframes and minis and onto PCs can not only make better use of them, but also theoretically reduce the upgrade frequency of the larger and more expensive machines.

What's Bad about Client/Server

Allthough there are a lot of positives concerning client/server, it has a number of negative things going for it too, however. It's hard to put them in order, but certainly near the top of any list is the amount of misleading information surrounding the whole idea. Client/server has been grossly oversold. And since it lacks a single, clear definition, the door is wide open to general misunderstanding. It's widely believed that client/server is a modern-day replacement for hierarchical computing solutions, for example. But as we discussed earlier, that's simply not true.

Another popular misconception is that client/server is inexpensive. Again, not true. It may use inexpensive PCs as clients, but when everything else is factored in—education, more demanding application development, security, systems management and maintenance—it often turns out to be more expensive than a comparably sized mainframe effort. But more than just increasing implementation costs, the special challenges associated with many of these same issues threaten the very success of a client/server project.

Heterogeneity also weighs heavily against client/server success. There's no guarantee that a database engine from vendor A will work with a client application built with a tool from vendor B if client and server are connected by a network supplied by vendor C—if it's Tuesday, and the moon is full. Seriously though, when you stop and take everything into account—operating systems, networking protocols, CPU designs—it's amazing that client/server works at all. It's the price we pay for living in an non–open systems world.

Client/server is still relatively new. Not only do we lack widespread experience, but there's an acute shortage of comprehensive tools. This is perhaps most evident in the areas of systems management and security. To date, few products can simultaneously monitor and control both mainframe and LAN-based systems—bad news for client/server, which often lies somewhere between the two. The state of client/server security is even less cheery. Apart from an almost complete absence of tools, client/server's "information for the people" philosophy flies directly in the face of historical security practices. This is certain to become the topic of much debate over the next few years.

But folks are using the client/server model, and many of them are deriving hard benefits from it. We examine four such cases in the next section.

Client/Server: Who's Using It

Client/server implementations are as varied as the organizations using them. In spite of this, there are some commonalities. As we've seen before, client/server usually means client/*data* server. And when it comes to data, either you can perform adjustments (transactions) on it, or you can query it, in order to gain information for decision support. Of the two, decision support is by far the most common use for client/server.

Banking on Client/Server

Neuberger and Berman Management, Inc., is a New York–based mutual fund provider. On a typical day, it receives about 1,000 requests for fund literature from prospective customers. To meet this need, the company relied on a contractor's mainframe-based order fulfillment system. In need of modernization, the contractor finally decided to overhaul the system and migrate it to OS/2. This meant that Neuberger and Berman would need to purchase new equipment, however. Already committed to NetWare and unsatisfied with a number of aspects of the new-order system's functionality, the firm decided to terminate its relationship with the contractor and go it alone.

The application would be used by various groups within the company. Marketing, for example, was interested in determining what percentage of literature requests resulted in a sale. With its sizable NetWare installation, Neuberger and Berman reasoned that it was well positioned to take advantage of a client/server solution to meet these different needs.

To construct the new order fulfillment system, the Information Systems (IS) group selected PowerSoft's PowerBuilder. PowerBuilder has a significant slice of the client/server tools market. Strictly speaking, it's a client tool that provides programmers with the ability to design and craft application screens and then connect up selected fields on these windows to information maintained by a number of popular database engines. Neuberger and Berman chose Sybase's SQL Server running in a NetWare NLM configuration.

No more than 30 workers needed to use the system. Concurrent usage would be only a small percentage of this. Data volumes weren't intractable either, meaning that the database and engine could be deployed on an Intel 80486-class server. This was convenient. It meant that the company didn't need to acquire new skills to support it.

Almost immediately, however, things started to go wrong. System response time was slow. But worse, the Windows application began crashing with alarming frequency. Desperate for a solution, Neuberger and Berman's development team acquired a number of software "patches" from the participating vendors. (Most post them on CompuServe, for example.) But as soon as one was applied, something else would fail. The team decided their problems lay with IPX or, more specifically, the IPX/SQL Server relationship. They believed that the database engine was unable to recognize when an IPX connection was terminated. Additional patching didn't improve things, so they moved from SPX/IPX to TCP/IP. The system is now in production.

Analysis

Does this prove that TCP/IP is better suited for client/server implementations than SPX/IPX? Not necessarily. One of the most vexing problems with client/server is its heterogeneity. A certain version of NetWare and a certain version of PowerBuilder and a certain version of Windows and a certain version of SQL Server may work well together, but change any one of these, and the result may be quite different.

Neuberger and Berman's reasons to go client/server are interesting. It needed an application that could cater to the needs of very different end users. One group needed to access the system to log customer requests; another needed it for shipment purposes. But Marketing wanted to get some idea of how successful the company's literature was at attracting customers. The uniqueness of each of these needs could be placed on the client side of the application. On top of this, the company already had many of the elements of a client/server solution in place—or so it thought. In the end, after considerable effort, it had to add a new networking protocol to the inventory. This demonstrates that even the smallest of client/server implementations may run into plenty of unexpected problems. It's an all-too-common story.

A World-Class Event

It's the world's largest single sporting event. Its final game drew a television audience 10 times the size of the Super Bowl. It's the World Cup, and in 1994, it was held in the United States for the first time.

On the face of it, the 1994 World Cup was a logistics nightmare. Over a one-month period, 24 teams would play 52 games at nine different cities spread across four different time zones. (See Figure 7.3.) Teams would move from city to city as they won their games and moved to the next level of competition. While all this was going on, results needed to be compiled and recorded, and the world press needed to get information out to the fans.

Then there was the matter of security. Soccer has a reputation of stirring up the passions of its fans—often to the point of violence. At several sites around the globe, altercations did, in fact, break out—some

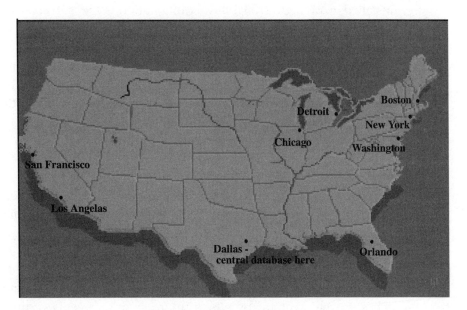

Figure 7.3 Games sites for the 1994 World Cup.

with tragic consequences. To restrict the movement of nonauthorized personnel, some means of tracking the 20,000-plus identification passes was required.

Planners wanted to make attending fans feel as connected to the games as possible. They envisioned kiosks, spread around the games sites, that could instantly provide historical and even personal information on the players. Image and video were favored for this job.

Although central control was called for, distributing functionality to the games sites would reduce network traffic and improve system response times. This pointed toward a client/server solution.

In exchange for advertising rights, Sprint, Electronic Data Systems Inc. (EDS), and Sun Microsystems partnered to deliver the system. Sprint provided all communications, Sun came through with the hardware, and EDS built the software to make it all work.

The central database (Sybase) was used for ticket management, security, the World News Service, and World Cup Bulletin connections to CompuServe and America Online. It's also where running game statistics, historical data, player information, security photos, and video clips were kept. Located in Plano, Texas, it sat on two SPARCcenter 2000s installed in a high-availability configuration. One server was active, while the other was a hot standby, mirroring the first in case of system failure.

Redundancy was an important consideration throughout the system design. Dual routers and dual T1 or T3 lines connected all the cities. The TCP/IP-based WAN employed a spiderweb design connecting each city with at least two data links.

The front end of the system was a graphical touch-screen application developed using Sybase's Gain Momentum object-oriented toolset. It ran atop Sun's Solaris (UNIX) operating system on an array of client stations composed of 600 SPARCstation 10s and approximately 1,000 SPARCclassic workstations. The SS 10s were located in the game center kiosks to provide image and video support. The SPARclassics were used by games administration staff and the world press.

By all accounts, the 1994 World Cup was a great success. And few would disagree that in no small part technology was a key contributor. It has set the standard by which future sporting events of this caliber will be judged.

Analysis

As applications go, this one was as about as mission critical as it gets for its users. It shows what can be done if you're willing to make the investment. (It's estimated that the participants spent somewhere in the neighborhood of $14 million to pull it off.)

Possibly one of the most interesting aspects of the project, apart from the glitz of the technology and take-no-prisoners manner in which it was implemented was the unusual degree of homogeneity among the hardware and software components. All the principal software and hardware components came from the same vendors. Contrary to our quest for open systems, selecting products from an array of manufacturers certainly would have complicated implementation. Since the system was to be torn down following the games, its designers weren't encumbered with concerns about single-vendor tie-in or product obsolescence.

Taking the Cure

Wisconsin's Department of Health and Social Services administers the state's $2.3 billion Medicaid program. Although the state has no such estimates, the federal government predicts that as much as 10 percent of this amount is paid out to unnecessary or all-out fraudulent claims. In order to get a better feel for such activities, the state has undertaken an ambitious program to overhaul its existing records-keeping system.

The Medicaid Evaluation and Decision Support system, or MEDS for short, will provide its users with decision and even artificial intelligence support. The project is expected to cost $5.8 million. The old system was antiquated, to say the least. Claims information was stored in flat files on a VAX. The problem was that the information was incomplete. Necessary supporting data was kept in a paper format. The system was also slow and difficult to work with. Little of it could be salvaged.

The new system is built around Oracle's database engine. It actually runs on two separate machines. A portion of the data is kept on a Compaq SMP server containing a dual Pentium configuration, 256 MB of memory and 20 GB of disk. Acquired as part of an earlier imaging project, it also has 144 GB of optical near-line storage. The server runs Windows NT and is part of a NetWare 4.1 network.

The other server is an HP 9000 workstation with four RISC processors. It has 640 MB of memory, 300 GB of disk, and 200 GB of optical archival. It directly attaches to the MEDS system through a 100Mbps FDDI backbone.

MEDS clients run Microsoft's Windows for Workgroups and intend to migrate to Windows 95 when it becomes available. The front end was built using Microsoft's Visual Basic. The design team chose it because of its gentle learning curve and quick prototyping capabilities. The VB application facilitates database access and orchestrates the standard office productivity tools used to analyze it.

If federal estimates are correct, $230 million of Wisconsin's Medicaid dollars are paid out inappropriately. If MEDS corrects even 10 percent of this, it will deliver a fourfold return on the $5.8 million investment in its first year alone. And if it does, watch for similar efforts to follow in other states.

Analysis

In this case, doing practically anything would have improved matters. The team chose a client/server solution to take advantage of office productivity tools already familiar to computer users in the department. With the vast amount of software being written for it, the PC is the most open platform we've got. MEDS starts there and then augments functionality with the two database servers. Why two? The department already has a capable Compaq server on site that it wanted to incorporate into the system, but it alone couldn't run the entire system.

Keeping Their PROMISe

Lockheed is one of the world's largest aerospace companies. The support mechanism needed to run an organization of its size is staggering. In a typical year, for example, more than 30,000 purchase requests pass through the system—the majority more than once. Lockheed used to use a complex, paper-driven request process that most users found frustrating and difficult to work with. As many as 75 percent of the total number of purchase requests had to be returned to their sources because of errors. As a result, a purchase request that should have taken days actually required an average of six weeks to be actioned.

Not unusual for an organization of its size and type, Lockheed has PCs, Macs, Sun workstations, and Digital DECstations on the desktops throughout the company. Any technological solution to the purchase request problem had to work with this existing base.

As it turned out, the company already had an automated purchase request system in place in one of its smaller divisions. The problem was that it ran on an aging VAX. Certain that something could be salvaged from it, Lockheed elected to construct a client/server solution around the VAX-based purchase request system that could integrate with the various desktops. They call it PROMIS: Procurement Online Management Information System.

But while a client/server version of the purchase request system might make the process more approachable, it didn't address its fundamental complexity of the process. Purchasing policies still required users to go through as many as 104 different checkpoints to get what they needed. So system designers added an expert system to the client/server solution. The expert system scans users inputs and prompts them if something's not quite right.

Designers selected Oracle's database engine for the back end of the application. It runs on a Sun UNIX/RISC server. While that was reasonably straightforward, the front end posed a challenge. The application had to run on a number of different client devices yet appear the same on each. For this, the client/server design team turned to Neuron Data's Open Interface Elements (OIE). OIE belongs to a family of products called code generators. Unlike PowerBuilder or Visual Basic, OIE assists in the development and construction of the screens only, generating C++ code for them. It's left to the developer to code them to the back-end database. The attraction is that OIE produces portable code.

The expert system was constructed with Neuron Data's Smart Elements, an object-oriented business-rule development tool designed for the client/server environment.

Does it all work? The results speak for themselves: A process that used to take six weeks has been shaved down to an average of 2.5 days. PROMIS's designers are confident that by streamlining the procurement process, the company will save several million dollars a year.

Analysis

This case demonstrates how a client/server solution can be adapted to a company's existing infrastructure. System designers used a code generator to construct a portable GUI that runs across several different client devices. The interface appears the same no matter what device is used.

It also demonstrates that existing software systems occasionally can be incorporated into a client/server design. PROMIS contains large portions of the original code from the older VAX-based purchase request system. This is actually a bit unusual. But because the designers weren't relying on a 4GL, such as Visual Basic or PowerBuilder, and instead were building everything themselves in C++, this was not only easier but desirable.

Finally, perhaps the most intriguing facet of this case is the use of the expert system. PROMIS's designers have not only delivered "information for the people," they've added knowledge delivery as well. Expert systems were popular a few years ago and then they sort of faded away. One reason why, might have been that business wasn't really ready for them. The concept of "boxing up" an expert's knowledge to have whenever you need it is a great idea, but workers need access to basic corporate information stores first. Once that's in place, then the notion of adding value with something like an expert system becomes worth considering.

Wrap-up

You might conclude from all the press it receives that client/server is a cure-all to the woes of computing. Not quite. It has its place, but it's a solution that must be chosen wisely. A shortage of tools, a lack of proven implementation practices, the complexities of distributed computing: all conspire to make client/server development a risky practice.

Client/server is also not a replacement for mainframe computing. There may be times when a business problem can be solved by either approach, but few organizations are about to sweep away their mainframe investments to embark upon a largely unproven and possibly even more expensive client/server alternative.

There are benefits to client/server, of course. Combining the presentation abilities of the personal computer, the flexibility of midrange servers, and the data processing talents of the mainframe, client/server can bring together the best of computing. It can be a bit of a challenge, but people are doing it.

Two things can be said about almost every client/server implementation discussed: It had to fit into the existing infrastructure, and it was hard to fit into the existing infrastructure. Even in situations that look dead-easy, something always happens, as in the case of Neuberger and Berman. Fortunately, the company had some good people on staff who were able to identify the problem. Many projects don't turn out as well.

Client/server can squeeze more out of your existing computer technology. This is where it shines. Adding to what's already there to leverage a company's investment is what client/server does best. We saw that in three of our four cases.

The World Cup application is an unusual one and not overly representative of how client/server is being used. But it gives us a glimpse into the future. As more affordable WAN technologies such as SMDS and ATM become available, imaging, video-on-demand and other high-bandwidth technologies certainly will follow.

What makes client/server development so complex? Why do so many client/server projects end in failure? We begin to get a better idea of the complexity involved in the next chapter, when we take a detailed look at the client, the middle, and the server.

Notes

[1] T. Collins, "Can You Afford to Adopt Client/Server?" *Computer Weekly*, June 1994, 10.
[2] R. Finkelstein, "Client/Server: Not a Cure-all," *Visual Basic Programmer's Journal*, Oct.–Nov., 1994, v4, 136.

Chapter 8

Executive Summary

At a high level, client/server systems have only three components: a client, a server, and something network-related that stands between the two. Clients are usually PCs, running a graphical user interface (GUI). This allows them to take on the presentation component of the application. Several GUIs are in use today, but overwhelmingly, the leading choice for client/server applications is Microsoft's Windows.

MS Windows is actually a memory-extender that happens to have a graphical interface. It works with DOS, the underlying operating system, to give programs access to extended or expanded memory beyond DOS's 640 KB memory "barrier." Windows relies on a number of unique methods to exchange information between programs running on top of it. The incredible success of the Windows has made it the de facto standard. Of its methods, OLE (Object Linking and Embedding) is probably of most interest to end users. OLE allows users to create Windows applications in which various parts can be created and edited seamlessly by other dedicated Windows applications. It shifts the end user's emphasis from applications to data.

In the client/server relationship, servers usually hold the data. Most often this is kept in a relational database management system (RDBMS). Relational databases are favored over other types because of their speed and their modular design. The only way to get at the data stored in a relational database is with Structured Query Language (SQL).

Because the ANSI standard for SQL has such limited capability, RDBMS vendors have been forced to add to it. This has led to a proliferation of incompatible SQLs. To insulate client/server programmers from the need to learn different versions, SQL translators have been proposed. The best known of these is Microsoft's Open Database Connectivity (ODBC).

Products like ODBC belong to often ill-defined category of software known as middleware. Although still popularly used as a catchall phrase, three official forms of middleware are gaining recognition: remote procedure calls, message-passing, and object-request brokers. Their arrival signifies an increasing maturity of the client/server computing model.

CHAPTER 8

The Client, the Middle, and the Server

Introduction

Although their exact functions can vary, clients generally are responsible for presentation and computation, while servers take care of the data. Once a client/server application is up and running, system tuning can take place. At that time, a portion of the computational load may be shifted over to the server to run alongside of the database engine if necessary.

Practically without exception, these database engines adhere to the relational model of database design. In this model, all data takes the form of tables. And also practically without exception, the language used to manipulate the data stored in these tables is the Structured

Query Language (SQL). For this reason, relational database management systems are often referred to as SQL-servers.

SQL is a standard specified by the American National Standards Institute (ANSI). But it's incomplete; the language has numerous inadequacies. This has compelled SQL-server vendors, such as Oracle, Sybase, and Informix, to extend SQL. As a result, there's no such thing as portable SQL. Since organizations often have more than one SQL-server kicking around, this is cause for concern. For many, an interim answer are SQL managers, such as ODBC from Microsoft and Independent Database Application Programming Interface (IDAPI) from Borland, IBM, and Novell. Part of the often murky dimension known as middleware, these products substitute a virtual SQL-server with its own virtual SQL for many of the more popular (actual) renditions on the market today.

Unlike the server RDBMS, or the chosen middleware, the identity of the client is one facet of the client/server equation that's unusually persistent. In the majority of cases, "client" has come to mean DOS/Windows client. This has nothing to do with some unusual technical prowess on the part of the duo: Far from it; DOS/Windows is a buggy union disliked by programmers far and wide. But in the "if you can't beat 'em, join 'em department," DOS/Windows vastly outsells any other would-be client operating system. That attracts more third-party vendors to it and, in turn, further perpetuates its own popularity.

The Client Side

Clients can be saddled with many tasks within a client/server application. They often perform calculations. They sometimes store data. But they're almost always responsible for the presentation of information.

Often employing a graphical user interface (GUI), edit lines, drop-down list boxes, push buttons, and other graphics make the job of using a computer more intuitive. And while there's nothing in the technical definition of client/server about GUIs, almost all clients use them; if you're going to go through all the trouble of getting data to a worker's desktop, it might as well look nice when it gets there.

When it comes to GUIs, none has the market presence of Microsoft's Windows. It is, without question, the dominant style of interface in client/server implementations today.

Microsoft's Windows

To say that Microsoft's Windows has captured the largest share of the GUI market is to put things mildly. It *is* the market. By the end of 1994, Windows outsold OS/2 and UNIX by more than 15 to 1. DOS, Windows' underlying operating system, held a market share 30 times that of OS/2 and UNIX.

That makes DOS the most widely used operating system in existence. A pity, because as operating systems go, DOS is pretty clunky. To this day, it still can't cope with memory requirements exceeding 640 Kb. That's a ghost from its past. When the original PC was being dreamed up, IBM went with Intel's 8088 CPU—and an empire was born.

The 8088 featured a 20-bit address bus, meaning that it could access as much as 1,048,576 eight-bit memory locations—a seemingly inexhaustible amount back in 1981. So the designers of that humble machine's first operating system, Microsoft, decided to limit the actual addressable space to 640 Kb (still thought to be plenty) and use the 400 Kb or so left over for video display and general housekeeping. It turned out to be an unfortunate move. Programmers ran into the 640 Kb barrier much sooner than anyone predicted.

Intel's 80286 helped out somewhat, by adding an additional 15 Mb of addressable memory in a region that came to be known as extended memory. When running DOS on an 80286, specially outfitted applications can access the extended memory by swapping data into, and out of, the basic 640 Kb space, which itself is known as real mode. The problem with this is that it comes with a performance penalty. It also made writing software for DOS a pain.

On top of all that, DOS often has problems with extended memory. So Lotus, Intel, and Microsoft came up with another idea: the Expanded Memory Specification, EMS. Software specifically written to the EMS standard can access as much as 32 MB of memory under DOS. (This figure is even higher with the Intel 80386 and greater.) Depending on the resident CPU and what kind of memory the system's got, Windows sits on top of DOS, making extended or expanded memory available to applications.

Officially, this makes Windows a DOS extender. It might look like an entirely new operating system, but underneath, it's still DOS, warts and all.

Windows exchanges information between applications running on top of it in some very unique ways. As the interface has become more entrenched in the computing world, these exchange mechanisms have become de facto standards. And as client/server applications strive to integrate the desktop with remotely held applications and data running on dedicated boxes, programmers and designers have had to become familiar with them.

Dynamic Link Libraries

Check any standard Windows 3.x setup, and you'll find 50 or so files with the extension "dll". DLL stands for Dynamic Link Library, a form of Windows executable program. Essentially, DLLs are libraries that contain functions and Windows resources. But they're not typical libraries. They offer a Windows application the possibility of dynamic runtime linking—something more efficient than traditional static (compile time) linking. During static linking, actual copies of the library functions are bound to the executable. If two or more applications happen to call the same functions, then there are that many copies of them bouncing around the system at the same time. When library functions are dynamically linked, routines are loaded only in response to end-user needs. It results in a better usage of available memory.

DLLs also encourage good programming style. Using DLLs, programs can be modularized, easing maintenance requirements. Instead of one large executable, an application can consist of a smaller main program and one or more supporting DLLs. (DLLs by themselves aren't executable.) This makes it easier for a group of software developers to participate on a Windows development project.

Most Windows-supporting compilers can create DLLs. And they're quite flexible; an application even can call a DLL function that was written in a language different from that of the calling program. DLLs are more challenging to build and implement than static libraries are, however. The resolution of DLL function calls, for example, demands the use of something called an import librarian. It assures the compiler that the identified function indeed exists and is available.

Various client side tool vendors, such as PowerSoft, allow programmers to augment functionality of their PowerBuilder applications through the use of DLLs. DLLs are one of those things that sounds great in theory; if you have some legacy code that can be recompiled as a DLL, it can be called, and essentially enveloped, into the PowerBuilder application. But in practice, it never seems to work that smoothly. DLLs are fussy things to work with.

DLLs are primarily of interest to programmers. Some of Windows' other data exchange mechanisms, such as DDE, are of more relevance to Windows users as well.

Dynamic Data Exchange

Dynamic Data Exchange (DDE) enables both Windows 3.x and OS/2 (Microsoft originally built it too, remember) applications to use another DDE-compliant program's data as if it were its own. This isn't cutting and pasting. DDE is fully automatic; once a link is established, data transparently "flows" between DDE-supporting applications. Microsoft came up with DDE while working on Excel, the company's well-known spreadsheet. It proved so handy, the company built it right into Windows 2.0. Today, any fully Windows-compliant application can participate in information-sharing via DDE.

Establishing data links in DDE-supporting applications usually is straightforward. It's relatively easy to set up a data link between MS Word and Excel, for example. In Word's main menu bar, there's an option called Insert. If the document's author wanted to dynamically embed the results of some spreadsheet calculation, he or she would invoke the Insert option at an appropriate point in the document and then select Field..."Auto" (or "Link" in Windows 3.x). The author would then fill in the field-code template providing Word with the target application, "Excel" (the spreadsheet name), and the row and column number of the spreadsheet cell. After that, whenever that cell's contents changed, it would be reflected automatically in the Word document.

DDE follows a client/server model for its data exchange. Clients, as Word was in the last paragraph, accept incoming data. Clients can access multiple servers, and a single Windows application even can act as both a client and a server.

DDE data interactions are called conversations. Clients initiate conversations by specifying the target, the topic, and an item, just as we did a moment ago. With the advent of Windows for Workgroups (Windows 3.11), clients and servers even can reside on different machines.

When using NetDDE, a client must include a node name in the server specification as well.

DDE has a questionable future, however. OLE, Microsoft's popular scheme for Object Linking and Embedding, used to sit on top of DDE. As data exchange was somewhat slow, the latest rendition of OLE (version 2.0) relies on remote procedure calls instead.

Objects of Desire

All of a sudden, everything's object-this and object-that. You might well wonder what all the fuss's about. Object-oriented programming (OOP) is a way of thinking, and programming, that holds the promise of reducing program development time through component reuse. From the end-user perspective, OOP applications work better together and will help to integrate our desktops in the process. Microsoft's Object Linking and Embedding (OLE), pronounced "o-lay," is intended to do just that.

PC users are application-focused—at least, so says Microsoft. To be more productive, the company believes users should be data-focused instead. OLE can help. It allows the creation of documents, spreadsheets, databases, and other Windows-based applications in which parts are creatable and editable by different Windows applications better suited for the immediate task. Double-clicking on an embedded or linked object seamlessly invokes the application that created it. The object then can be updated in a separate window that's intimately tied to the original Windows application. If an Excel spreadsheet (an "object" in this case) were embedded in a Word document (the "container"), for example, a double-click on the spreadsheet would launch Excel, with its cells populated with the relevant data. When complete, the object is reembedded or relinked back into that application. In many respects, OLE is sort of like "DDE-plus."

Embedding an OLE object creates a copy of the source document, while linking, like DDE, just establishes a reference to it. This means that embedding is static. Linking is dynamic.

Some of the confusion around OLE's object-orientedness stems from its dual nature; OLE is both a Windows interface standard—a set of protocols really—and an assemblage of data and code in the object-oriented tradition, a tradition that has finally taken hold after going through spurts and stalls since the mid-1960s.

For as long as folks have been programming computers, there has been talk about code reusability. It makes sense; how many times has a programmer, even the same programmer, written a chunk of code that does essentially the same thing as something he or she wrote before? If all those chunks were stored in a library somewhere, the programmer wouldn't need to keep on reinventing the wheel. Development time would drop off—and possibly even melt away. This is the holy grail of object-oriented programming.

Why don't programmers reuse code? There are lots of reasons, but generally, they just don't program in a way that allows it to be done easily. When programmers tackle a task, they see the solution as one big "thing"—oh, they might lay out functions and subroutines, but it's still a "start here, step, step, step, and end there" design. If programmers remember that a piece of code they're about to write feels similar to something they've done before, first they have to find the program they built it in and then locate the code fragment they want. After that, they have to copy it and then shoe-horn it into the current application. This all takes a lot of time, and often it's just easier to recode it from scratch.

Reusing code their colleagues built is even less likely. There are two problems here: First of all, how does a programmer know that someone else wrote what is needed? And if so, will that person be able to find it? Will he or she have the time to find it? Will it be exactly what the programmer needs? Usually it's just not worth the effort. As for the other problem, it has to do with a curious little facet of programmer behavior: Programmers hate using other programmer's code. And it's not just an attitude thing. Everyone has his or her own programming style. By the time you've familiarized yourself with someone else's, and confirmed the logic flow, you could have written it yourself.

Enter object-oriented programming. OOP addresses these issues on several fronts. First, it encourages the use of small, modular pieces of code. This code performs a fundamental task—something more basic than a traditional function or a subroutine would. Object-oriented programs are assembled from these building blocks, inspiring many to draw the analogy of working with pieces of Lego.

The code inside these modules also is shielded from view. Only the programmer who built the module knows exactly what's inside. Other programmers, wishing to use it, need only know what it does, and how to make it do it. These modules of code are the definition for "objects."

In OOP, the term "object" is used just as it is in the real world. Cars, vases, planes, pancreases: They're all objects. So are you and I. Beyond that, we're unique examples of the notion of a "person." This more abstract concept is referred to as a class. Classes define generic objects. They're like templates. The definition of a generic automobile, for example, might go something like this:

an automobile has an engine
an automobile has wheels
an automobile has windows
an automobile has doors
an automobile is a color
an automobile can accommodate passengers
an automobile moves
an automobile stops
an automobile accelerates
an automobile decelerates
an automobile refuels

Some of these describe automobile behavior, while others generally describe what it looks like. Together, they're the class definition. This is another unique thing about object-oriented programming: Data and the actions executable upon it are treated as a single package. This prevents the possibility of the data from getting out of sync with the "programs" (slices of code really) that work with it.

Moving from the general to the specific leads to the notion of the class hierarchy. (See Figure 8.1.)

The Legend and Sierra are instances of the class "automobile." They do most of the same basic things, and they use the same data definitions. In OOP-speak, these two characteristics are referred to as methods and instance variables (or attributes). Methods are pieces of code that manipulate the instance variables (the data). They represent all of the actions that an object can perform.

In spite of their similarities, trucks and cars are different, however. That's reflected by the additional method for the Sierra (carry payload). All the other methods are inherited from the class definition above it. This is another feature of OOP, one that also can significantly impact program development. If a fundamental change needed to be made

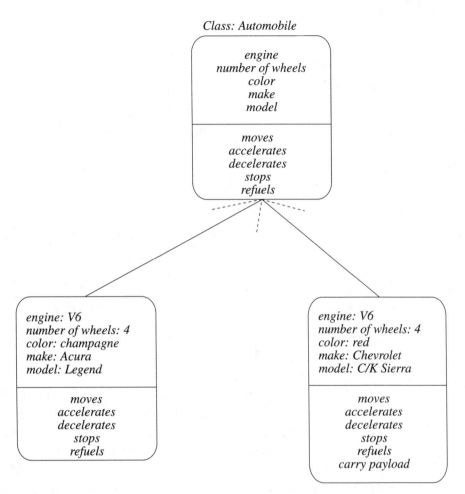

Class: Automobile

Figure 8.1 A class hierarchy for automobile.

to an object-oriented program, rather than adjust each method for all the objects in a system, only the higher-level (common to all) methods need to be modified. The modifications trickle down to all the objects beneath them in the hierarchy.

Objects communicate with each other by message passing. The messages are aimed at the methods contained in the object. (See Figure 8.2.)

This is the only way objects interact with each other. The execution of an object-oriented program is really a set of messages being exchanged between objects.

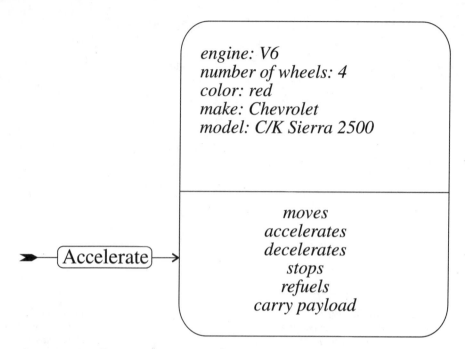

Figure 8.2 Telling an object to accelerate.

Instead of automobiles, what if we were modeling human behavior? We all do many of the same basic things, but often we do them differently. We all eat, but some of us use a fork and knife, while others use chopsticks. While the method "eat" would exist in the person class definition, in the inherited objects lower in the hierarchy, each would have a customized version of the method to reflect this individuality. The same message would be used to initiate the action in all, but the details of how to execute that action are left up to the object itself. This goes under that rather grandiose title of polymorphism.

Objects should be stored in a corporate class library. This library must be well documented, closely controlled, and easy to get at and use. The ultimate success or failure of code reusability demands it. But this has less to do with the idea of objects and classes than with good old-fashioned discipline. The construction of a class library is an obvious requirement, yet most organizations tend to drop the ball when it comes to class library development and maintenance. Programming techniques and languages can go only so far; it's up to organizations to establish an OOP regimen and then to stick to it.

Speaking of languages, the grand old language of object-oriented programming is called SmallTalk. It was invented in the 1970s at Xerox's Palo Alto Research Center (PARC). SmallTalk sticks pretty close to the notion of OOP. Programmers are required to work in terms of messages, objects, and methods. It's a reasonably easy language to learn, certainly in comparison to C++, the most widely used of the object-oriented languages. C++ is an object-oriented extension to C, a fact that contributed to its widespread acceptance in the programming community; experienced C programmers theoretically can make the jump to this new language with relative ease. But it's a good news, bad news kind of thing. There's nothing within C++ that forces programmers to follow the object-oriented style of programming. It's completely possible to take a C++ compiler and write good old procedural C code. Not so in SmallTalk.

Just a few years ago, it looked as if SmallTalk didn't have much of a future. It created slower executables than C++ and ran on few platforms. Now things appear to be turning around. IBM, for one, has thrown its weight behind SmallTalk, leaving some to speculate that it's destined to become the next Cobol. Perhaps, but C++ has some powerful backers too—both Microsoft and Borland are strongly committed to it—and it enjoys a considerable following among programmers. Both languages undoubtedly are destined to have a substantial impact on future program development.

Getting back to our original discussion, in spite of all the hype surrounding it, OLE has a number of shortcomings. Relying on Windows' clipboard for its data dealings, it can cope with only so much data. Linking or embedding very large objects can lead to lost data and "out-of-memory" errors. Currently OLE can't exchange data between networked applications either, but a networked version is in the works.

OLE is a big part of Microsoft's desktop strategy. The company intends for it to become the standard for dealing with compound documents. Judging from all the third-party interest in it, this just might happen. But OLE is being challenged by OpenDoc. Jointly developed by Apple, IBM, Novell, Oracle, and Xerox, OpenDoc, like OLE, allows applications to be combined seamlessly on demand, to create documents containing text, image, and even video. Most believe it to be technically superior to Microsoft's offering. The OpenDoc consortium itself positions it as a superset of OLE. But OLE has one clear advantage over OpenDoc: It's been on the market longer and has established a solid beachhead. Once again, it all comes down to timing.

OLE, DDE, and DLLs may make Windows a better operating platform, but try as it might, Windows 3.x can never make up entirely for the failures of DOS. But, as you read this a new Windows is emerging, one that's a full-blown, standalone operating system: Windows 95.

Windows 95: DOS Need Not Apply

DOS is doomed. As Microsoft rolls out Windows 95, its successor to its enormously popular Windows 3.x line, we see, for the first time, a version of Windows that's a true operating system—a separate version of DOS isn't required.

Windows 95 features preemptive multitasking (meaning it can do more than one thing at a time, through CPU timesharing). It comes with out-of-the-box networking support for TCP/IP and SPX/IPX, and, in addition to the newer 32-bit Windows applications, it runs DOS and Windows 3.x applications as well. Windows 95 isn't processor independent like NT though; the Intel CISC line is the only target CPU. Also unlike NT, Windows 95 doesn't support symmetric multiprocessing. In a nutshell, Windows 95 is a new operating system designed for the role of the client.

Windows 95 sports a new object-oriented user interface—one that's said to be familiar to Windows 3.x users, while being even more approachable to new PC users than anything that came before it was (that might be open for debate, however). This is directly aimed at the folks over at Apple. We've all smirked at their witty commercials slamming PCs (and Windows especially) for their unfriendly demeanor. Windows 95 will go a long way to addressing that.

If Windows 95 proves only half as successful as Microsoft predicts, it will do extremely well. According to *ComputerWorld* magazine, Microsoft expects to ship 50 million copies of Windows 95 in the first 12 months.[1] Industry watch groups aren't as optimistic. The Gartner Group estimates the number will be closer to 30 million—still incredible—while Dataquest and IDC peg it at 20 million and 12 million. DOS is still more widely used than Windows 3.x, and many of those who have made the move to Windows haven't had time to recoup their investments in it yet. Combine this with a natural hesitance to go with a new operating system, and you can understand why many are leaning toward the more conservative figures. But things ought to be interesting, to say the least.

Practically everyone concedes that Microsoft has taken over the desktop. It's actually rare to hear of a case in which DOS/Windows isn't the client these days. That kind of presence has propelled it, and everything it's associated with, toward de facto standardom.

Things aren't quite as certain in the space between the client and the server, however. While it's true that almost all client/data server applications use SQL to query the database and extract information, in this business, there's almost always more than one way to denude a feline.

The Middle

Structured Query Language

There are plenty ways to store data. A basic, flat file works fine. The problem is that when you have a lot of data, it becomes hard to find something in a hurry. So over the years several methods have been invented to make the whole process more efficient. Of the bunch, the relational model is currently the most popular.

Relational database management systems (RDBMSs) use a simple, straightforward technique for storing data. Everything is held in two-dimensional tables (sort of like a spreadsheet). And for getting around these tables, and getting data into and out of them, the language of choice is the Structured Query Language.

IBM invented SQL back in the 1970s. Today it's used in IBM's DB2 line of databases and just about everybody else's database as well. In its basic form, SQL allows users to:

- Create tables
- Select data from tables
- Adjust table entries
- Store new data in tables

SQL is always easy to recognize. Using the sample table from a customer database, shown in Figure 8.3, to list off all of the names and addresses of the company's customers, you'd use the command

```
SELECT  NAME, ADDRESS
FROM    CUST;
```

the Customer Table

CUSTNO	NAME	ADDRESS	BALANCE	CODE
94-0031	S. Johnson	123 Rosemount, Austin, TX	205.10	SUS
94-0032	C. Wong	48-1200 Bay Road, Buffalo, NY	1034.60	NUS
94-0033	A. Harish	86 Sky Way, Toronto, ON	0	CAN
94-0034	D. Reel	25 Wiser St., Chicago, IL	300	NUS
94-0035	J. Lee	12 Park St., Halifax, NS	56.75	CAN

Figure 8.3 A sample RDBMS table.

The semicolon marks the end of the query. Notice that apart from telling the database manager what table to use ("CUST"), nothing was said about how to actually get to the data. This is SQL's strength: it leaves navigational details up to the database engine (the SQL-server).

SQL was once touted as a language easy enough for average people to use. It hasn't turned out that way, though. For one thing, anyone querying the database has to know all the cryptic column and table names used by the database programmer. More than that, however, queries simply can become too cumbersome for just anyone to use:

```
SELECT      NAME, ADDRESS, PDATE
FROM        CUST, DETAIL
WHERE       CODE = 'CAN'
AND         BALANCE BETWEEN 500 AND 1000
AND         CUST.CUSTNO = DETAIL.CUSTNO
ORDER BY    ADDRESS;
```

In this case, two tables are being queried for information: the CUST table—a "master" table—and DETAIL, another table containing further (detailed) information on customer purchases, or something like that. The fifth line into the query establishes a "join" between the two tables; CUSTNO, some internal customer number, is common to both tables.

Some shy away from calling SQL a programming language. It's not programmable, as is C or Cobol. Officially, SQL is a query language; it provides a way for users to tell the database engine what to do, without requiring them to specify how to do it.

The story of SQL is a little like that of UNIX; although all database vendors offer it, they're all different. This is a bit puzzling at first; there is an ANSI standard for SQL, after all. The current one is ANSI SQL92. As it exists, however, SQL92 really is capable only of retrieving and editing data. It's of no help in formulating a report, for example—something you would probably want to do when working directly with databases. ANSI is working on a version of SQL that does this, but it's not expected for a couple of years. In the meantime, vendors have been forced to add their own functionality to standard SQL to meet their customer's needs. (I like to think they all would have used a standard version of SQL if it were comprehensive enough.)

As a result of vendor add-ons, no rendition of SQL can truly call itself portable. This fact presents yet another challenge to data consolidation at the desktop; if you need to access data from an Oracle, Sybase, and Informix database, you need three different versions of SQL. With any hope of resolving this rift at least several years away, some have taken matters into their own hands.

ODBC

It's unusual for an organization to have just one database product within its software inventory. Most have three or four. Because of this, programmers are confronted with several different flavors of SQL in the move to client/server. For several years now, the SQL Access Group (SAG) has been trying to come up with a SQL standard designed to meet the needs of client/server computing. But it's a tall order. There are different clients, different servers, and different networking protocols to come to grips with—on top of the profusion of SQL versions.

Some vendors aren't willing to wait. There's too much at stake. One of the first one out of the blocks was Microsoft. Its Open DataBase Connectivity, ODBC, is designed for organizations needing to access data held in multiple sources.

Accessing a particular RDBMS generally is accomplished with the aid of an SQL driver. ODBC is like a switchboard that "plugs in" the correct driver for the target data store. Microsoft, in fact, refers to ODBC as a driver manager.

The attraction of ODBC is that programmers only need to learn one set of database calls. ODBC takes these calls (to a "virtual database") and then maps them to the product-specific calls of the target database engine. But on the down side, ODBC adds an additional layer of overhead. For lightly utilized decision-support systems, it might not be an issue. Transaction-intensive client/server applications, on the other hand, probably should use native SQL drivers directly.

Challenging Microsoft in this arena is Borland, IBM, and Novell, with their IDAPI, the Independent Database Application Programming Interface. IDAPI does pretty much the same thing as ODBC, except it does it for different operating systems. IDAPI works with OS/2, Windows, NetWare, and AIX, whereas ODBC is exclusively Windows-centric.

Before the arrival of ODBC 2.0, IDAPI was generally considered to have the technical upper hand. ODBC has narrowed the gap and has the momentum behind it; recently IDAPI has begun to fade into the sunset.

ODBC and IDAPI are generally thought to belong to a murky side of client/server known as middleware. To many, middleware is simply something that stands between the client and the server that magically makes the two capable of exchanging data. Lately, however, as client/server has begun to mature, the term has started to gain respectability.

It's Everyware

Just what we need—another one of those "ware" terms. "Middleware" has become especially popular with buzz-term spouters. For a long time, no one really knew what "middleware" was, which allowed the term to be thrown around with impunity. But lately middleware has actually become a tangible "thing" to contend with.

The idea behind middleware is simple: Since we don't have real open systems, let's introduce translators to connect up clients and servers that otherwise don't communicate so well. It will shield applications and application programmers from platform- and network-specific details.

For the most part, client/server implementations have adhered to what's sometimes referred to as the remote model: a single database server, doling out data to a number of clients. But many yearn for something more sophisticated: a patchwork of multiple clients and multiple servers. This introduces some stiff challenges and is exactly what middleware is intended for.

Identifying precisely what middleware is can be tough. This is partly by design; middleware works in the background, freeing programmers from the details of the underlying system complexity. It's supposed to be invisible. Furthermore, the middleware of today often ends up as part of somebody's operating system tomorrow. But generally speaking, there are three types of middleware: remote procedure calls (RPCs), message passing, and object request brokers.[2]

We encountered RPCs earlier, when discussing the OSF's Distributed Computing Environment (DCE). Computer programs usually make sub-routine, or function, calls during their execution. With RPCs, those routines now can reside on remote hosts. DCE, which is largely based on Hewlett Packard's Network Computing System, depends heavily on RPCs. They are the most popular form of middleware: Clients issue RPCs that are directed to, and then interpreted by, remote database servers.

Alongside of RPCs, message-passing middleware is gaining in popularity. Message-passing is an asynchronous type of middleware. Whereas RPCs are intended to operate in "real time," message-passing uses a store-and-forward approach. If a server is unable to respond immediately to a client's request, the message-passing middleware logs the message and then posts it to the server later when it's free. This is better than having the client sit and wait if the server is unavailable. Even though we're not be talking about long periods of time here, at least in human terms, message-passing wouldn't be well suited to the needs of on-line transaction processing.

Yet a third form of middleware is emerging. Object Request Brokers adhere to a specification laid out by the Object Management Group (OMG) for object sharing. Known as CORBA, the Common Object Request Broker Architecture, it's backed by more than 180 vendors and establishes a groundwork for distributed computing with portable objects.

As we discussed earlier, objects are pieces of code that carry their own data. They communicate with each other through messages. As long as messages can reach each other and can be interpreted, objects can be distributed. The challenge becomes knowing where the objects are and what they're able to do.

Getting distributed objects to work together is a bit of a sore point for object-oriented technology. All the same old issues apply: different servers, different clients, different networking protocols, and even different compilers. CORBA defines Object Request Brokers (pieces of software) that sit on each networked client and server. They take care of all the low-level stuff. CORBA further defines what the ORB interfaces should look like. CORBA 2.0 takes this further, to the point of describing how the ORBs should communicate, so progress is being made. As client/server matures, we'll hear a lot more about CORBA and Object Request Brokers.

Middleware deals directly with issues of interoperability. Once systems and information sources are connected, businesses can begin to look at new ways of using corporate data to their advantage. They can begin to apply computer systems to the flow of work.

Workflow Management

Workflow managers are software systems that not only cope with all the details of hooking up clients and servers but also "understand" how work moves between them. They're sort of like "smart middleware." But whatever else they are, workflow managers are a hot application for client/server computing.

Workflow management tools have their roots in the imaging world. It was an obvious next step; once documents were converted into an electronic form, they had to be conveyed somehow throughout the workplace. But why stop there? Image is just another data type, after all. Why not use workflow managers to orchestrate *all* the tasks of a business process? So goes the current thinking, at least.

Workflow management promises to do to the office what efforts such as "just-in-time" manufacturing did to the shop floor. Workflow management means control. With it, managers can identify bottlenecks and instantly determine who's doing what. It makes for a tight ship, and a tighter ship often needs fewer hands to sail it. Organizational downsizers and reengineering folks love it.

There's been a lot of talk about the failure of computer technology in the workplace. The return on the massive IT investment that's been made over the years is downright miserable. Although output has gone up, so has the capital outlay to support it. The net result is an almost-unbelievable increase in productivity over the past 20 years of less than 1 percent.[3] Workflow management is different from past computerization efforts in that it addresses collective business practices.

Riding this idea all the way to the bank is Lotus, with its popular Notes product. Strictly speaking, Notes belongs to a related slice of the computer business known as groupware. Although the demarcation is fuzzy, groupware is more ad hoc in nature, whereas computer-based workflow management tends to focus on the minute-by-minute activity of well-defined business flows.

So with middleware, SQL drivers, ODBC, or IDAPI, clients can get to the server. But what do they find when they get there?

The Server Side

Serving Up Data

Relational database engines holding the middle ground, the so-called SQL-servers, define the state of the art in data serving. Market leaders are names long known in computing: Sybase, Oracle, Informix, and Ingres (now owned by Computer Associates). Competition in the SQL-server business centers on four areas: performance, concurrency, consistency, and client/server support.

SQL is a declarative language. Actual data access paths are left up to the database engine. Its effectiveness at doing this defines SQL-server performance. Defining data access paths is the job of the optimizer. The optimizer compiles all possible routes to the requested data and assigns each a cost. It then selects the least expensive one. We tend to think of databases as existing only on one machine—the server—and most do. It's becoming more common, however, for data to straddle several machines, a fact that complicates the optimizer's job: In addition to all the regular stuff, the optimizer has to account for network data exchange rates and associated costs as well.

For a database to be of any value, its users must be confident about the data it contains. That's what concurrency and consistency are all about. Concurrency recognizes the fact that people use data—often lots of people. If they're all updating, deleting, and reading it at the same time, pandemonium can erupt unless proper care is taken. Usually this involves data locking. A lock is a claim that an application places on a piece of data. In one extreme, that piece could be the entire database or, more correctly, all of the tables it contains. This wouldn't do much for concurrency; only one person could use the data at that time. At the other extreme is record- (or row-) level locking. This allows lots of people to use the data, but it comes with a performance cost. In practice, the chosen granularity is dictated by a number of things, including table size; large tables may lend themselves better to page-level locking (an intermediate between table locking and record locking). Smaller tables are better suited to locking at the record level.

Database consistency is actually a requirement of the relational database model itself. As noted before, relational databases store data in related tables. If two or more tables are joined—such as in the case of a master-detail relationship—action must be taken to insure that the tables remain synchronized if records are deleted. SQL-servers do this in a number of ways.

One method is "referential integrity," which refers to a lock-step relationship between the data columns of related tables. A common method for accomplishing this is through the use of "database triggers." Triggers are small SQL routines that automatically execute whenever a table modification is attempted. Triggers might be used to guarantee that information in a master table isn't deleted, "orphaning" data a detail table somewhere else in the database.

Transactions—modifications to database data—unfold in discrete increments. Because of this, it's possible for a system failure to occur before a transaction is complete. If this should happen, the database, and specifically a component of it known as the transaction manager, must "roll-back" the affected changes and return the data tables to their state before the transaction began. Database consistency is an all-or-nothing type of thing.

A few years back, Sybase introduced the concept of the "stored procedure." Really just the server end of a remote procedure call, stored procedures are small SQL routines that reside in the database. They have become an essential element of many client/server applications.

Rather than issuing SQL queries from the client to the server one after the other, in some circumstances a single call can be made to a stored procedure, spurring it to execute a number of server-stored commands instead. Once initiated by the client, the stored procedure operates on its own and returns only a result. This not only frees up the client to do other work, but it also directly impacts on the amount of network traffic moving between the client and the server.

Stored procedures offer choices for computation placement. It's just not logical to usher thousands of rows of data down a possibly over-burdened communications line to a client, when all the user wants is an average or something. Stored procedures can move that computation to the server.

All of the leading SQL engines now contain stored procedures and triggers. So the search for product differentiation has taken a new direction: BLOBs. Binary large objects are large "bit buckets" that can hold images, sound, video, and text. They can range in size from a few kilobytes to more than a gigabyte.

The early lead in BLOB support went to Informix. Oracle and Sybase have been quick to catch up though. All three use pointers to outside files where the BLOBs actually are stored. Only in this way can the relational model cope with them. Relational databases are designed for highly structured, alphanumeric data—quite unlike the kind of stuff found in a BLOB. This means they can't be manipulated in the same way as regular relational data can. No triggers, no stored procedures—just a pointer to a file. To do anything with a BLOB—present it, magnify it—requires the use of some additional software not normally included as part of an SQL engine.

One of the fundamental edicts of client/server is to put data closest to where it's used the most. While this makes sense, it may require the data be synchronized across several sites. Database replication is a particularly vexing aspect of distributed computing and has become another battlefield for RDBMS differentiation.

Database replication can be synchronous or asynchronous. Synchronous database replication involves an up-to-the-minute relationship between a number of distributed data stores. This is accomplished with something called two-phase commit (2PC).

In Figure 8.4, data store "H" and data store "R" are identical. If, during a 2PC, any of the necessary steps can't be performed for one reason or another, nothing gets committed. While this is good for database consistency, it might not always be efficient. If "H" sat at head office in Atlanta, and "R" was a regional office in Toronto, there could be unproductive wait periods in either of the sites if network traffic or general system failures caused a two-phase commit to be abandoned.

In cases like this, asynchronous replication may be more appropriate. It's a simple idea: Instead of continuously proliferating database

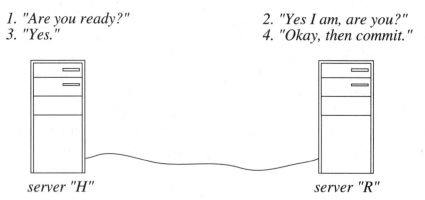

1. "Are you ready?"
3. "Yes."

2. "Yes I am, are you?"
4. "Okay, then commit."

server "H"   *server "R"*

Figure 8.4 Two-phase commit.

modifications across the network, copies of changes are transmitted to the distributed stores only at specified times. Sometimes called snapshot replication, it's appropriate only if transactions, and the data they apply to, aren't overly time-sensitive.

With asynchronous replication, updates can be scheduled for times when network traffic isn't as heavy. And if a WAN separates the databases, updates can be performed when transmission rates are cheaper.

Another version of asynchronous database replication uses a store-and-forward approach similar to e-mail and message-passing middle-ware we saw earlier. Instead of posting modifications at specific times during the day, table changes are passed as messages and queued at the target servers. Although store-and-forward demands an additional dedicated server to oversee things, it's a better scheme, since snapshot replication is unable to cope with downed target servers at the time of update.

Support for multithreading is another hot topic in the database business. With multithreading, a database server assigns queries to threads that can be swapped in and out of a waiting state. When a query is idle, perhaps during an input/output operation, it's swapped out of its thread—its small chunk of the available CPU slot—and replaced with the next waiting query in the queue. That's for computers with just a single CPU. Multithreading substantially boosts database performance in devices capable of symmetric multiprocessing. In these cases, queries

Symmetric multiprocessing

Multiprocessing devices contain two or more CPUs attached to a high-speed data bus within the same chassis. It's a way of gaining more CPU power for a marginal investment. Symmetric multiprocessing makes each of the CPUs available for any process to use, while asymmetric multiprocessing dedicates the processors to specific tasks. The operating system is responsible for assigning the processors and ensuring that each doesn't overwrite the memory space of the others. Windows NT, OS/2, and several versions of UNIX currently support symmetric multiprocessing. Both Sybase and Oracle also have introduced database engines that can take advantage of symmetric multiprocessing systems.

can be executed simultaneously on separate CPUs. Sybase takes its own approach to multithreading, while Oracle and Informix rely on multithreaded operating systems, such as some versions of UNIX, or NT, to do the job.

Wrap-up

At a high level, the technical notion of client/server is simple: There's a client, a server that provides services (usually data) to that client, and something that links the two together. When you dig a bit deeper, however, there's plenty to contend with.

One of the few constants of client/server design is the identity of the client. Ninety percent of the time, it's DOS/Windows. Because of this, there are reasonably well-proven implementation practices in place for the client side.

Getting from the client to the server is another matter. Here there are a raft of choices—not all of them solid—depending on the specific needs of the application. Raw SQL queries can be passed over the target database engine's SQL driver to the store. Generic SQL queries can be handed over to a product such as ODBC to first translate them into the appropriate format before transfer. Remote procedure calls can be used to interact with the server. To a lesser extent, message-passing software or object request brokers can be invoked.

The choice depends on what needs to be done. If an application is heavily transaction-based, raw SQL, ORBs, or RPCs might be appropriate. For occasional decision-support use, ODBC or message-passing might be best.

On the server side, we're confronted with more choices. What degree of data locking is right? Should triggers be used to enforce consistency? Is synchronous or asynchronous replication required across distributed data stores? Should computations be moved to the server? Does the application call for symmetric multiprocessing?

The good news is that we've got choices. The bad news is that we've got choices. With each comes the risk of something going wrong later. In Chapter 9 we take a closer look at the ramifications of many of these decisions as we delve into client/server development.

Key Terms and Ideas Appearing in This Chapter

BLOB:

Binary Large OBjects. BLOBs are unstructured "bit buckets" that can contain text, image, sound, or video. Most imaging applications rely on BLOBs, attached to databases, for storage. But because of the non-relational structure of the data, RDBMS applications can't directly do anything with BLOBs.

CORBA:

Common Object Request Broker Architecture. An emerging standard from the Object Management Group. CORBA is intended to assist in the intercommunication of networked objects. In its first rendition, it specifies what ORBs (object request brokers) should generally look like. CORBA 2.0 further defines how they should communicate. ORBs are a new form of middleware that are beginning to make their presence felt.

DDE:

Dynamic Data Exchange. A Microsoft Windows "standard" for information exchange between Windows applications. Say you wanted to link a Windows spreadsheet to a document. You would set up the DDE link between the two specifying the spreadsheet application name, the name of the spreadsheet, and the desired rows and columns you wanted to embed. Then whenever a change was made to that portion of the spreadsheet, it would be reflected automatically in the linked document. Windows for Workgroups can do this over a network with NetDDE.

DLL:

Dynamic Link Library. Another Microsoft Windows "standard." This one's used for sharing Windows resources (graphics and stuff like that) or small pieces of executable code. Most Windows-compliant compilers can create DLLs. They're more than a typical library, however. DLLs are copied once (on demand) and shared among calling programs. Compare this to "static linking," in which whole libraries are attached to programs at compile and link time. If three programs need a certain library, there are then three copies kicking about the system.

groupware:

Also variously called workgroup computing and ad hoc workflow, groupware is sometimes considered to be a part of workflow management. It concerns itself with tasks and processes that are unstructured in nature as compared to production, "heads-down" workflow management. Lotus' Notes product leads the groupware market.

IDAPI:

Integrated Database Application Programming Interface. Similar to Microsoft's ODBC. IDAPI is multiple database access software created by Borland, Novell, and IBM. Unlike ODBC, IDAPI can access both SQL and navigational (xBASE) databases, and of course, it's not limited to Windows. IDAPI made it to market after ODBC. This may have killed it.

middleware:

A nebulous little term for anything that stands between a client and a server to help communication. There are three types: remote procedure calls (RPCs), message-passing schemes, and object request brokers (ORBs). Getting down to tangibles, DCE, ODBC, and IDAPI fall into the middleware category.

ODBC:

Open DataBase Connectivity. ODBC is part of the Windows Open Services Architecture (WOSA). It's intended for multidatabase access. ODBC adds its own layer to database application programming interfaces (APIs). With this additional layer comes the necessity of dealing with only one group of function calls that can access different databases. The result is less variation between application source code for different databases. Underneath, ODBC takes the function calls, translates them, and directs them to the appropriate database API. It takes a lowest-common-denominator approach. One drawback with ODBC is that it runs under Windows only.

OLE:

Object Linking and Embedding. A way of sharing information among Windows applications. When linked, the host application, also known as a container, contains only a reference to the object, but when embedded, the application contains an actual copy. OpenDoc is OLE's biggest competitor. It's a network-enabled compound document standard developed by Apple, IBM, Novell, and Xerox. OpenDoc reached the marketplace well after OLE.

OOP:

Object oriented programming. OOP is a different way for programmers to model the physical world—one claimed to be closer to reality. Many people think that OOP is just an extension to modular programming because it encourages the use of small chunks of code to define the objects and their associated methods. But OOP is more than that. It rests on three "principles": encapsulation (information hiding), inheritance, and polymorphism. One of the goals of OOP is to construct small, reusable pieces of software. To enforce this, the code used to define objects generally is not available to the outside world for review. This black-box approach encourages programmers to accept the object's contents and focus on how to interact with the object instead. That's what encapsulation is all about. Taking a real-world view, OOP also allows objects to inherit features from others they're related to. For example, a programmer could define a "car" and then create a specialization of that—sports car—that inherits all the attributes of the "parent." Polymorphism is a little stranger than the other two OOP principles. We know that, again, in the real world, different "objects" do the same thing differently. How an object does what it does is left up to the object, but the message sent to the objects is the same. That's polymorphism.

RDBMS:

Relational DataBase Management System. There are a few different ways in which data can be stored and accessed logically: the hierarchical model popular in bygone days, the network model, the object model, and the relational model. Relational database engines represent data as a series of two-dimensional tables. SQL is used to create, manipulate and extract data from these tables. Most industrial-strength database engines, such as DB2, Oracle, Sybase, Informix, InterBase, SQLBase, and Ingres, are relational.

SQL:

Structured Query Language. SQL is a data-access language invented by IBM. It removes the navigational responsibilities from the user. (You don't have to know exactly where things are.) Most of the newer, larger database engines are SQL-based. A standard version of SQL set out by ANSI is available, but it is kind of limiting. It contains little in the way of data reporting, for instance. This means vendors need to add their own functionality to the base. Oracle, for example, calls its rendition of SQL SQL*Plus. It adds approximately 40 additional commands. SQL is commonly embedded in programs written in languages such as COBOL and C for database access.

SQL driver:

A piece of proprietary software that hooks up clients to database engines. The SQL driver takes care of much of the low-level stuff, such as the networking protocols. It also works at a higher level, linking the client application to the database. Every database has its own SQL driver, since every relational database has its own implementation of SQL.

two-phase commit:

A synchronous data replication strategy. Whenever one data store is updated, a related one is too. During a two-phase commit, the database engines first confirm to each other that they're ready. If they are—and there can be more than two of them involved in this process—the data is officially modified. The problem with two-phase commit is that network latencies or all-out system failures can leave one (or more) of the parties waiting. Asynchronous replication is becoming popular because it avoids this problem.

Windows 95:

Unlike all previous versions of Windows, Windows 95 is a full operating system, very much like OS/2—not surprising, since Microsoft helped create it too. All agree that if it turns out to be even half as popular as Microsoft expects, OS/2 (and every other operating system vying for the desktop) is in trouble.

workflow management:

Many are pointing to this as the big application for client/server computing. Workflow management is middleware that knows how work moves around the workplace. Beyond being able to link up clients and servers and mainframes, it also can be programmed to route pieces of work. Some organizations are looking to workflow management to revolutionize their businesses. The leaders in this field are long-time information technology leaders such as Xerox, Wang, Digital, and IBM.

Notes

[1] W. Brandel, "Users Unwilling to Gamble on First Release of Chicago," *ComputerWorld*, June 27, 1994, v28, 1.

[2] E.U. Harding,, "Middleware Emerges as the Next Battlefield," *Software Magazine*, April 1994, v14, 21.

[3] T. Koulopoulos, *The Workflow Imperative*, (Delphi Publishing, Boston, 1994).

Chapter 9

Executive Summary

Client/server development really differs from other types of software development only in the implementation phase. It's there that we come to appreciate the challenges of distributed computing. Applications residing on a client must interact smoothly with a database engine on a remote server. With a network standing between the two, programmers and system designers must, often for the first time, become knowledgeable in the workings of data communications.

New technological solutions often call for new tools. This is certainly the case when it comes to client/server development. But the wrong choice can subject programmers to an unreasonable learning curve or even lead to all-out project failure if the chosen tool cannot provide some (later-understood) needed functionality.

Development tools are part of either the third or fourth generation of programming languages. Third-generation languages, such as C and C++, offer flexibility at the expense of steep learning requirements. Fourth-generation languages can be likened to "macros" (built from a third-generation language) constructed with a specific purpose in mind. Many exist exclusively to facilitate the development of client/server applications. But while fourth-generation languages may sound like the appropriate choice, it must be understood that they are limited by their builder's implicit development philosophy. When a project's needs fall outside of that philosophy, solution designs may need to be adjusted.

Beyond programming, client/server's distributed nature introduces an operational aspect into the development process. Will a client/server solution fit into the existing infrastructure? The question has far-reaching ramifications. All too often, the answer is a definite maybe.

CHAPTER 9

Client/Server Development

Introduction

Client/server is just a model of computing. It has no special development methodology associated with it. Software development proceeds just as it always has.

The first thing investigators do is determine what the problem is. This is sometimes called the requirements analysis phase. Once it's complete, a solution is proposed. This is where client/server may come in.

Solution architects must ask themselves what computing model best meets the needs of the business unit. Problems involving multiple data sources or that decision-support emphasis often lean toward client/server. But there's much that needs to be considered. Are the requisite skills available? Does the existing infrastructure lend itself toward the inclusion of a client/server solution? Can the system be managed? An-

201

swers to these questions, and others like them, form the basis for a cost estimate against which benefits can be weighed.

Once the decision to proceed with a client/server style of solution is made, its distributed nature deviates development away from the norm. In principle, development is straightforward. Programmers construct client screens (often under a graphical user interface such as Microsoft's Windows) and then connect selected fields on these screens to a database located on the server. Simple maybe, but making it all work is another matter. In the end, there may be new tools, new network protocols, new operating systems, new hardware, and new database technology.

Software Development

There is no special client/server development methodology. Client/ server is just another technological solution, and in the initial phases of problem resolution, technology should be put aside. As with any other software development, the goal is first to find out what the problem is.

It may turn out that technology isn't even necessary. Instead, the problem may lie with the business process in question. In accordance with fundamental business process reengineering practice, don't immediately look to technology to fix everything.

But if the need for a technological solution has been established, the next step is to decide, at a high level at least, what that solution looks like. Is a mainframe-based solution? Is it LAN- or workgroup-based? Is it client/server?

How do you decide if a problem is suited to client/server or not? There are two ways to answer this (and both should be used): First dissect the problem and ask yourself if it would benefit from having functionality—especially presentation—distributed across more than one computer. Second, draw on the public record of client/server case studies looking for one close to your problem. Other things to consider include whether there is a data component to the problem; where the data is located now—exclusively on the mainframe, or sitting in xBASE files; whether the data is located in more than one source; whether you can get to this data easily; and whether the data is used by more than one person. While none of these questions by itself will lead to yes-or-no answer as to the suitability of client/server, all usually are part of the decision process.

If a client/server solution appears most appropriate, you next have to ask whether the investment in this type of technology is justified. Client/server is expensive, and it can be risky. The degree of each depends on the organization and the problem to be tackled. Just because a problem appears simple doesn't mean that a client/server solution will be a snap.

The most important factor in this part of the decision process is cost. Once this is roughly worked out, information technology representatives can sit down with members of the business area to construct an estimate of probable benefits to weigh it against. To give you some idea of what you're in for, I've scoped out some typical client/server costs in Table 9.1. They pertain to a hypothetical pilot implementation of approximately 10 seats (a rather small system).

The actual development and deployment costs, of course, could be quite different depending on the application and on your organization. For example, I've included an entry for client desktops. An organization might already have PCs in place. So maybe they just need to be upgraded. I've also assumed that developers use a client/server

Table 9.1 Some Sample Client/Server Project Costs

Training	developers, networking people, DBAs, and end users	$250/person/day
Consultants:		$500 – $1,000/day
Hardware:	server clients cabling	$25,000 $ 3,000/user $ 1,000
Software:	RDBMS client development tools mainframe gateway	$20,000 $ 3,000/developer $40,000
Development costs:		$400/developer/day
Project Management:		$450/day

Programming languages

The first generation of programming languages was machine code. This was just cryptic strings of 1s and 0s tacked together in a manner understandable to the CPU. Assembly language was an improvement over this. In this second-generation computer language, terse statements replaced the binary sequences. Assembly language programming is still linked to a particular CPU type, however, which effectively prevents programs written in assembly languages from being moved easily between different processors. So next came the third generation of languages, the "3GLs." A program written with a 3GL is portable, although it probably needs to be recompiled for a particular CPU. Well-known 3GLs include FORTRAN, Cobol, and C. Object-oriented languages such as C++ and SmallTalk also are considered to be part of the third generation, although it may be fairer to place them somewhere in between the third and fourth. Fourth-generation languages usually are built for a certain task, such as constructing programs for database access. Each generation is built on the one that comes before; many 4GLs are written in C, for example. Tools such as PowerBuilder and Visual Basic are regarded as being 4GLs.

development tool, such as PowerBuilder or SQLWindows. If an organization has some highly proficient C or C++ programmers on staff (and available), either language might be used instead. I've also assumed a three-tier client/server solution and included a mainframe server link. Your problem might not involve mainframe participation.

Given all these assumptions, a small pilot project with two full-time developers, one full-time consultant, one half-time project leader (all for a period of about a half a year), and 10 end users would cost approximately $250,000. This investment has to be weighed against a possible x percent (whatever your team comes up with) increase in end-user productivity—a speculative number, at best. You won't know the actual productivity gain—if any—until several months after the system has been built and put into production.

Finally, we come a step in the process that is uniquely client/server. Assuming the project receives the go-ahead, designers must begin to decide on the location of the data and computations. This is called application partitioning.

As we've seen, data and computations can reside on the mainframe (if one's involved), the desktop client, on the "server," or on all three. To start off with, however, simplest is probably best. Many pilot client/ server implementations are actually two-tiered (just a few clients and a single server) and assign data to the server (which could be a mainframe) and computations and presentation to the client. Later, once everything is working, the system can be "tuned" by moving some of the computations to the server (using stored procedures) if network loadings or system response times dictate. Having said this, some computations obviously belong on the server—frequently updated calculations that every client must access, for instance.

A two-tier implementation may be easier, but the three-tiered client/ server model offers distinct benefits. Rather than incur a security risk by exposing actual corporate database to system users, a working copy can sit on the server. This might be only a portion of the corporate (mainframe-based) database relevant to a department served by this midlevel device. At the end of each working day (or at some other times during the day), modifications can be posted to the mainframe and a fresh image replaced on the server. (See Figure 9.1). This is a logical way to blend the strengths of both computing environments.

Ultimately, the decision whether to use a two- or three-tier version of client/server depends on the experiences and skills of the organization. If you don't have a mainframe, it's not relevant; if you do, remember that melding it into a client/server application is easier if the resident mainframe database is relational (such as DB2). If it's a nonrelational database, melding it is considerably harder (although there are tools around, especially from database vendors, that can help).

Very probably (unless you intend to use an existing data store exclusively), the next thing that you'll need to do is to lay out the design of the server database. This is the same as in any other relational database design; representatives from the business area work with programming staff to define relevant data fields. This design can occur in parallel, to some degree, with the design of the client interface.

Most client/server applications use a graphical user interface. Building them involves two things: "painting" the actual screens and connecting up designated areas on those screens to fields in the database.

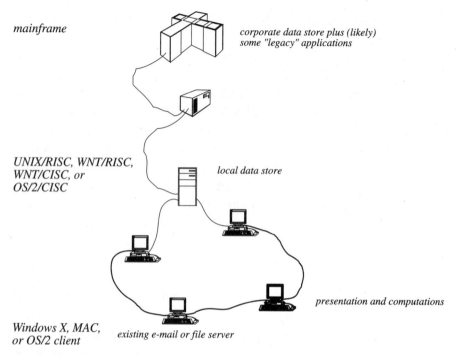

mainframe

corporate data store plus (likely)
some "legacy" applications

UNIX/RISC, WNT/RISC,
WNT/CISC, or
OS/2/CISC

local data store

presentation and computations

Windows X, MAC,
or OS/2 client

existing e-mail or file server

Figure 9.1 The three-tier client/server model.

This is where client programming begins. This is also where the old 3GL-versus-4GL debate rears its head. With a Windows or OS/2 application programming interface (API) in hand, practically any good third-generation programming language can be used to construct the screens. C is popular. C++, an object-oriented extension of C, is probably a close second.

Procedural (C-like) versus object-oriented languages is a whole other issue. And it's not just C versus C++. SmallTalk, another object-oriented language, also is attracting supporters. Of the three, it's probably the most approachable—certainly more so than C++. Just a few years ago, SmallTalk substantially trailed C++ in overall usage. Recently, to the surprise of many, the gap has begun to close. IBM, among others, has identified SmallTalk as a strategic future programming language.

If your organization is about to embark upon its first client/server project, but has never dabbled with object-oriented programming (OOP), it may be a good idea to forget about it—at least for now.

Client/server by itself is tough enough. Tossing in something else for the developers to come to grips with probably isn't a good idea.

But no matter which 3GL you choose, building screens is slow, demanding work. It's getting better though. Companies such as Borland, producers of C and C++ compilers, have taken some of the drudgery out of screen building by providing resources—precreated graphical push buttons and the like—to simplify construction somewhat. Not so long ago, programmers had to build everything themselves.

Going beyond what compiler manufacturers provide, a number of companies produce code generators. Neuron Data's Open Interface Elements (OIE), for one, can be used to create interfaces for a number of different client platforms. It's then up to the interface designers to bolt the generated code (for the push buttons and other graphics that have been laid out on the screens) onto the database interchange software they've developed themselves in some 3GL (usually C++ or C).

Code generators offer the attraction of portability. If you have several different client types in house (PCs, Macs, and Suns, for example), products such as OIE can be used to produce consistent interfaces for your client/server applications across all of them.

Once the screens are built, it's time to grab the data. By this time, the database designers, with the aid of business area representatives, will have architected the database. They may even have seeded it with data for testing purposes. The only way to get information out of an RDBMS is with Structured Query Language (SQL).

SQL can be embedded either statically or dynamically into both 3 and 4GLs. (We'll talk about 4GLs in a minute.) When statically embedded, blocks of SQL are "flagged off" within the 3GL code, to be dealt with by a precompiler at a later point. The problem with static SQL is that programmers must anticipate all possible end-user requests. Sometimes it's better to let users pose their queries to the database themselves (with appropriate controls). Using dynamic SQL, programmers can design things so that the end user is prompted at run time to enter an SQL command of his or her choosing. It can be anything, as long as it's syntactically correct. The down side of this is that end users must be knowledgeable in SQL. To get around this requirement, many programmers design client-side applications in a manner that allows end users to create syntactically correct SQL queries on-the-fly from a series of menus or other graphics.

From a performance perspective, dynamic SQL is optimized at run-time. Static SQL is optimized prior to execution, so it can be more efficient. Database traditionalists prefer it for this reason. (Some database administrators refuse to allow dynamic queries altogether.)

When working with static SQL, code containing the SQL must pass through a precompiler. Every SQL-server has one—a unique one, not surprisingly. That's because, as we saw in the last chapter, every SQL-server maker has its unique twist on SQL. The precompiler strips out the SQL commands from the 3GL program and ushers them over the network to the server. There they are actually stored in the database in an optimized form. The precompiler then creates a series of function calls to retrieve and execute them later, during execution. After the SQL statements are stripped out, the rest of the 3GL code proceeds through a compiler as usual.

At a lower level, client applications and database engines need to be connected in order to push the data across the lines. This is the realm of middleware. As we saw in Chapter 8, there are many different types of middleware, some established, some still emerging. For decision-support systems—the kind of application client/server is deployed for initially most often—the best-known way of connecting clients and servers is via a group of library calls called an application programming interface (API). SQL*Net is Oracle's access API, for example. Generically speaking, this type of software is called an SQL driver, and both the client and the server need it in order to communicate.

Using a 3GL with embedded SQL to develop client/server applications is time consuming—even for experienced programmers. And it's challenging; you really have to know what you're doing. The alternative is to use a 4GL. 4GLs are languages/environments designed with a specific type of application in mind, usually a database application. They're like "macros," built from 3GLs underneath. They're faster, easier to use, and much easier to learn. But once you elect to use any 4GL, you've also implicitly adopted a method for solving your problem. And there are going to be times when that method lets you down. When it does, that's too bad. Maybe the vendor will add your needed feature in its next release. Maybe not. Starting from scratch, using a 3GL, may take longer, but you end up with exactly what you want. No compromises or "work-arounds" in the face of a 4GL shortcoming. Build it or buy: It can be a tough decision.

In the early days of client/server, you had no choice; there simply weren't any tools around. Now, there are almost too many choices. Take even a quick look at what's out there, and very soon, all 4GLs will start to look the same. And the three that everyone seems to want to look like are PowerSoft's PowerBuilder, Gupta's SQLWindows, and Microsoft's Visual Basic.

PowerSoft's PowerBuilder

Timing is everything. Back in 1990 when PowerSoft (a company now owned by Sybase) launched PowerBuilder, the client/server movement was just picking up speed. Now PowerBuilder is the leading client/server 4GL.

PowerBuilder is described as a graphic PC-based client/server application development environment. It provides an easy-to-use facility for designing and painting screens as well as a logical procedure for embedding SQL statements.

It's semi-object-oriented, allowing programmers to inherit screens. This eases them into the OOP waters. However, experienced object-oriented programmers often find PowerBuilder too restrictive. It's hard to please everybody.

PowerBuilder works like this: Programmers lay out screens using a palette of graphical objects (called controls in Windows lingo). The list of possible controls includes longtime GUI staples such as push buttons, drop-down list boxes, checkboxes, and something new in PowerBuilder's case, a control called a DataWindow (more about that in a moment). Controls have characteristics: how big, where on the screen, what color, stuff like that. They also can possess scripts—small programs, written in PowerSoft's PowerScript, a proprietary language—that give the controls their functionality. An "Exit" button would have PowerBuilder's "Close" function as part of its script, for example.

DataWindows are special entities that can be used to manipulate, update, and present data. There are actually two of them: one you see on the screen, called the DataWindow *control*, and another that does the bridging between the on-screen control and the data store, the DataWindow *object*. DataWindow objects can retrieve data via static SQL, SQL with arguments (sort of a semidynamic SQL), or a server-based stored procedure.

PowerSoft's PB 4.0, its fourth version of the product, expands its horizons to include other operating systems and CPUs in addition to Windows on Intel. At the same time, close ties to Windows have been reaffirmed with support for OLE 2.

PowerBuilder is used mostly for department-size decision-support systems. Many wonder if it can go beyond that to step up to enterprise-wide client/server solutions. That's doubtful. But that's probably fine with PowerSoft; most of the client/server activity is at the low-to-medium end right now anyway. One thing that is sure is that PowerSoft has captured the lead in this very competitive slice of the computer business.

Gupta's SQLWindows

PowerBuilder's most immediate competition comes from Gupta Corp's SQLWindows. Like PowerBuilder, SQLWindows is a graphical client/server application development system. Gupta's latest release, version 5.0, is a well thought out design.

PowerBuilder's success forced Gupta to rethink some previously held convictions. In the early PowerBuilder days, Gupta held that client/server programming was not for the novice. If programmers were going to take on this kind of stuff, they had to learn the basics, and that included SQL. Gupta scoffed at PowerSoft's attempts to minimize programmer exposure to the query language. This philosophy extended throughout the entire look and feel of the company's early products; while thorough, SQLWindows didn't seem to provide much advantage over good old C coupled with embedded SQL.

All that changed with Gupta's version 4.0. Have a simple data access requirement and not want to type a single line of SQL? No problem. Using an embedded version of its popular ad hoc database query tool, Quest (in a graphical form called QuestWindows), Gupta claims that sophisticated master-detail applications can be constructed with almost no knowledge of database programming whatsoever. Perhaps. It's more likely that QuestWindows serves as a starting point for more complicated applications, however; once the programmer has used it to lay out the basic application, it can be built upon using SQLWindow's proprietary language, SAL (SQLWindows Application Language).

SQLWindows consistently gets high marks for its robust multideveloper facility. Draped around a dictionary-driven central repository (that uses SQLBase, Gupta's low-end SQL-server) is a sophisticated tracking and updating scheme. SQLWindows also receives high praise for its thorough implementation of OOP fundamentals: encapsulation, polymorphism, and even multiple inheritance. While this is available for the more experienced programmer, novices needn't worry about such things. Pilot systems can be constructed in pseudo-object-oriented style, allowing programmers to wade into the OOP waters at their own speed.

While PowerBuilder has a larger market share, it and SQLWindows invariably run neck and neck in product reviews. Generally, SQLWindows requires programmers to write more code than PowerBuilder, but it has better project management facilities.

Visual Basic

Visual Basic (VB) is a general-purpose Windows application-construction tool. In spite of this, Microsoft insists that its primary use is for client/server development. That being Microsoft's position, it's easy to understand why the company has continued to improve upon database support in its product over the years. Nevertheless, out of the box, Visual Basic just isn't in the same league as PowerBuilder or SQLWindows. It might suffice for small client/server (10 seats or so) applications, but for anything more, additional software support is strongly recommended.

In some respects, it's not fair to compare VB to PowerBuilder or SQLWindows. Both of those products are dedicated exclusively to the task of building client/server applications. On the other hand, you can use VB to build practically any Windows-based application you like. And you can do it faster than with just about any other Windows-building tool.

Programming in Visual Basic is very much like programming in PowerBuilder and SQLWindows. You select what you want from a palette of graphical objects and place it on the screen. You can then size it, change fonts, or adjust its color. Double-clicking on any of these graphical objects "drills down" to an area for constructing fragments of supporting code in the VB language.

If you remember the Basic language, you'll be pleasantly surprised at Microsoft's re-interpretation of it. All those annoying line numbers are gone, and there's a whole new assortment of conditional statements and loops. It has matured into a highly sophisticated programming language more reminiscent of C than Basic.

VB has caused quite a sensation in the computing business. A name for the phenomenon is related to its overwhelming success: "component(sigh)ware." The "components" are chunks of VB executable code, called VBX's, and just about everyone's producing them for just about anything you can think of. These custom-made pieces of code actually become part of the Visual Basic development environment. The functionality these tools offer can save programmers from having to write hundreds of lines of their own code.

Microsoft, which would prefer programmers to use OCXs (OLE Custom controls), is attempting to persuade people to give up on VBXs, however. OCXs are new 32-bit controls destined for the upcoming version of Visual Basic (4.0, expected to become available at the same time as Windows 95). OCX controls can be embedded in any application able to act as an OLE container and are more versatile than VBXs. A lot of folks in the programming community aren't happy about the switch, however.

Visual Basic's out-of-left-field success surprised even Microsoft. At last count, there were over 1 million official copies of the product in circulation.[1] PowerSoft and SQLWindows, by comparison, have far fewer devotees. It is fast becoming the preferred Windows programming language.

Putting It Altogether: System Integration

Almost as soon as you've decided to make the move to client/server computing, someone invariably asks how you intend to maintain current services to the new client/server end users. "Legacy systems," people call them. And that doesn't necessarily imply only mainframe stuff. Existing LAN-based services are just as much a part of an organization's legacy.

The question of maintaining existing services is really one of integration; how well will the client/server solution fit into the existing infrastructure? The answer depends on what type of client/server system it is and what the organization's infrastructure looks like.

To better understand the integration requirements, let's imagine a typical organization, one that has a mainframe and a LAN-based (NetWare in this case) e-mail system. Members of an information technology investigative team recommend a client/server solution to a pressing business need. This solution must complement the existing systems; users still need e-mail and occasional mainframe access for applications outside of the scope of the proposed client/server implementation.

As system design unfolds, the team decides that a UNIX/RISC box is the most appropriate choice for the role of server. But this introduces a problem. The mainframe "talks" SNA; the UNIX server, TCP/IP; and the PC client, SPX/IPX. How is everything glued together?

Taking things one step at a time, let's first get the PC platform (the eventual client) connected to the server. One of the most painless ways of linking up NetWare PCs and TCP/IP hosts is to employ dual protocol stacks on the PC. (See Figure 9.2.) This permits the PC to continue its NetWare relationship while at the same time acting as a client for the new UNIX host. To do this, the company requires either NDIS or ODI drivers (software) in each of the PC clients. You may recall from an earlier discussion that Novell (and Apple) invented ODI so that LAN administrators could "bind" multiple protocols to a single LAN adapter card. Before ODI, if you needed to support several different networking protocols, many separate adapter cards were required for each client. But with ODI, a PC can have both the NetWare shell and an ODI-compatible version of TCP/IP loaded at the same time. NDIS does the same kind of thing for Microsoft's LAN Manager.

So the PC needs a LAN adapter, an ODI or an NDIS driver, the TCP/IP protocol suite (for DOS—assuming the PCs are running DOS/Windows), and the usual LAN access software. This allows the PC to continue to run NetWare applications plus be able to get at and run new ones on the UNIX server as well.

The UNIX server is also where the SQL-server sits. Let's assume that, because of information-sharing requirements, our hypothetical

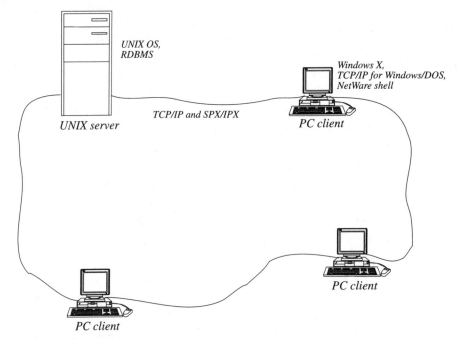

Figure 9.2 First get the PCs connected to the UNIX server.

organization has opted to use database replication. Modifications to the server-based working database are time-posted to the mainframe data store at set intervals throughout the day. The information used within the client/server application also is used by other departments outside of this group, but it's not overly time-sensitive. Asynchronous replication will suffice.

That brings us to the mainframe. In traditional SNA communications, a front-end processor (a 37xx communications controller sometimes called a FEP) sits in front of the host. This device runs NCP, the Network Control Program. The communications controller subsequently attaches to a 3 × 74 cluster controller to which peripherals (327x terminals and printers) can be connected. (See Figure 9.3.)

Through software, UNIX platforms can emulate 3 × 74 cluster controller behavior. As far as the FEP is concerned, the UNIX machine *is* a

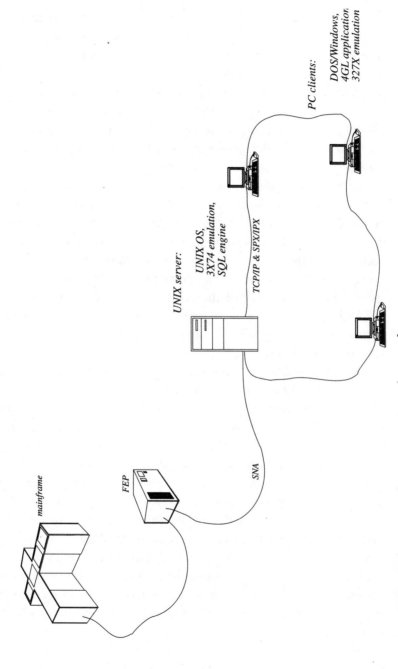

Figure 9.3 Next connect the UNIX server to the mainframe.

mainframe

FEP

SNA

UNIX server:

UNIX OS,
3X74 emulation,
SQL engine

TCP/IP & SPX/IPX

PC clients:

DOS/Windows,
4GL application,
327X emulation

cluster controller, albeit an expensive one. But cost comparisons aren't really fair. Actual controllers are dedicated devices. They have no ability to process applications. But the UNIX box, of course, does—it's running the SQL-server for one thing.

With the appropriate emulation software in place, a link is established between the UNIX server and the mainframe. If each of the PC clients also runs 327x software emulation, such as Attachmate's Extra! for Windows or Wall Data's Rumba, they can, if they need to, pass right through the server to get to the mainframe.

At this point, the clients have everything they need to be able to access LAN applications, native UNIX applications (such as the SQL-server), and mainframe applications as well. But it's a choppy arrangement, users always having to flip between different operating systems; something a bit more cohesive would certainly make their jobs easier.

This is where tools such as PowerBuilder, SQLWindows, and Visual Basic shine. Using any of these, programmers can create a client application that presents users with a consistent interface into the entire system. For the purposes of our example, let's assume that the company selects Visual Basic.

After designing the screens and connecting the relevant controls to fields in the server database, end users are able to obtain controlled access to the working data. Underneath the Visual Basic application is the RDBMS's SQL driver. It takes care of establishing the physical connection between the client application and the database over the chosen networking protocol (TCP/IP in this case).

Several options provide end users with seamless access to existing mainframe applications via the same client interface. One of the simplest is to use a special application programming interface called EHLLAPI (Emulator High-Level Language Application Programming Interface). EHLLAPI is an IBM protocol that sits on the PC and rides atop 327x emulation software to enable PC-to-mainframe communications. The main attraction of this approach is that it doesn't require any modification to the mainframe side. A number of third-party VBXs provide EHLLAPI functionality for Visual Basic.

EHLLAPI is designed to simulate a 327x terminal session. Also known as screen scraping, it's based on the known layout of a mainframe application's screens. EHLLAPI allows a programmer to extract and feed necessary information to, and from, those screens (even though they aren't actually visible). The information then can be directed to a graphic on a screen—a drop-down listbox or something. To the end user of the face-lifted application, it looks like something all new is happening. Really, though, it's still just the same old 327x dialog. (For many, this can be a first step toward client/server. Although it does little in the way of off-loading mainframe cycles, it is a quick way to breathe new life into an old application.)

There is a down side to screen scraping, though. For it to work, mainframe applications must remain stable. If the position of any required field changes without also modifying the EHLLAPI-enabled application, the results can be unpredictable. It's also not a particularly efficient way to get PC and mainframe applications communicating.

A better way to get at mainframe data is to use APPC (IBM's Advanced Program to Program Communications). Before communication can begin, the mainframe-designated Logical Units (LUs) of the participating applications on the mainframe and on the client must be connected logically. Once they are, direct program-to-program communication can take place. But there's a drawback here too. Using APPC, mainframe applications do require a bit of retooling. IS managers like to avoid this, since mainframe programming is usually expensive, and what's more, few programmers possess the requisite APPC skills.

Wrap-up

Client/server introduces some new challenges into the software development process. Being a distributed computing model, solution designers must decide on the best locations for data and supporting computations. This has far-reaching ramifications. With a network standing between client and server, the inappropriate location of either can aggravate system response time or, at worst, saturate the network. Client/server systems must be designed with postimplementation tuning in mind.

Programmers also face new challenges under client/server. They may have to become skilled in a new computer language. They may have to learn about object-oriented programming and to adjust their past programming practices to begin to think in an object-oriented fashion. They also may have to learn something about art; the design and development of graphical user interfaces is very much an artistic endeavor. Surprising amounts of time go into the creation of a user interface that fits the way end users work. And much of this has to do with how the windows look.

There's also an operational challenge. Making client/server systems "work"—work with the existing infrastructure, work as they're supposed to, work well enough to satisfy end-user demands—is sometimes enough to make you ask if you truly need a client/server solution. And if all this weren't enough, additional issues of performance management and client/server security must be contended with. As we'll see in the next chapter, here's where some real client/server challenges lie.

Key Terms and Ideas Appearing in This Chapter

EHLLAPI:

Emulator High-Level Language Application Programming Interface. An IBM API that provides a way for programmers to "scrape" information from 3270 (green) screens. It's not elegant, but it works, and it allows a graceful transition away from all those applications on the mainframe. Screen scraping reads data off of specific green-screen locations and fires it off to a GUI to be displayed on a PC. But if the screen changes, things get crazy.

4GL:

Fourth-generation language. A higher-level language usually constructed upon a 3GL (such as C). 4GLs are especially prevalent when it comes to databases. Client/server (client really) development tools such as PowerBuilder and SQLWindows are 4GLs.

ODI:

Open Data Link Interface. Software that allows multiple communication protocol stacks to use a single LAN adapter. ODI was invented by Novell and Apple to allow users to load and access several protocols concurrently, meaning that they could access file servers and hosts that employ different protocols. SPX/IPX and TCP/IP could be used simultaneously, for example, if both the NetWare shell and some DOS-based implementation of TCP/IP were installed on the client. They call this dual-stacking.

OOP:

Object Oriented Programming. OOP is a different way for programmers to model the physical world—one claimed to be closer to reality. It rests on three "principles": encapsulation (information hiding), inheritance, and polymorphism. One of the goals of OOP is to construct small, reusable pieces of software.

PowerBuilder:

Currently, the leading (low/medium-size) client/server development tool. PowerBuilder is a 4GL that can be used to "paint" end-user screens with graphics and data fields and then connect these fields up to any of a number of databases.

RDBMS:

Relational DataBase Management System. Data can be stored and manipulated in several different ways. Currently the favorite is a series of linked (related) two-dimensional tables. SQL is used to create, manipulate, and extract data from these tables. Most leading database engines are relational.

Screen-scraping:

Using IBM's EHLLAPI mainframe application program interface to grab data fields off of 3270 green screens and representing these fields in a graphical format. Often this is an organization's first humble step toward client/server computing.

SQL:

Structured Query Language. SQL is a data-access language designed to remove the navigational responsibilities from the user. (You don't have to know exactly where things are).

SQL driver:

A piece of proprietary software that hooks up clients to database engines. The SQL driver takes care of much of the low-level stuff, such as the networking protocols. It also works at a higher level, linking the client application to the database.

SQLWindows:

A client/server development product, much like PowerBuilder. Although it doesn't have the same market penetration as PowerBuilder, many contend that it is a technically more sophisticated offering.

3GL:

Third-generation language. In the beginning there was machine code: 1s and 0s. Not a lot of fun to work with. Then came assembler. It was an improvement but still left much to be desired. It was pretty terse stuff. The third generation introduced "languages." There are a lot of them around, but the most popular ones are Cobol, FORTRAN, C, and Pascal. The newer object-oriented languages, such as C++ and SmallTalk, generally are still considered to be 3GLs as well, but it might be fairer to call them 3.5GLs since they build on lower-level constructs. Computers still speak 1s and 0s, so compilers must step in to translate.

VBX:

Visual Basic control. A small executable chunk of code conforming to Visual Basic's interface standards. Essentially, VBXs are clamp-on components that developers (often VB developers) add to Visual Basic in order to draw on their functionality as needed. To add an encryption routine, for example, a VB programmer could use (often for a fee) someone's VBX instead of writing his or her own from scratch. 4GLs such as PowerBuilder and SQLWindows can access and use VBXs too. The code inside the executable doesn't even need to be written in VB; some C++ compilers can generate VBXs.

Visual Basic:

Microsoft's enormously popular Windows development tool that is easier to learn than PowerBuilder or SQLWindows and certainly easier to learn and use than C++. Many are turning to Visual Basic in order to develop small client/server applications.

Notes

[1] Charles Babcock, "Visual Basic Creeps Up on IS," *ComputerWorld*, September 5, 1994, v28, 6.

Chapter 10

Executive Summary

Client/server management can be split into performance management (and maintenance) and security management. Client/server performance management suffers from a shortage of Information Systems professionals skilled in the workings of distributed, heterogeneous networks. Further aggravating matters is the fact that practically no comprehensive tools permit operators to monitor events on heterogeneous networks. What exists follows one of two possible approaches: extend traditional mainframe management tools to oversee the operation of non-SNA nodes, or expand the scope of workstation-based tools upward, to include mainframe management. The latter, based on the Simple Network Management Protocol, looks the most promising.

Much about the client/server model stands contrary to network security. It seeks to increase data access and favors distributing the data. To lessen the threat that accompanies these client/server credos, technologies such as RAID (Redundant Arrays of Independent Disks) and data encryption are necessary. But no network can be made completely safe. Combining client/server with the tried-and-true security practices of the glass house can help.

CHAPTER 10

Client/Server Management

Introduction

The idea of distributing computations, and data, over networks throughout organizations makes sense under certain circumstances. But such distribution has to be managed. Management is one of the most pressing problems associated with the client/server model; as you're about to see, network management currently leaves much to be desired.

Wrapped within the label of network management is network configuration, performance monitoring, fault tracing, the prevention of breakdowns, and protecting the network from unauthorized, intentional, or accidental intrusion. All too often, client/server supporters overlook these fundamental needs, sluffing them off to "backroom activities." Yet if ever there was a client/server showstopper, network management could be it.

223

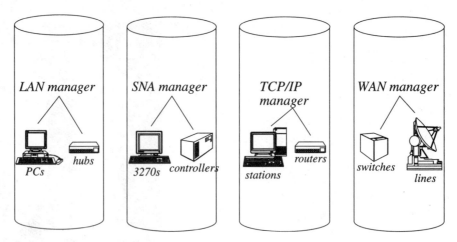

Figure 10.1 Management stovepipes.

Heterogeneous network management—exactly the kind of stuff you'd expect to run into in a client/server application—is still pretty green. There's little cohesion among different environments to begin with. And few IS professionals are experienced in dealing with them. Tools are limited—both in number and in what they can do. This leads to a series of network management stovepipes with little cross-over between them. (See Figure 10.1.) No single, off-the-shelf solution meets today's enterprise-wide network management needs.

Clearly separate management options isn't too efficient. More than that, it clashes directly with the integration aims of client/server; until internetworks can be managed collectively from a single point, there can be no effective enterprise-wide information sharing. There are two efforts under way to change this: one from the top-down and another from the bottom-up. In the top-down approach to enterprise network management, IBM proposes to extend its successful mainframe network management environment to embrace both SNA and non-SNA entities alike.

NetView/390: The Top-down Approach

IBM has long been the leader in systems network architecture (SNA) management. That may seem natural, but the company hasn't exactly had the field all to itself. It continues to face stiff competition from both Systems Center Inc. (now a division of Sterling Software) and Legent. But IBM was not prepared to lose this fight. Leadership in SNA management is vital to the company because it gives IBM a means to control the direction of network management while maintaining close ties to its customer base.

As you would expect, traditional SNA management is a centralized affair. To participate in the process, networked devices are expected to have sufficient intelligence to permit them to gather their own statistics and then shunt them up to the mainframe, where operators monitor collective SNA performance.

There are three components to IBM's SNA management architecture: focal points, entry points, and service points. Like most SNA entities, these are more logical than physical things. Focal points provide mainframe-based network management for all devices connected to that network. NetView is IBM's flagship product in this category. But there are other focal points as well. Secondary to NetView are packages like NDM, the NetView Distribution Manager, used for downloading software throughout the network.

Entry points are SNA nodes that support peripheral devices. Cluster controllers are perhaps the best example, but there are others. Outfitted with the appropriate software, PCs and AS/400s can act as entry points.

Not all SNA-networked devices possess sufficient statistics-gathering intelligence. Service points are used to help them out. (See Figure 10.2.) NetView/PC is IBM's primary service point product. Running on a PC, NetView/PC is sort of like a gateway. After a programmer codes the necessary monitoring software for the non-SNA device, data collected by it is passed to NetView/PC, which, in turn, forwards alerts to the mainframe management system on its behalf. Service points are a key element in IBM's strategy to grow NetView, now generally referred to as NetView/390, beyond the immediate reach of the mainframe.

There are a couple of snags to this strategy, though. For one, a PC must be dedicated to service point duty. But beyond this, "what-to-do" information for the NetView/390 operators when confronted with non-SNA device failures has to be provided. If the networked device is part of the traditional IBM family, NetView/390 simply accesses a centralized look-up table to provide the operator with the suggested response action. However, this table usually doesn't contain entries for non-SNA devices. Recognizing that networks are destined to heterogeneity, IBM

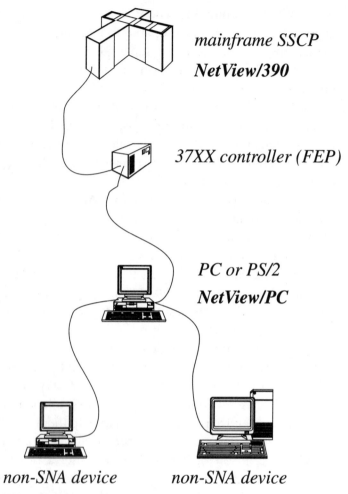

Figure 10.2 NetView/390.

has opened up NetView to manufacturers of non-SNA devices through its generic alert capability.

Generic alerts permit remote devices, both SNA and non-SNA alike, dynamically to provide operators with detailed information regarding probable causes of failures and recommended actions. It's a significant step toward opening NetView to enterprise-wide network management.

In recent years, IBM has evolved SNA away from a mainframe-centric posture. (We saw this in Chapter 5.) With APPN, Advanced Peer-to-Peer Networking, SNA becomes a much more democratic style of networking. But even here the idea of focal points remains valid.

Network alerts can be directed to a specific node designated as the SNA focal point. Even with distributed networks, control still needs to be centralized.

Although IBM has groomed NetView/390 for enterprise network management, the company also comes at the problem from the other side. In addition to NetView/390, it manufactures LAN NetView, NetView for Windows, and NetView/6000 (a version originally slated for TCP/IP networks) as well. Unfortunately, for the time being, at least, each operates in isolation. But IBM's diversification of NetView demonstrates that the company may be willing to concede that network management isn't always best done on a mainframe. And this brings us to the "bottom-up" approach to network management.

SNMP: The Bottom-up Approach

We ran into SNMP, the Simple Network Management Protocol, earlier, when talking about TCP/IP. (It's one of the generic applications that's often a part of most implementations.) It's the foundation for the three best-known toolsets for the management of heterogeneous networks: Sun's SunNet Manager, HP's OpenView, and IBM's NetView/6000.

SNMP is a polling protocol used to obtain performance and status information from networked devices. It's often said that the protocol can be used to manage everything from supercomputers to toasters. Not only is it simple, as its name suggests, but more important, from the point of view of market acceptance, it's vendor-neutral. It was developed at the University of Tennessee and then transferred into the public domain. It's free. Ultimately it became one of TCP/IP's Application layer protocols, but SNMP isn't restricted to TCP/IP networks, as many believe. It can run over practically any appropriately configured connectionless communication protocol. Today it's available for TCP/IP, DECnet, AppleTalk, NetWare's IPX, and even raw Ethernet. Manufacturers of WAN products are moving quickly to support SNMP as well.

SNMP is a protocol for query and response. But that's all it is; SNMP is not a network management tool by itself, just the foundation for one. And its expectations are meager; SNMP doesn't assume that the networked devices to be managed are intelligent enough to gather their own statistics (as NetView/390 does). Instead, it places most of the responsibility, and the bulk of the code that goes with it, on the management end of the relationship. All that's expected of the remote device is the ability to run the small SNMP "agent" program. (See Figure 10.3.) In cases where it can't even do that, a proxy agent can act as a go-between.

The fact that SNMP has kept agent program requirements to a bare minimum has made it a favorite among manufacturers of network control equipment. It's clearly favored over the Common Management Information Protocol (CMIP), once thought to be its eventual successor. An emerging ISO standard, CMIP offers more control over networked devices than does SNMP. But along with this comes greater network overhead, something that both network component manufacturers and LAN administrators would rather avoid. Under TCP/IP, SNMP relies on only the User Datagram Protocol and the Internetwork Protocol. CMIP, on the other hand, uses the entire OSI protocol stack. Just a few years ago SNMP supporters were locked in a fierce battle of words with CMIP backers. Now CMIP is hardly mentioned at all. You could say that, in the end, the choice was "simple."

SNMP is a polling protocol; the SNMP manager queries networked devices in turn to request performance information. When it does, it grabs information from an agent's Management Information Base (MIB): a list of browsable device-specific functions that are sometimes referred to as objects. SNMP-compliant devices adhere to a standard set of MIB objects. A recent enhancement to SNMP allows its manager to go beyond simply reading the MIB to actually adjusting the values it contains. It's the difference between monitoring and managing.

Within the last few years SNMP-based network managers have begun to reach up as well as out, to take over SNA management too. This has some important implications; not only does it offer the promise of one day managing both SNA and non-SNA networks from a single graphical device, but it also off-loads precious CPU cycles from the big iron. NetView/390 is demanding; it uses up approximately 10 percent of a mainframe's total compute capacity. This has motivated companies such as Peregrine Systems Inc. and NetTech Inc. to try to "downsize" it. Although their products can't perform all of NetView/390's functions, they do handle most of the major stuff.

Even IBM is getting into this act. Through a gateway (known as SNA/6000), NetView/6000 can extend its reach to include SNA

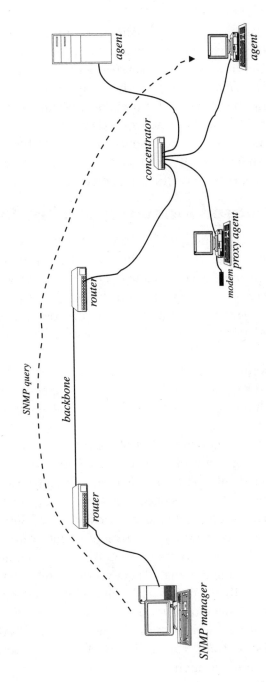

Figure 10.3 SNMP-based management.

networks in addition to SNMP-supporting nets. Unlike Peregrine's Open/SNA or NetTech's Review/6000, however, NetView/6000 still requires NetView/390 to remain resident on the mainframe.

But there may be limits to how far SNMP can go. Although some are moving to enhance it,[1] it remains a polling technology. This works fine when the number of networked devices isn't too great, polling one of thousands of networked devices is unworkable.

Nevertheless, SNMP remains the leading choice and the best hope for heterogeneous network management.

SNMP-based Management: The Big Three

The vendor community clearly prefers SNMP. There's a daily migration away from proprietary solutions toward the protocol. But that's only one part of the network management solution. Something has to sit at the center of it all able to poll the MIBs of the networked devices. That something is the management "platform," and today, three vie for its leadership: Sun's SunNet Manager, HP's OpenView, and IBM's NetView/6000.

It's worth noting that, as comprehensive as these platforms are, none provides end-to-end network management right out of the box. Instead, all rely on third parties to supply missing pieces to complete the picture.

SunNet Manager, the oldest of the big three, boasts the largest third-party following. But even with all its available add-ons, SunNet Manager really is suited only to the management of small networks. And although it retains the lead in terms of market share, its piece of the pie is eroding.

Sun has just completed a major overhaul of SunNet Manager.[2] The rebuild is part of a new management architecture called Encompass, which takes a broad approach to network configuration, performance, and security. Admitting that it's been slow to respond to encroachments from HP and IBM, SunSoft is hoping that object-oriented technology will put its management tools back into contention. Encompass not only does all the normal things expected of an SNMP-based management platform, it also can distribute software to networked nodes—a welcome feature at upgrade time.

While Sun struggles to get back on track, HP has had nothing but success with its management product. OpenView literally changed the face of network management. "Open" was the driving theme right from the word go. In a bid to attract as much supporting vendor interest as possible, OpenView is designed to allow easy third-party access. More approachable and versatile than anything that came before it, OpenView has set the standard for SNMP network management.

Ten times larger than SunNet Manager, OpenView features an extensive graphical user interface. This includes tools such as an MIB browser. Like Encompass, with the latest release of OpenView it's possible not only to monitor network devices but to configure and distribute application software to them as well.

Like IBM's network management suite of tools, there's really no single product called "OpenView." Instead, there is an OpenView for UNIX, an OpenView for Windows, and an OpenView for NetWare. Teaming up with Peregrine Systems, OpenView for UNIX now can even manage SNA networks too. To help tie all this altogether, HP has developed the OpenView OperationsCenter.[3] It's just one of a number of initiatives the company has on the drawing board to bring sanity to the management of multivendor, multiplatform, multiprotocol infrastructures.

IBM was so impressed with HP's open platform concept that it licensed the OpenView core as the basis for its NetView/6000 product. Then IBM added to it—so much so that NetView/6000 now is generally seen as the most technically sophisticated SNMP-based management platform available.

NetView/6000 got a big boost in 1993 when Digital dropped its own network management line and selected IBM's platform to replace it. Resold under the name Polycenter NetView/6000, it's capable of managing both TCP/IP networks as well as Digital's proprietary DECnet implementations.

Many are surprised at how quickly NetView/6000 carved out a piece of the market for itself. Only a short time ago, it looked as if Sun and HP had network management in the bag. The truth is, however, the market hasn't really taken off yet. As client/server and distributed networks grow in popularity, demand for heterogeneous network management platforms will intensify.

NetView/6000 differentiates itself from OpenView in a number of ways. Its API (Application Programming Interfaces) set, part of its so-called General Topology Manager (GTM), is more sophisticated than OpenView's. Applications written to the GTM API end up closely tied to the management platform. This permits the GTM to manage TCP/IP, SPX/IPX, DECnet, SNA, and APPN networks from a single, graphical topology map. And where does this map come from? you might ask. From NetView/6000 itself. The product automatically "discovers" what's on the networks and produces a schematic—a map—showing routers, computers, and LAN segments. This is where NetView/6000's other best-in-class feature shines. Although both SunNet Manager and Open-View use graphical displays, NetView/6000's displays are considered some of the easiest to understand and most efficient to use. Network administrators especially like being able to watch performance plots of several networked devices at the same time.

At one time, the Open Software Foundation (OSF) was supposed to still the troubled waters of network management with its Distributed Management Environment (DME). It never happened. Coming up with a scalable, open, easy-to-use, sophisticated network management platform that everyone could agree on turned out to be much more difficult than the OSF first thought. Although the OSF continued to hang on to the idea even after many pronounced it dead, it now appears that it's finally slipped away.

With all the activity surrounding it, it seems certain now that SNMP-based management eventually will dominate. It may be a few years away, but heterogeneous, corporate-wide network management is an achievable goal. And nothing intrinsic to the client/server model precludes it. The same can't be said when it comes to network security, however. Client/server's philosophy of information for the people directly contradicts most corporate data security practices. This presents a formidable challenge to system designers.

Client/Server Security

How much is information worth? Here's an interesting bit of trivia: It's been estimated that 70 cents of every dollar invested to bring a product to market goes to information gathering, sharing, and management. Those old clichés are right: Information does appear to be an organization's most important resource. Protecting it is serious business.

Viruses, hackers, fire, earthquakes, terrorist attacks, tornadoes, mechanical failure, corporate espionage, floods, disgruntled employees: There are plenty of threats around to keep network and database administrators up at night. Yet the greatest menace to corporate data is the threat from within—from the well-meaning end user who modifies or erases something by accident. Client/server is bent on giving end users more access to more data. While this makes sense from the point of view of productivity—with more information, employees can make better, and possibly even faster, decisions—it flies directly into the face of corporate security.

To some, "client/server security" is practically a contradiction in terms. Not only does it seek to establish greater data access, but client/ server also pushes for the distribution of data and applications throughout the workplace. Top it all off with a limited selection of tools and proven security procedures, and you can understand why few are willing to field mission-critical applications on the model.

But the situation is not hopeless. Certain things can be done to improve the situation, at least. To lessen the risk, security must be designed into client/server solutions right from the word go. But before you take that plunge, it might be a good idea to first get a handle on your organization's existing security exposure.

Assessing Your Risk

How exposed is your data? There's no shortage of high-priced experts around who are only too happy to help answer that question for you. But often they're not really necessary; it's just a matter of common sense. (See Table 10.1.) Organizations often can assess their own security risk.

To start with, where are the corporate data sources? If your organization has a mainframe, likely it contains several databases. There might be additional data stores on NT, UNIX/RISC servers, or AS/400s. Novell file servers are able to support database operations through Net-Ware Loadable Modules. There are also probably a number of xBASE databases (dBASE, Paradox, and Fox Pro) scattered throughout the organization. But that's not all. That's just the database-held stuff. It's a good bet that every PC in your organization has some unique data on its hard drive. Although not as formal, it's still data that would have to be reproduced somehow if lost.

Table 10.1 Assessing Security Risk

1. List all corporate data sources.
2. Estimate costs of rebuilding lost data.
3. List all possible threats.
4. Assign probabilities to threats.
5. Estimate costs of effective prevention.
6. Compare to current security investment.

That leads to the next step: estimating the cost of rebuilding lost data. Usually this involves person-hours only, but if the corporate data includes test results or manufacturing statistics, there could be additional test facility costs too.

The third step in the exercise is to list the data threats. Some threats are regional: Coastal sites are at greater risk of hurricanes than inland sites; earthquakes generally occur along known fault lines. Many threats are common across the board, however: accidental loss, viruses, acts of sabotage. And as we saw in Oklahoma in 1995, in the United States we're not immune from acts of terrorism either. Some threats have a higher likelihood of occurrence than others; based on past experience plus a bit of gut instinct, try to come up with an estimate of the probability of occurrence for each.

Prevention is the most effective countermeasure. In the next step of the assessment, first list and then cost out effective preventive measures for each threat. As an example, to reduce the occurrence of viruses, a company might consider the exclusive use of (floppy) diskless PCs.

Finally, compare all this to the organization's ongoing security investment. Often it is sobering to see how poorly the current investment compares to the cost of rebuilding lost data. Figure 10.4 illustrates what these relationships often look like for a typical organization.

If your risk assessment uncovers some glaring holes, you might want to think twice about handing over more data to an even more-

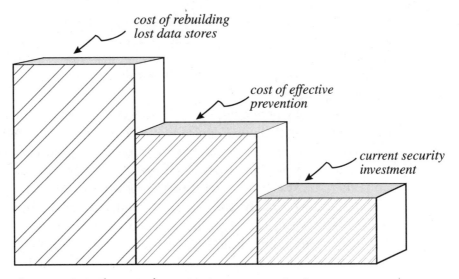

Figure 10.4 The typical situation in most organizations.

difficult-to-secure client/server system—at least until you patch things up.

With all the challenges that go along with an organization's first deployment of client/server, security often gets overlooked. Yet even in non-mission-critical applications, the system still has to be responsive and available; security is still an issue.

As noted earlier, to be effective, client/server security must be designed into the system right from the beginning. Bolting something on later is harder and usually more expensive. Because of the complexity involved, many prefer to break the problem down and tackle security issues one piece at a time.

Layers of Client/Server Security

When it comes to client/server security, there are three primary concerns: the physical protection of both the clients and the server(s), the logical protection of clients and server(s), and the protection of the data itself.

Overall, clients are the hardest to protect. There are lots of them, and they can be almost anywhere in the corporation. Physically they're not that hard to secure, although everyday corporations report thefts of PCs. It's relatively easy to deter this kind of thing—at least when it comes to desktop machines. (Safeguarding notebooks, of course, is a lot tougher.) Most PC supply stores sell devices that can be used to physically secure PCs to desks. Assemblies that attach to the rear of the PC chassis are probably best; out of sight, they're less likely to rile honest employees.

But physically protecting client devices costs peanuts, and is simple compared to the challenge: logically protecting them. DOS/Windows, the most-used client operating system, offers little in the way of password protection. While it is possible to set up a keyboard lock with the aid of the DOS system disk, third-party products are generally easier to install and to work with. The down side is that they take up memory, and sometimes can cause problems when running memory-intensive Windows applications. (It doesn't take much to disturb Windows 3.x.) OS/2 and Windows 95 offer password protection out of the box. In fact, because Windows 95 platforms are remotely accessible, the operating system requires both a valid user name and password to access the system (as do most UNIX devices). The problem with each of these solutions, of course, is that they require PC users to remember their passwords.

We've all heard the horror stories surrounding password use— everything from users writing them on the bottom of their keyboards to slapping them right on the side of their monitors with a yellow sticky note. They're annoying, but passwords are an unfortunate side effect of life in the information age. To save employees from having to remember them, some vendors have come up with physical keys, cards, and other such paraphernalia. One of the more interesting of these, designed for user authentication in client/server systems, is Secure Dynamics Inc's SecureID SmartCard. The credit card–size device (held by the user) generates and displays a random six-digit code every 60 seconds. To access a server, the user would first be prompted for a PIN (a short, easy-to-remember sequence known only to that person). Then, if recognized, the server would next request the random digit sequence displayed on the SmartCard. Synchronized with the card, the server knows what it should be. If the user gets that right, he or she is in. But the process is a lot to go through, and the card is just another thing for people to lose. There's no perfect solution.

And what about the data and applications held on the clients? How do you protect them from mechanical breakdown? Although they're improving, hard drives still fail. And when they do, you can bet something important is going to be lost. The solution is simple: Back it up. But that takes time, and it's a hassle, especially if backing up to floppies, so people rarely do it. To make backup easier, several vendors have developed automatic, remote backup procedures that can be initiated from a server. These procedures require that employees leave their PCs on 24 hours a day, since it's the kind of thing you'd do off hours. Another solution is simply to provide enough disk space on file servers so that users can keep all their important files there. If you do, make sure you take the time to explain the merits of server storage to end users. If they don't cooperate, nothing's been gained.

Client PCs are the most common doorway for viruses. The National Computer Security Association believes that 90 percent of all viruses are transmitted by floppy disk. Employees exchange data, programs, and yes, games every day. And many times a virus goes along for the ride. In short order, nearly every machine in the organization can be infected. The result can be lost data, slow response times, or at best just some irritating message.

Virus-scanning software should be part of every client's startup routine. As new viruses crop up practically every day, the software has to be kept current. To further reduce viral threat, it's also a good idea never to boot a PC directly from a floppy disk. Viruses like to hide in system boot-up files. Some system administrators see the prevention of floppy disk use altogether as the best way to thwart the spread of viruses. The problem with that approach is that "sneakernet" sometimes is the only way to physically exchange information in this non–open systems world of ours. In the end, perhaps the best deterrent to viruses is education. Employees must be made to understand the threat and how to deal with it.

Security is a bit easier on the server side. There are fewer of them, and they can, and should, be locked away. When locating servers, by the way, apply a bit of common sense: Don't place them next to other electrical equipment or directly under sprinkler heads. Also, don't plug them into the same power strip as laser printers. Laser printers need to reheat their fuser elements periodically, and when they do, the electricity they draw fluctuates (or "bounces"). This fluctuation causes a small electrical surge for any devices sharing the same outlet, which can damage disk drives over time.

If a read/write head crashes into the disk, the server, and the services it provides, can be off-line hours or even days. Keeping servers up and running is what fault tolerance is all about.

Fault Tolerance

Fault tolerance is a matter of degree. It can be simple or quite complex. It all depends on how much you want to spend. The first level of redundancy is disk mirroring. (See Figure 10.5.). Rather than rely on a single disk, everything is simultaneously written to two. If the primary disk should then fail for some reason, the secondary (mirrored) disk can take over automatically. Disk mirroring is expensive though: You end up with only half the available disk space that you actually paid for. Since data can be read from different portions of both disks at the same time, read performance is usually quite good. But, on the down side, having to write everything twice is a real drawback.

Write performance can be improved by taking the next step in fault tolerance: disk duplexing. Here, as with mirroring, there are two disks, but each has its own dedicated controller. That too adds another level of redundancy.

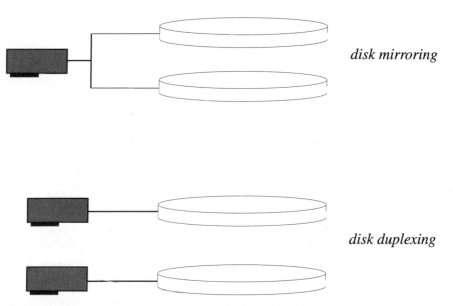

disk mirroring

disk duplexing

Figure 10.5 Disk mirroring and disk duplexing: Elements of business recovery.

Redundancy has taken a big step forward in the form of RAID: Redundant Array of Inexpensive Disks. RAID gets a lot of press, and there's significant market to back it up. LAN implementations of RAID are expected to top the $1 billion mark by 1996.[4]

RAID is a nonstandard set of redundancy levels for the simultaneous use of multiple disks. It starts off at RAID 0. Well, actually, RAID 0 has no fault tolerance. In fact, it's less dependable than a single, large disk. Intended for high-performance applications, different portions of a file are written, and read from, several disks at the same time. If one fails, the entire unit goes down.

Fault tolerance really begins with RAID 1. This is the same as disk mirroring. And everything after it is an attempt to get around the 100 percent overhead of requiring a dedicated second disk.

RAID 2 spreads data across multiple disks at the bit level. (The first bit is written to the first disk, the next to the second, and so on.) RAID 2 was designed for mainframe and supercomputer use and doesn't usually make its way down to most client/server implementations.

RAID 3 is similar to RAID 2 except that it was designed for microcomputer use. It sets aside one entire disk for parity (a mathematical representation of the data held on all the other disks in the array) and simultaneously writes the data to an even number of disks in the pack. If any disk should fail, its contents can be reconstructed from the information held on the parity drive. Like RAID 1, a single read request grabs different pieces of the data from all of the drives at the same time. However, since all the drives operate in lockstep, only one input/output action can occur at a time. RAID 3 is good for applications requiring fast sequential access of large data files (such as in imaging).

RAID 4 improves on RAID 3 by reading and writing whole data blocks to different disks in the array. This gives them a degree of independence from each other. If attached to a multitasking operating system, read rates are increased in step with the number of disks in the array. RAID 4 still uses a single dedicated parity drive, however. And since every write is accompanied by an update to that drive, write operations can hit a bottleneck.

RAID 5 does away with the dedicated parity drive and instead distributes parity information across all of the disks in the array. This gets around the single-write bottleneck. The only trick is ensuring that par-

Which level of RAID should you buy?

Selecting the appropriate type of RAID can be a bit confusing. Descriptions for the various levels are only generally accepted; many vendors don't adhere strictly to them. Not only that, the hard drive market is currently undergoing a significant change. IDE, a less expensive alternative to SCSI, has been enhanced, permitting drive capacities to extend beyond their previous 528 MB limit. The reduction in drive costs is shifting the market back in favor of RAID 1.

ity (rebuild) information for a disk is not written onto the same disk to which it pertains. Since both read and write transactions can be performed simultaneously, it's faster than other forms of RAID. This makes it a popular choice.

Protecting data and applications from mechanical failure is an ongoing concern. Appropriate levels of redundancy can lessen the threat significantly. Significantly more difficult to deal with, however, is data loss and damage inflicted by human beings.

Defending against Intruders

Like the client, the server operating system should offer logical (password) protection. NetWare, UNIX, OS/2, and NT all do. Many even go beyond this to offer single-point logon. NetWare 4.x, for example, allows users to log on once and gain access to all servers for which they are authorized, rather than having to log on separately to each one as required. With only one password to deal with, users are less likely to lose it or to write it down someplace where others can find it.

Many people feel that something even a bit more stringent is called for, however. This is the motivation behind authentication schemes like Kerberos. As we saw in Chapter 6, Kerberos grants time-limited, and very specific, authentication privileges to known end users. It's available as part of the OSF's Distributed Computing Environment as well as from a number of third parties as dedicated security software. But Kerberos only tells the requested service that users are who they say they are. It's still up to the target application to grant user authorization.

And unauthorized access is a growing problem. Illegal system entries cost U.S. companies at least $500 million per year.[5] Of course, all such incidents aren't reported; on the contrary, many organizations go to great lengths to keep security breaches a secret. Some even hire the perpetrators as "security consultants."

Aggravating matters further is the fact that many organizations are turning increasingly to the Internet for workgroup computing, general commerce, and remote e-mail. As we saw in Chapter 5, the Internet is a huge network of networks spanning the entire globe. No one really knows how many users are attached to it, but safe estimates are in the tens of millions. Internet access, and remote computing in general, poses special problems to network security.

Hackers used to be joy-riders. But today's more sophisticated intruder often has something more diabolical in mind. We discussed IP spoofing in Chapter 5. In another, equally crafty approach to intrusion, a hacker first sets out to compromise a local Internet node. But that's not their ultimate goal. Security experts believe that approximately 80 percent of all unauthorized accesses are performed by individuals "inside" the organization. Their status supplies them with information they need to guess, or somehow otherwise obtain, legitimate passwords. Once on their local Internet node, they set up a "sniffer" program. Sniffers monitor network traffic (and are usually used for legitimate purposes). The sniffer allows hackers to trap remote logon information and collects user ids and passwords for remote nodes on the Net. With that information, they're free to go where they please. This practice has become so widespread that CERT (Computer Emergency Response Term), an Internet security agency, issued a general advisory against it in early 1994.

With this kind of thing going on, and with all the rumored viruses roaming about, it's little wonder that many organizations have serious misgivings about connecting up to the Internet. But in spite of this, even though dial-on-demand is more secure and often all an organization really needs, many find the attractions of a direct link to the Net too tempting to resist. Thousands of organizations already have them, and the number increases daily.

If you're going to connect to the Net directly, make sure that a firewall stands between it and you, in order to minimize your risk exposure. Firewalls are intelligent network entities, such as a router (from companies such as Cisco or Bay Networks), that stand between the Internet and the rest of an organization's network. They can be programmed to block certain types of data traffic. For example, some firewalls permit only e-mail transfer. Others may allow only an in-to-out flow of information. In concert with an attending computer, they also can log activity and alert security personnel about selected threats.

But firewalls, user authorization, and user authentication aren't enough. To help further thwart intruders, data encryption is needed.

Data Encryption

The most effective means of keeping sensitive information from falling into the wrong hands is to use data encryption. Scrambling transmissions (or files on a hard drive) so that they can be read only by the intended recipient was in use long before computers were around. The ancient Romans commonly scrambled written transmissions to keep their enemies in the dark.

Central to modern cryptography is the idea of private and public keys. In private key cryptography, the sender and receiver of an encrypted message use the same secret key. (See Figure 10.6). If Bill wanted to send an encrypted message to Mary, he would first scramble it with their mutual secret key. She would use the same key to decrypt it.

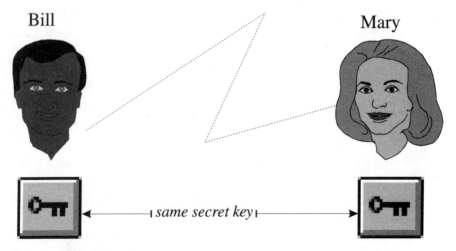

Figure 10.6 Secret key encryption.

But if the key falls into the wrong hands, security is breached. And that's the problem: If the sender and receiver are geographically distant from each other, how do they share the key in a manner that they both know is secure?

In 1976 Diffie and Hellman introduced the idea of public key cryptography to address this. Here all senders and receivers get two unique keys: a private one and a public one. The public key is known to all and is used to encrypt a message for a specific recipient. It can be decrypted only with that recipient's corresponding private key—known only to the recipient. So now when Bill wanted to send an encrypted message to Mary, he would first look up her public encryption key. (See Figure 10.7.) He would use this to encrypt the message and then send the result along to her. On Mary's side, the message would (only) be decrypted with her private key.

Since the secret key is never exchanged between communicating parties, a public key/private key cryptosystem offers greater security. But it requires management of the keys, and it's slower than pure secret key encryption. And what's more, even it isn't completely bulletproof.

In 1977 a team of RSA Data Security Inc. (a principal provider of private key/public key technology) engineers issued a challenge to any comers to try to break the 129-digit key used to encrypt a simple message. They predicted that the feat would take more than

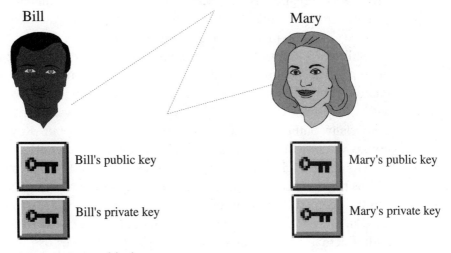

Figure 10.7 Public key encryption.

50 years. But within only eight months, a team of 600 researchers, led by engineers from Bellcore Labs, managed to do it. This didn't trouble RSA though. They expected it could be done, they just hadn't anticipated such a massive effort would be mounted to try to do so. To quell customers' concerns regarding the encryption method, RSA would merely resort to a longer (and much harder to crack) encryption key.

One of the most widely adopted secret key data encryption algorithms is DES, the Data Encryption Standard. It's extensively used by nonmilitary wings of the U.S. government. DES uses a 56-bit private key cryptographic system. In contrast to the RSA experience, DES has never been broken. Nevertheless, not everyone is convinced that it's secure. As computers become more powerful, the day approaches when DES eventually will be cracked (within a reasonable time period). Banks, also common users of the DES cryptosystem, have started to "triple-DES" transmissions to put that day significantly off into the future. Applying the DES algorithm to transmissions three times in succession is approximately the same as doubling the length of the secret key to 112 bits, making it substantially more difficult to crack.

But the federal government views the practice of triple-DESing with some concern. DES is a publicly obtainable encryption algorithm. There's nothing to stop individuals or groups from using it to pass information of threat to national or local security. Triple-DESing might provide lawbreakers with a secure way to carry on criminal activities. The government prefers that organizations use elements of its controversial "Capstone project" for data encryption.

Still under development, Capstone has four elements: a bulk data encryption algorithm, a digital signatures algorithm (DSS), a key exchange protocol, and a hash function. The data encryption scheme is called Skipjack. It uses an 80-bit public key cryptosystem that runs on a specially outfitted encryption chip known as Clipper. Keys for the cryptosystem would be managed by a U.S. federal agency.

Going through a federal agency to acquire public encryption keys means that the government could selectively listen in on any communications deemed important to national security. This is the controversial bit. But only the government and companies directly doing business with it actually are required to use Skipjack. All other use will be discretionary.

Which scheme is better, a secret key cryptosystem like DES, or a public key/private key system like RSA's? It's not really a question of "better." Both have their place. Public key cryptosystems usually are positioned as complementary to pure secret key systems. It's common practice, for example, to encrypt a message with a secret key cryptosystem like DES and then encrypt the randomly chosen DES key with a public key system. The encrypted message and the publicly encrypted key then are sent to the intended recipient. In another application, to encrypt the information on a client's or server's hard drive—for example, DES alone—might be fine.

While DES is still the most widely used cryptosystem, public key offerings, especially those from RSA, are in demand. VISA and Microsoft, for example, are developing a secure system for electronic commerce over the Internet.[6] Scheduled for deployment sometime in 1995, many are concerned that the system, built on RSA's encryption technology, will run only on Windows platforms. Many RDBMS vendors such as Oracle also are turning to RSA's public key system to encrypt transmissions between clients and data servers. RSA's product is certainly the most talked about encryption technology at the moment.

Encryption will foil all but the most capable of hackers. But do you encrypt everything? Probably not. Doing so would simply be too slow and add too much overhead to data transmissions. Thus hackers may still occasionally hit pay dirt whenever they break into organizations. So security comes back to prevention, sealing up holes before someone gets in. To locate these holes, many companies are invoking SATAN.

The Devil Only Knows

Invoking SATAN to find weaknesses in an organization's networks may sound a bit rash. But we're not talking about devil-worshipping here. SATAN is an acronym for Security Administrator Tool for Analyzing Networks, an easy-to-use facility for probing networks for openings.

Running from a computer outside of the target network, SATAN mimics intruders, looking for ways they could get in. If it finds any, it then explains the vulnerability and how hackers might exploit it. While the product was intended to help network administrators determine their degree of exposure, many fear that potential hackers will use it for something less constructive. User-friendly, the product could, quite conceivably, give those with little knowledge of break-in techniques the information they need to become dangerous. And the fact that SATAN is available free of charge over the Internet only tosses more fuel on the fire.

SATAN is essentially an expert system. Rules gleaned from security experts form its core. In its current manifestation, the product doesn't actually break into sites—only point out potential risks. But its developers are working on enhancements that take SATAN further; a future version will have the ability to act on its findings and penetrate the network to demonstrate just how easy doing so is.[7]

Should you be worried about SATAN? If you're directly connected to the Internet or otherwise accessible from the outside world, yes. What should you do about it? Get the product, use it as it was intended, and act on its advice to patch up any openings it finds. Only by doing so can you avoid any threat from the product.

Wrap-up

Client/server has been largely a grass-roots reaction. Frustrated with the backroom nature of mainframe politics, workgroups went out on their own and began stringing their PCs together. But most corporate data sits on the mainframe. To do their job, the people in the groups still had to get at it. The solution? Client/server, of course.

By its very definition, client/server often results in heterogeneous computing environments. But while the spirit is willing, the tools are weak. The technology simply hasn't matured to the point where large, mission-critical, enterprise-wide applications can be managed on heterogeneous client/server networks yet.

But there is reason to take heart. Vendors clearly understand the need and are moving quickly to meet it. While management tools are fragmented today, within a few years many of them will have become integrated. And although there have been numerous contenders, it seems now that most will be built on the SNMP protocol.

Client/server security is another matter. There are no obvious quick fixes here. Protecting computers and networks is difficult enough. But client/server seeks to increase accessibility and to spread data throughout the organization, close to where it's needed most. This can be a frightening specter for those charged with maintaining the company's security and will form a sizable component of client/server's hidden cost.

Many of the security measures we've discussed in this chapter aren't new; they've been used in mainframes for years. And in some respects, it seems foolish to try to duplicate them on a network if a mainframe installation is already in place. Established mainframe security practices is a good reason to consider the three-tier client/server model, which really just blends the new and the established; client/server excels in the presentation of information and collaborative computing, the mainframe excels in security and in its ability to perform transactions. A marriage of the two just seems to make sense.

Adoption of a three-tier client/server model doesn't mean that fault-tolerance measures such as RAID and intruder-protection schemes such as encrypting the data aren't necessary; you still have to protect the data, and the systems it is processed on, out on the floor. Even if a rigorous server-to-mainframe data replication procedure is followed, there may come a time when a server crashes before it's had the opportunity to replicate the latest data changes to the mainframe in the glass house.

Can client/server systems be managed? Some can—certainly the small ones. Others prove (unfortunately) later on, after they've entered production, that they can't. If there's any advice you should take away with you from this book, it is not to overlook security and performance management in client/server design.

Key Terms and Ideas Appearing in This Chapter

Capstone project:

A government-initiated effort to establish encryption methods for all government dealings. It has four components: a bulk data encryption algorithm called Skipjack, a digital signatures algorithm, a key exchange/management protocol, and a hash function. Skipjack runs over a special chip called Clipper. Only companies doing business with the government and the government itself are required to use Capstone.

Cryptography:

The study of data encryption. Cryptosystems, highly mathematical undertakings in general, follow either a private (secret) or a public key system. Private key cryptography is the most common. The best-known algorithm is called DES. It requires that both the sender and the receiver of an encrypted message use the same secret key to encrypt it. The key is changed routinely to prevent others from cracking the code. But this causes a problem: How do you safely share keys? An alternative scheme is to use a public key system. In this form of cryptography, everyone has his or her own public and private keys. To send a message to person A, it would be first encrypted with his or her specific public key. It then can be decrypted only with A's (permanent) private key. The most popular public key algorithm is RSA's algorithm, licensed from Public Key Partners, a group that manages the patent rights of Hellman and Diffie, who invented public key cryptography.

CERT:

Computer Emergency Response Team, a group of computer professionals based at Carnegie-Mellon University. Their purpose is to seek out computer-based threats in order to bring them to the attention of the general public. They also often issue advisories (available from the Internet) on suggested actions to take in order to make your networks more secure. It's a good idea to review these routinely.

CMIP:

Common Management Information Protocol. An ISO standard for the monitoring and control of networked devices. CMIP isn't terribly popular with makers of networked devices because it's top-heavy. This means that low-end networked entities such as repeaters have difficulty accommodating it. It also places a burden on network communications, so administrators aren't thrilled with it either. Still emerging, the protocol may be too late anyway. SNMP has become so popular that it appears impossible to unseat.

DES:

Data Encryption Standard. An ANSI standard published by the National Institute of Standards. DES is a private cryptosystem. It uses a 56 bit key, considered too long for current computers to crack in a reasonable amount of time. But as computers get faster, cracking it will become more likely. Many predict that DES will one day be replaced or overhauled in favor of a public key system.

Disk duplexing:

A fault-tolerant technique for coping with mechanical failure. Usually used in servers, disk duplexing simultaneously writes data to two disks. Each disk further has its own controller card. One of the disks is designated as the primary; if it should fail, the secondary disk takes over.

Disk mirroring:

Also known as RAID level 1, disk mirroring is very much like disk duplexing, except that a single controller card is used. Disk mirroring offers good read performance—both read heads can grab different portions of the file at the same time—but doesn't exhibit very good write performance—everything needs to be written twice.

Entry point:

One of those logical SNA things. Entry points are SNA nodes that serve as connection points for other SNA nodes. Cluster controllers are the archetypal entry point. These devices are equipped with the necessary smarts to allow them to collect their own management information. They pass this information on to the mainframe.

Firewall:

A way of isolating networks. Many intelligent devices can act as firewalls, although routers are generally the favorite. With the growth of interest in the Internet, the term often has come to mean some device that controls the flow of information between an organization's networks and the Net. They can be programmed in a variety of ways: Some only allow the flow of e-mail, for example. If your networks are connected to the Internet or can be accessed in any way from the outside, you should have a firewall in place.

Focal point:

Another SNA logical notion. Focal points are management software that accept incoming data from SNA network nodes and compile it for presentation to a human operator. NetView/390 is IBM's best-known focal point.

Kerberos:

Kerberos is a user authentication system, designed and developed at MIT. It uses a "ticket" system to establish user identities. The whole idea behind Kerberos is first to have users prove who they are and then to limit them to specific services on the network. If users wish to access a data server, for example, their Kerberos ticket is valid only for that server and no other. That would require the acquisition of another ticket. Kerberos has nothing to do with authorization. It doesn't check to see if a user does indeed have the right to access that data server— that's left to that server. Kerberos is part of the OSF's DCE (Distributed Computing Environment).

MIB:

Management Information Base. Used with SNMP, the Simple Network Management Protocol. When SNMP polls networked devices, it reads information stored in its MIB (a table of relevant performance data unique to that device). A more recent version of MIB allows SNMP to change entries as well.

NetView/390:

IBM's premier mainframe focal point product. NetView is a strategic product that helps IBM attract and then hold onto mainframe customers. The company is trying to extend the reach of NetView/390 to include non-SNA devices as well. The effort is fast losing ground to SNMP-based heterogeneous network management, however.

NetView/6000:

A version of NetView based on the SNMP protocol. Although originally intended for TCP/IP nets, the adoption of SNMP by others, such as IPX, has extended the possible reach of IBM's NetView/6000. Referred to as a network management platform, NetView/6000 provides a highly graphical environment from which to monitor and manage remote devices. Although it has a smaller market share than Sun's SunNet Manager, NetView/6000 is garnering a great deal of attention these days.

OpenView:

Hewlett Packard's OpenView was the first network management platform to take an open, highly graphical approach. It set the pace for SNMP-based network management. Even IBM's NetView/6000 was based on it originally. HP is working to bring the many versions of OpenView (for Windows, for UNIX) under a single umbrella. Called OperationsCenter, efforts such as this hold the promise of enterprise-wide network management in the not-too-distant future.

RAID:

Redundant Array of Independent Disks. A nonstandard set of levels for the use of multiple disks. It's a fault-tolerant scheme that tries to lessen the overhead of dedicating an entire second disk for the storage of data (RAID 1). There are at least six levels of RAID: 0 to 5 plus RAID 10 (sort of a cross between 1 and 0); but as it is nonstandard, vendors are completely free to call anything they like RAID or even to make up levels.

SATAN:

Security Administrator Tool for Analyzing Networks. SATAN is a highly graphical expert system designed to identify security risks in networks that is available free of charge over the Internet. (Even the source code is available.) Many people worry that SATAN will be used for nefarious activity. The solution is to act first. Get the program, use it, and act on its advice to close any openings.

Service point:

An SNA node that acts as a bridge to non-SNA nodes for management purposes. This is IBM's primary means for growing NetView/390 control beyond traditional SNA networks. NetView/PC is the main service point product. It runs on a PC.

Sniffer:

Software that's used to monitor and analyze network traffic. Although often designed for legitimate purposes, system intruders use sniffers to trap user ids and passwords.

SNMP:

Simple Network Management Protocol. A polling protocol adopted into the TCP/IP suite of protocols. SNMP doesn't need to run over IP, however. Any connectionless protocol, such as Novell's IPX, for example, is just as good. SNMP has become very popular for the control of networked devices. The leading SNMP management platforms are IBM's NetView/6000, HP's Openview, and SunSoft's SunNet Manager.

SunNet Manager:

The most widely used SNMP-based network management platform. Sun's product fell behind offerings from HP and IBM, but in a move to catch up, the company recently has released Encompass, a more comprehensive object-oriented management platform. It's too early to tell if it will turn the tide back in Sun's favor, however.

Notes

[1] R. Adhikari, "MIS Anxious for Systems, Networks to Tie the Knot," *Software Magazine*, June 1994, 78.

[2] Y. Lee, "Sun Finally Set to Deliver Encompass Suite," *InfoWorld*, Jan. 16, 1995, 8.

[3] T. Cahoon, "An OpenView of the Future," *HP Professional*, May, 1994, 56.

[4] C. Bauer, "RAID Subsystems," *Government Computer News*, March, 1994, 83.

[5] R. Adhikari, "Unresolved Security Issues Blunt Distributed Hoopla," *Software Magazine*, Feb. 1995, v15, 44.

[6] K. Rodriguez, "Microsoft-VISA Software Will Allow Secure Credit Card Purchases on the Internet," *InfoWorld*, Nov. 14, 1994, 8.

[7] J. Levitt, "Not the Devil Incarnate," *InformationWeek*, April 3, 1995, 15.

CHAPTER 11

Some Final Words

A Few Words of Advice

Just because something's new doesn't necessarily mean that it's better. Client/server is not a replacement for mainframe computing. On the contrary, in many shops, it's a bridging technology, a way of blending PCs, LANs, and the mainframe into a cohesive whole.

Not only is the newness of client/server not better; its newness actually works against it. The skills and tools (especially for network management) aren't completely in place yet. Nowhere is this more evident than in the areas of performance and security management. These are perhaps the biggest concerns Information Systems managers have about the computing model. And rightfully so. At this time there are no satisfactory solutions for the enterprise-wide management of computer networks.

253

But in spite of all this, client/server does have its place. Under the right circumstances, it can improve end-user productivity greatly and give organizations a competitive edge.

Tools are improving, skills are improving—many of the risks to client/server development and deployment will reduce over time. But it's safe to say that using client/server always will be more involved than developing hierarchical computer solutions.

Until tools and skills mature, there are some things you can do to reduce your risk.

- Use consultants—but only as mentors.
- Train staff adequately. Use the just-in-time approach wherever possible.
- Start small.
- Use 4GLs for the first implementation.
- Prototype a system to get a handle on network loadings.
- Use remote procedure calls.
- Limit vendors, database engines, operating systems, and protocols.
- Consolidate servers.
- Think about security right up front. Design for it from the beginning.

Use consultants, where appropriate, but don't get too attached to them. They're an expensive lot. Set them up as mentors so that they can pass their expertise on to staff.

Don't skimp on training dollars. With the amount of change surrounding even the most humble of client/server applications, it's essential to train all staff involved adequately—designers, project leaders, programmers, and end users.

Start small. If this is your first client/server implementation, keep it to as few seats as possible. To turn this advice around: If there's a business need for a client/server solution, and the application involves more than 100 seats, be careful.

Use 4GLs. In spite of their shortcomings, a 4GL can provide some much-needed guidance when constructing your first client/server application. Easier to learn and simpler to use than 3GLs like C, they make it possible to construct a client/server application in relatively short order.

These benefits generally outweigh the risks of vendor lock-in. Just stick with a mainstream toolset.

Although often it's only of marginal help, prototyping—building a small proof-of-concept system—can pinpoint areas of potential trouble. The problem with prototypes is that often they don't scale up that well. But any help can be useful.

Remote procedure calls offer choices in the placement of computations. Design with RPCs in mind, even if you don't use them in your first release. If the application is sluggish or network loadings become a concern, you can try tuning the system by moving some of the computational load to the server.

Although it's contrary to our quest for open systems, given the state of the technology, sometimes it's best to limit the number of vendors and different products involved—particularly on your first application. By doing so you'll have a better chance that everything will work together. Just be sure to take care not to become completely tied to a particular vendor. Stick to whatever standards there are.

Don't become too "distributed-minded." Although one of the big attractions of the client/server model is the ability to tie together information from a variety of different sources, it simply stands to reason that the more sources there are, the more things can go wrong. As the client/server model continues to mature, multiserver implementations will become more common.

Finally, design for security right from the word go. Don't try to add it in later. Some security systems, such as Kerberos, are tied very closely to the application. It's almost impossible to bolt those on later when everything is up and running.

Good luck.

Vendors Mentioned in This Book

Apple

Who is it?

For years Apple was always "the other desktop company." While sales never matched those of "IBM compatibles," few would deny that Apple has been an influential force on the computing landscape. Now, with its new PowerPC line of Macs, Apple is poised to increase its share of the desktop market. With so many things happening in the computer business, few stopped to note that IBM and Apple had joined forces in the delivery of the new chip. Apple has consistently ranked in the top 10 in Datamation's top 100 North American IT companies.

What does it produce?

Apple produces its own hardware and software.

How do you contact the company?

Apple Computer Inc.
20525 Mariani Avenue
Cupertino, CA 95014
408.996.1010

Bay Networks Inc.

Who is it?

Bay Networks is a leader in the production of LAN and WAN supporting technology. Bay Networks represents the merger of two well-known players in the networking business: Synoptics and Wellfleet.

What does it produce?

The company produces hubs, routers, switches, and practically anything you'd need to set up a LAN or WAN. It is focusing on ATM switching these days.

257

How do you contact the company?

Bay Networks Inc.
4401 Great America Parkway
Santa Clara, CA 95054
408.988.2400

Borland

Who is it?

Borland is a world leader in the development of PC development tools. Its C++ compiler is known across the industry. Although the company has fallen on hard times over the last several years, some see new hope for Borland as it streamlines operations.

What does it produce?

Borland produces compilers (C++, C, and Pascal) and office productivity tools (databases). It is earning high marks for is new Delphi client/server development tool. According to all reports, this one could knock PowerBuilder off top spot.

How do you contact the company?

Borland Inc.
P.O. Box 660001
Scotts Valley, CA 95067-0001
408.438.5300

Cisco Systems Inc.

Who is it?

Cisco Systems is a leader in the production of LAN and WAN supporting technology.

What does it produce?

Cisco produces much the same kind of product line-up as does Bay Networks. It tends to be better known for its routers though.

How do you contact the company?

Cisco Systems Inc.
170 West Tasman Drive
San Jose, CA 95134
408.526.4000

CompuServe Inc.

Who is it?

CompuServe is the largest of the value-added Public Data Networks. It is a division of H&R Block.

What does it produce?

CompuServe is an information service provider. In addition to its own extensive service, the company has significantly increased Internet access over the past months. It also has just acquired Spry Systems Inc., maker of Mosaic (a WWW browser) in a Box.

How do you contact the company?

CompuServe Inc.
5000 Arlington Centre Blvd.
Columbus, OH 43220
800.848.8199

Digital

Who is it?

Digital is another of those big hardware and software companies, à la IBM.

What does it produce?

Although it produces warehouse-loads of software, Digital, like IBM, is perhaps best known for its hardware. And these days, Digital hardware features the Alpha RISC chip. Although the fastest available chip in the industry, the performance of platforms constructed around it have been disappointing. Digital is moving to fix that. Digital has a close working relationship with Microsoft and intends to phase out its VMS operating system in favor of Windows NT. It already runs on Alpha boxes.

How do you contact the company?

Digital Equipment Corp.
146 Main Street
Maynard, MA 01754
508.493.5111

Gupta

Who is it?

Gupta is a maker of client/server support tools and databases. It generally is regarded as PowerSoft's greatest nemesis.

What does it produce?

Gupta has focused on the PC client/server market. Its SQLWindows product rivals or surpasses PowerBuilder—depending on whom you talk to.

How do you contact the company?

Gupta Corp.
1060 Marsh Road
Menlo Park, CA 94025-1020
415.321.9500

Hewlett-Packard (HP)

Who is it?

After IBM and Digital, HP is the next biggest North American hardware/software vendor.

What does it produce?

Like IBM and Digital, HP is best known for its hardware. Of course, tops on that list are its laser printers. Workstations are a close second—

HP Apollo, as they're often called (after HP acquired Apollo some years back). The HP Apollo 9000 line has done well and earned the company the reputation of being a serious workstation contender. It has joined up with Intel to produce the P7, successor to the P6.

How do you contact the company?

Hewlett-Packard Co.
3000 Hanover Street
Palo Alto, CA 94304
415.857.1501

IBM

Who is it?

IBM is one of the world's leading software and hardware companies.

What does it produce?

It is perhaps fair to say that IBM is better known for its hardware than its software (although the company appears to be out to change that—they recently acquired Lotus). On the hardware side, it makes PCs, workstations (RS/6000), minicomputers (AS/400), and mainframes (ES9000). IBM is also challenging the Intel empire with its new PowerPC RISC chip. As for software, among other things, it produces OS/2, a well-known, and respected, desktop and server operating system. Its NetView/6000 product is fast becoming the favorite SNMP-based network management platform.

How do you contact the company?

IBM
Old Orchard Road
Armonk, NY 10504
914.765.1900

Informix

Who is it?

Informix is another leader in relational database design. It has been very innovative, especially in its inclusion of imaging support (BLOBs). This has quickly moved the company into the "inner circle" of database vendors.

What does it produce?

Informix makes a range of database engines and decision-support tools. Its NewEra client/server development tool is gaining a following.

How do you contact the company?

Informix Corp.
4100 Bohannon Drive
Menlo Park, CA 94025-1032
415.926.6300

Insignia

Who is it?

Insignia is one of the leading producers of Windows and DOS emulators. It is known for its UNIX utilities. DEC, IBM, and, yes, even Microsoft use Insignia's products.

What does it produce?

It produces DOS (SoftPC) and MS Windows (SoftWindows) emulation software.

How do you contact the company?

Insignia Solutions Inc.
1300 Charleston Road
Mountain View, CA 94043
415.694.7600

Microsoft

Who is it?

Microsoft is the world's largest software company.

What does it produce?

You name it: operating systems (DOS, Windows 95, NT), spreadsheets (Excel), word processors (Word), databases (FoxPro, SQL Server), development tools (Visual Basic, Visual C++), middleware (ODBC)... Just about anything Microsoft touches turns to gold, or so it seems. In many cases its products aren't the best, but still become de facto standards anyway. The next target areas for the company appear to be finance and education.

How do you contact the company?

Microsoft Corporation
One Microsoft Way
Redmond, WA 98052
206.882.8080

NetTech Inc.

Who is it?

NetTech is a maker of workstation-based SNA management tools.

What does it produce?

Founded by a group of ex-IBMers, NetTech is concentrating on off-loading mainframe cycles consumed by management software. Its product is called EView/6000.

How do you contact the company?

NetTech Inc.
3214 Spring Forest Road
Raleigh, NC 27604
919.878.8612

Neuron Data

Who is it?

Neuron Data made its mark in the expert systems market and has turned much of that experience toward client/server.

What does it produce?

The company produces code generators for the development of graphical user interfaces. Currently, its Open Interface Elements v3.0 supports NT, OpenVMS, OSF/1, SCO UNIX, Solaris, Mac, and DOS/Windows.

How do you contact the company?

Neuron Data
156 University Avenue
Palo Alto, CA 94301
415.321.4480

NeXT Computer Inc.

Who is it?

NeXT was Steven Jobs's follow-on project after Apple. It started out making hardware and a unique suite of object-oriented tools that ran upon it, but eventually had to drop the hardware line. Its operating system has caused quite a stir in the industry.

What does it produce?

Today the company produces NeXTStep, a highly capable object-oriented operating system. The latest version is release 3.x for Intel. Sometime during 1995, the company promises version for PA-RISC (HP) and SPARC (Sun) platforms also.

How do you contact the company?

NeXT Computer Inc.
900 Chesapeake Circle
Redwood City, CA 94063
415.366.0900

Novell

Who is it?

Novell is fast becoming one of the big players in the software world. Best known for its NetWare Network Operating System, the company has diversified. (Some say too much.) Novell purchased the UNIX core from AT&T in 1992. It also owns WordPerfect.

What does it produce?

Novell produces network operating software (NetWare), the UNIX core OS, UNIXWare, DR DOS, word processors (WordPerfect), e-mail systems (GroupWise), and spreadsheets (Quattro Pro—once owned by Borland).

How do you contact the company?

Novell Inc.
122 East 1700 South
Provo, UT 84606-6194
801.429.7000

Oracle

Who is it?

Oracle is the world's leading database vendor. It was the first to bring a commercial SQL engine to market.

What does it produce?

Oracle produces database engines for practically every platform, from PCs to mainframes. It also produces an array of supporting tools, including "client/server" (products that range from PowerBuilder-alikes to enterprise-wide solutions) tools and case tools.

How do you contact the company?

Oracle Corporation
20 Davis Drive
Belmont CA 94002
415.598.8000

Peregrine Systems Inc.

Who is it?

Peregrine is a maker of workstation-based SNA management tools.

What does it produce?

Its flagship product is Open/SNA, but it has been making mainframe-based network management tools for years. HP has teamed up with Peregrine to acquire its SNA management capability.

How do you contact the company?

Peregrine Systems Inc.
1959 Palomar Oaks Way
Carlsbad, CA 92009
619.431.2400

PowerSoft

Who is it?

PowerSoft is the leading producer of "client/server" tools. In late 1994 Sybase bought PowerSoft in what turned out to be the second-largest acquisition of any software company. (Novell's acquisition of WordPerfect was the largest.) Although the move grabs Sybase a big piece of the client/server pie, many PowerBuilder customers are concerned about such close ties to a database vendor (especially those that don't use Sybase).

What does it produce?

PowerSoft makes PowerBuilder as well as two supporting products: PowerViewer and PowerMaker. Both are stripped-down versions of PowerBuilder intended for quasi-programming staff and end users.

How do you contact the company?

PowerSoft Corporation
70 Blanchard Road
Burlington, MA 01803
617.229.2200

SCO (the Santa Cruz Operation)

Who is it?

A longtime manufacturer of UNIX operating systems, SCO has been in the business since 1983, with production of their "Xenix" OS. SCO is known for its Windows-friendly approach; recognizing that MS Windows has captured the desktop, the company has positioned its products as a compatible server.

What does it produce?

SCO UNIX System V—designed exclusively for Intel 80 × 86 processors

SCO Open DeskTop (ODT)—a version of UNIX with an integrated GUI. This product comes in three forms: regular, lite, and server.

How do you contact the company?

Santa Cruz Operation
400 Encinal Street
Santa Cruz, CA 95061
1.800.SCO.UNIX

Secure Dynamics Inc.

Who is it?

Secure Dynamics is a manufacturer of products designed to enhance the security of networks and computer systems.

What does it produce?

Its best-known product is its SecureID smart card. The size of a credit card, this simple device generates a random access key every 60 seconds. Synchronized with a server, it can be used to identify who's attempting to log on to the system.

How do you contact the company?

Security Dynamics Inc.
One Alewife Center

Cambridge, MA 02140
617.547.7820

Sun Microsystems

Who is it?

Sun is one of the world's leading UNIX software and RISC hardware companies. In 1993 Sun was the leader in UNIX workstation sales.

What does it produce?

Sun got its start in the UNIX business. With its software and its SPARC line of RISC processors, Sun has captured the biggest piece of the UNIX pie. In addition to operating systems (Solaris) and hardware, the company produces an array of UNIX-related software. SunNet Manager, the biggest-selling SNMP-based network manager, is another of Sun's world-class products.

How do you contact the company?

Sun Microsystems
2550 Garcia Avenue
Mountain View, CA 94043
415.960.1300

Sybase

Who is it?

Sybase is a dynamic force in the database business. Its inclusion of stored procedures into its database engines was a boon to client/server development.

What does it produce?

Sybase produces relational database engines and a range of supporting (application development) tools. It is known for its leadership in RDBMS design. It now owns PowerSoft too, giving it the edge in small-to-medium client/server development.

How do you contact the company?

Sybase Corp.
6475 Christie Avenue
Emeryville, CA 94608-1050
510.922.3500

Xcellenet Inc.

Who is it?

A client/server software vendor.

What does it produce?

RemoteWare is a suite of client/server communications and applications tools used to streamline and automate information exchange with remote and mobile users.

How do you contact the company?

Xcellenet Inc.
Suite 200
5 Concourse Parkway
Atlanta, GA 30328
404.698.8650

Glossary

access method:

Software used to get at network resources. VTAM consolidated a growing number of access methods into one when SNA was introduced in 1974.

Alpha:

The Alpha DECchip line is a RISC design that's claimed to be the world's fastest chip. It is Digital's first RISC chip; earlier platforms used chips from MIPS. While Alpha may be fast, platform designers haven't been as successful in getting information on, and off, of it. In actual tests, it usually trails Pentium-powered machines. Digital's working on the problem.

APPC:

A marketing term for LU6.2. APPC (Advanced Program to Program Communication) is intended to assist programs running on different computers to communicate directly and exchange data. It is used by many generic IBM transaction services.

APPN:

Advanced Peer to Peer Networking, the new SNA. Unlike hierarchical SNA, APPN doesn't require a mainframe—but mainframes aren't excluded either. Although APPN is still SNA (a radical extension of it) the term often is used on its own.

Archie:

A file/directory locator designed to complement FTP. Archie works in a client/server fashion to track down files and directories in anonymous

FTP sites on the Net. It knows nothing about the contents of these things, however. It searches based on a user-provided sequence that's part of the actual file name or directory.

AS/400:

IBM's mid-range computing platform. It runs the OS/400 operating system and comes with a built-in relational database engine known as SQL/400.

ATM:

A high-speed form of packet-switching. ATM uses small (53-byte), fixed-size packets running over optical fiber to reach speeds of 155 Mbps and beyond. ATM is sort of a cross between analog transmission (continuous, wave form) and packetized bursty LAN transmissions. Because of this, it can accommodate both voice and data with the same approach, over the same carrier. We examine ATM in Chapter 4.

bandwidth:

The difference between the highest and lowest frequency that can be transmitted over a line. The higher the bandwidth, the more information can be pumped over the carrying medium.

baseband:

A style of networking popularly used in local area networks (LANs). In baseband networks, only one signal can occupy the communication medium at a given moment. Ethernet and Token-ring are the two most widely used examples of baseband network.

BLOB:

Binary Large OBjects. BLOBs are unstructured "bit buckets" that can contain text, image, sound, or video. Most imaging applications rely on BLOBs, attached to databases, for storage. But because of the non-relational structure of the data, RDBMS applications can't directly do anything with BLOBs.

broadband:

Another type of LAN. Unlike baseband, a broadband network can accommodate more than one signal at a time. This is accomplished by time or frequency division multiplexing. It requires modulation of the signals at the sending and receiving ends, making broadband more expensive than baseband. Broadband also can be used for backbone transmissions between baseband LANs.

BSD:

Berkeley Software Distribution. The version of UNIX developed at the University of California at Berkeley. It was especially popular on university campuses. BSD x was the first to bundle the TCP/IP suite of protocols right into the OS.

caching:

A technique used in NetWare to speed file access. Each time a file is called for, it is copied to an area of server memory set aside for file caching. The theory is that if one person wants a file, the chances are good that somebody else might too. First-time access won't benefit (since it comes from disk), but subsequent requests for the same file will be much faster, since it now resides in memory. Files dumped to the cache are time-stamped. They're time-stamped again each time they're reaccessed. When the server runs out of cache memory, files with the "oldest" time stamp are dropped for files accessed for the first time.

Capstone project:

A government-initiated effort to establish encryption methods for all government dealings. It has four components: a bulk data encryption algorithm called Skipjack, a digital signatures algorithm, a key exchange/management protocol, and a hash function. Skipjack runs over a special chip called Clipper. Only companies doing business with the government and the government itself are required to use Capstone.

CCITT:

Comité Consultatif Internationale de Télégraphie et Téléphonie—a European organization that recommends international communication standards. It's most notably known for its V series (V.34, V.42) and X series (X.25, X.500) standards.

CERT:

Computer Emergency Response Team, a group of computer professionals based at Carnegie-Mellon University. Their purpose is to seek out computer-based threats in order to bring them to the attention of the general public. They also often issue advisories (available from the Internet) on suggested actions to take in order to make your networks more secure. It's a good idea to review these routinely.

CISC:

Complex Instruction Set Computing. Intel's 80×86 line is the archetype for CISC designs and, of that group, the Pentium is the state of the art. CISC designs use more detailed instruction sets—covering practically every imaginable requirement—than do RISC chips. If it were just a matter of instruction size, though, it wouldn't be at all clear why RISC generally is faster than CISC. RISC designers have introduced a number of technical innovations into chip design—many of which are now being adopted by CISC designers as well. Although these innovations lend themselves more easily to the simpler style of instruction set used in RISC, CISC chips such as the Pentium also have made considerable gains in speed because of them. When it comes to integer calculations, for example, the latest generation of Pentiums are as fast, or faster, than many RISC chip out there.

CMIP:

Common Management Information Protocol. An ISO standard for the monitoring and control of networked devices. CMIP isn't terribly popular with makers of networked devices because it's top-heavy. This means that low-end networked entities such as repeaters have difficulty accommodating it. It also places a burden on network communications, so administrators aren't thrilled with it either. Still emerging, the protocol may be too late anyway. SNMP has become so popular that it appears impossible to unseat.

CORBA:

Common Object Request Broker Architecture. An emerging standard from the Object Management Group. CORBA is intended to assist in the intercommunication of networked objects. In its first rendition, it specifies what ORBs (object request brokers) should generally look like. CORBA 2.0 further defines how they should communicate. ORBs are a new form of middleware that are beginning to make their presence felt.

COSE:

Common Open System Environment. An informal grouping of approximately 70 UNIX vendors aimed at bringing greater harmony to the OS as a whole. Really, however, it was seen as a response to the introduction of Microsoft's Windows NT—a possible UNIX killer. The COSE effort has been largely adopted by the revised OSF.

Cryptography:

The study of data encryption. Cryptosystems, highly mathematical undertakings in general, follow either a private (secret) or a public key system. Private key cryptography is the most common. The best-known algorithm is called DES. It requires that both the sender and the receiver of an encrypted message use the same secret key to encrypt it. The key is changed routinely to prevent others from cracking the code. But this causes a problem: How do you safely share keys? An alternative scheme is to use a public key system. In this form of cryptography, everyone has his or her own public and private keys. To send a message to person A, it would be first encrypted with his or her specific public key. It then can be decrypted only with A's (permanent) private key. The most popular public key algorithm is RSA's algorithm, licensed from Public Key Partners, a group that manages the patent rights of Hellman and Diffie, who invented public key cryptography.

DCE:

The Distributed Computing Environment. DCE is a set of operating system–independent services for the development and use of distributed applications. Designed and developed by the Open Software Foundation (OSF), DCE contains Distributed File Services, Naming Services, a time service, system management services, and security services, the latter of which is based on MIT's Kerberos authentication system.

DDE:

Dynamic Data Exchange. A Microsoft Windows "standard" for information exchange between Windows applications. Say you wanted to link a Windows spreadsheet to a document. You would set up the DDE link between the two specifying the spreadsheet application name, the name of the spreadsheet, and the desired rows and columns you wanted to embed. Then whenever a change was made to that portion of the spreadsheet, it would be reflected automatically in the linked document. Windows for Workgroups can do this over a network with NetDDE.

DES:

Data Encryption Standard. An ANSI standard published by the National Institute of Standards. DES is a private cryptosystem. It uses a 56 bit key, considered too long for current computers to crack in a reasonable amount of time. But as computers get faster, cracking it will become more likely. Many predict that DES will one day be replaced or overhauled in favor of a public key system.

directory bashing:

Another technique for improved file access. NetWare keeps records of all files stored in its directories. When a file is requested, rather than sequentially searching the identified directory, NetWare looks up the file's location in its records, goes directly there, and grabs it.

disk duplexing:

A fault-tolerant technique for coping with mechanical failure. Usually used in servers, disk duplexing simultaneously writes data to two disks. Each disk further has its own controller card. One of the disks is designated as the primary; if it should fail, the secondary disk takes over.

disk mirroring:

Also known as RAID level 1, disk mirroring is very much like disk duplexing, except that a single controller card is used. Disk mirroring offers good read performance—both read heads can grab different portions of the file at the same time—but doesn't exhibit very good write performance—everything needs to be written twice.

DLL:

Dynamic Link Library. Another Microsoft Windows "standard." This one's used for sharing Windows resources (graphics and stuff like that) or small pieces of executable code. Most Windows-compliant compilers can create DLLs. They're more than a typical library, however. DLLs are copied once (on demand) and shared among calling programs. Compare this to "static linking," in which whole libraries are attached to programs at compile and link time. If three programs need a certain library, there are then three copies kicking about the system.

EHLLAPI:

Emulator High-Level Language Application Programming Interface. An IBM API that provides a way for programmers to "scrape" information from 3270 (green) screens. It's not elegant, but it works, and it allows a graceful transition away from all those applications on the mainframe. Screen scraping reads data off of specific green-screen locations and fires it off to a GUI to be displayed on a PC. But if the screen changes, things get crazy.

elevator seeking:

Yet another method for faster file access. It's a way of prioritizing file access with respect to the read/write head position of the disk drive.

Rather than jump all over the disk, picking up files as they're asked for, NetWare looks at the pending accesses and sorts them relative to their physical distance from the current position of the read/write head. The result is faster overall access and less wear and tear on the disk.

entry point:

One of those logical SNA things. Entry points are SNA nodes that serve as connection points for other SNA nodes. Cluster controllers are the archetypal entry point. These devices are equipped with the necessary smarts to allow them to collect their own management information. They pass this information on to the mainframe.

Ethernet:

A contentious networking scheme in which network nodes compete for line access. Following a model known as CSMA/CD (Carrier Sense, Multiple Access with Collision Detection), nodes monitor packets after transmission to ensure their safe arrival. If something goes wrong and a data collision occurs, the transmitting nodes take steps to resend the data. Ethernet is efficient at moderate network loads. Its top speed, as specified by the "Ethernet protocol" (DIX or IEEE 802.3), is 10 Mbps. The Ethernet protocol corresponds to the two lower layers of the OSI model.

FDDI:

An ANSI standard for high-speed fiber optic LANs. According to the FDDI specifications, top-communication speed is 100 Mbps. FDDI is implemented in two ways: as a high-speed alternative to Ethernet or Token-ring LANs, or, more often, as a backbone for connecting such networks. When moving from Ethernet and Token-ring LANs ("802" networks) to an FDDI backbone, a bridging device is required. The bridge either encapsulates the packet (sticks the 802 packet into an FDDI packet) or translates it into an FDDI packet. Translation is a "more open" option; there are no standards in place for data packet encapsulation.

file server:

A file storage device, usually an actual computer, accessible to nodes on a local area (or even wide area) network. More than simply a remote disk drive, a file server contains special software that manages its resident files.

Firewall:

A way of isolating networks. Many intelligent devices can act as firewalls, although routers are generally the favorite. With the growth of interest in the Internet, the term often has come to mean some device that controls the flow of information between an organization's networks and the Net. They can be programmed in a variety of ways: Some only allow the flow of e-mail, for example. If your networks are connected to the Internet or can be accessed in any way from the outside, you should have a firewall in place.

Focal point:

Another SNA logical notion. Focal points are management software that accept incoming data from SNA network nodes and compile it for presentation to a human operator. NetView/390 is IBM's best-known focal point.

frame:

Datalink frames are groups of bits containing data and tombstone information. While the terms "frame" and "packet" sometimes are used interchangeably, TCP/IP definitely distinguishes between the two. Using Ethernet, Token Ring and FDDI at the Datalink and physical layers, a frame is the actual bit grouping that is transmitted across the medium.

frame relay:

A streamlined successor to X.25. Frame relay is also a CCITT standard. It's a popular packet-switching WAN option that starts in at 2 Mbps but will soon reach T-3 speeds (44 Mbps). Frame relay is now seen as the next logical step toward ATM.

4GL:

Fourth-generation language. A higher-level language usually constructed upon a 3GL (such as C). 4GLs are especially prevalent when it comes to databases. Client/server (client really) development tools such as PowerBuilder and SQLWindows are 4GLs.

FTP:

File Transfer Protocol. Another of the upper-layer TCP/IP protocols. FTP is used to transfer files between hosts, regardless of platform type or resident operating system.

Gopher:

Gopher servers scattered about the Net form what's often referred to as Gopherspace. Gopher servers contain all kinds of information and they're all linked; you can logically move from one server to another in the pursuit of information. Gopher, the application, runs in a client/server fashion to help people get around Gopherspace.

groupware:

Also variously called workgroup computing and ad hoc workflow, groupware is sometimes considered to be a part of workflow management. It concerns itself with tasks and processes that are unstructured in nature as compared to production, "heads-down" workflow management. Lotus' Notes product leads the groupware market.

high-speed Ethernet:

Several high-speed Ethernets are emerging. Full-duplexed Ethernet, for example, allows nodes to send and receive data at the same time, effectively doubling capacity. Switched Ethernet uses a star topology wired to a switch in the center. Each participating node has full access to the maximum available bandwidth. Finally, 100 Mbps Ethernet is strongly vying for low-level protocol dominance. There are two contenders, however: Hewlett-Packard's 100VG-AnyLAN and the Fast Ethernet Alliance's 100BASE-T. HP's offering is a completely new networking scheme that can support both traditional Ethernet and Token-ring traffic. The Fast Ethernet Alliance's 100BASE-T, on the other hand, acts like good old Ethernet, only faster. It's currently the industry favorite.

IAB:

The Internet Advisory Board, a volunteer organization that manages the Internet. The IAB recently came under fire for suggesting that IP be dumped in favor of the Connectionless Network Protocol (CLNP). One of the reasons it did so was to avert Internet address exhaustion, now predicted to occur sometime before the year 2000.

IDAPI:

Integrated Database Application Programming Interface. Similar to Microsoft's ODBC. IDAPI is multiple database access software created by Borland, Novell, and IBM. Unlike ODBC, IDAPI can access both SQL and navigational (xBASE) databases, and of course, it's not limited to Windows. IDAPI made it to market after ODBC. This may have killed it.

The Internet:

A massive, global internetwork spanning every continent. The Internet may have as many as 750,000 computers directly attached to it. It's used every day by tens of millions of people. E-mail is the most popular application, but the Internet is an important information resource as well. It contains databases on practically every imaginable subject. The Internet is the offspring of ARPANET. Funded by the U.S. Defense Department, ARPANET was a test bed for battle-tolerant communication networks. TCP/IP was the communication protocol designed to run it. Its use continues today in the Internet and in thousands of private communication LANs and WANs.

Internet address:

Initially defined by the ARPANET and now used on the Internet and every TCP/IP network as well, Internet addresses are 32 bits long. They come in five classes, of which only the first three, Classes A, B, and C, are commonly used. Class A has the following form: N.H.H.H (where N represents network and H represents host). Class A favors an internetwork with few networks containing many hosts. Class B is of the form: N.N.H.H. It's the most popular. On the Internet, Class B addresses are in danger of being exhausted within the next few years. To cope with this, a revised form of IP has been proposed. Known as IPng, it is designed to create more address space. Class C is applicable to internetworks with many networks each containing few hosts and takes the form: N.N.N.H. On the Internet, aliases are used in place of decimal or binary addresses.

IP:

Internet Protocol. Corresponding to the Network layer in the OSI model, IP takes care of packet creation and routing. It is a connectionless, unreliable packet delivery system.

IP Spoofing:

The modification of the address portion of IP packets in order to fool firewalls into believing they originate from a trusted source.

IPX:

Internet Packet Exchange. Novell NetWare's OSI Network-layer protocol. Like the IP part of TCP/IP, IPX is an unreliable, connectionless packet delivery protocol. Reliability is left up to SPX, higher up the stack. IPX takes care of such things as forming packets, addressing them, and routing them along their way.

ISDN:

Integrated Services Digital Network. ISDN is designed to permit the simultaneous transfer of voice, data, and image over the same network. It uses two separate channels: B (bearer) channels for data and voice that run at up to 64 kbps, and a D channel that carries control information. ISDN has been talked about for a long time and is only now arriving.

Kerberos:

Kerberos is a user authentication system, designed and developed at MIT. It uses a "ticket" system to establish user identities. The whole idea behind Kerberos is first to have users prove who they are and then to limit them to specific services on the network. If users wish to access a data server, for example, their Kerberos ticket is valid only for that server and no other. That would require the acquisition of another ticket. Kerberos has nothing to do with authorization. It doesn't check to see if a user does indeed have the right to access that data server—that's left to that server. Kerberos is part of the OSF's DCE (Distributed Computing Environment).

LU6.2:

A special Logical Unit designed for program-to-program communication. An API is necessary in order to use LU6.2.

MIB:

Management Information Base. Used with SNMP, the Simple Network Management Protocol. When SNMP polls networked devices, it reads information stored in its MIB (a table of relevant performance data unique to that device). A more recent version of MIB allows SNMP to change entries as well.

middleware:

A nebulous little term for anything that stands between a client and a server to help communication. There are three types: remote procedure calls (RPCs), message-passing schemes, and object request brokers (ORBs). Getting down to tangibles, DCE, ODBC, and IDAPI fall into the middleware category.

Motif:

The graphical user interface designed and marketed by the OSF. It was inspired by Microsoft Windows (which Apple, in turn, says was modeled after the Mac). Motif is now the dominant UNIX GUI.

MSAU:

Multistation access unit, a device used in Token-ring networks. The MSAU acts to preserve the ring if any node on the LAN should go off-line by establishing a bypass around that node.

multithreading:

The simultaneous execution of different parts of the same application, often on different CPUs. OSF/1 is a multithreaded operating system.

NCP:

NetWare Core Protocols. The NetWare shell, resident on the client, determines whether requests are directed to the server or the client. If they are for the server, the request is passed to NCP. NCP sets up connections between the client and the server.

NDS:

NetWare Directory Services. NDS is a network-wide distributed look-up table that contains information on every networked resource. New to NetWare 4.0, NDS assists in internetwork management and offers users "one logon, one password" functionality.

NetView/390:

IBM's premier mainframe focal point product. NetView is a strategic product that helps IBM attract and then hold onto mainframe customers. The company is trying to extend the reach of NetView/390 to include non-SNA devices as well. The effort is fast losing ground to SNMP-based heterogeneous network management, however.

NetView/6000:

A version of NetView based on the SNMP protocol. Although originally intended for TCP/IP nets, the adoption of SNMP by others, such as IPX, has extended the possible reach of IBM's NetView/6000. Referred to as a network management platform, NetView/6000 provides a highly graphical environment from which to monitor and manage remote devices. Although it has a smaller market share than Sun's SunNet Manager, NetView/6000 is garnering a great deal of attention these days.

NetWare:

More than just a stack of communication protocols, NetWare is a highly modular network operating system. At its core does sit communication protocols—IPX, SPX, and NCP—but attachable to it are chunks of code that take care of file and print serving. Other code adds additional functionality as needed. Novell calls these NetWare Loadable Modules (NLMs).

NFS:

Network File System. An upper-layer TCP/IP protocol. It makes remotely stored files appear to reside locally. It was invented by SUN Microsystems in 1985.

NLM:

NetWare Loadable Module. A piece of software that can be added to the NetWare kernel. NLMs are available for communications (e.g., T-1 support), databases (almost every leading database vendor has one), groupware (e.g., Lotus has an NLM version of its popular Notes application), and a whole bunch of other things. Novell customers can add NLM functionality on an as-needed basis.

NOS:

Network operating system. A NOS is an environment that usually complements a client operating system, endowing it with networking functionality. Usually this extra functionality is just file and print serving. Newer NOSs such as NTAS extend this to application serving as well, however.

ODBC:

Open DataBase Connectivity. ODBC is part of the Windows Open Services Architecture (WOSA). It's intended for multidatabase access. ODBC adds its own layer to database application programming interfaces (APIs). With this additional layer comes the necessity of dealing with only one group of function calls that can access different databases. The result is less variation between application source code for different databases. Underneath, ODBC takes the function calls, translates them, and directs them to the appropriate database API. It takes a lowest-common-denominator approach. One drawback with ODBC is that it runs under Windows only.

ODI:

Open DataLink Interface. ODI is a set of guidelines that, if adhered to, permit multiple protocol stacks to use a single LAN adapter. In the "old days," if you wanted to access a host on TCP/IP and a printer, say, on AppleTalk, you required separate protocol support for each and dedicated network cards as well. Apple and Novell got together to come up with ODI. To work, you need a network card and driver software written to the ODI "standard." In the business, loading up two protocols onto a single LAN adapter is called dual-protocol stacking.

OLE:

Object Linking and Embedding. A way of sharing information among Windows applications. When linked, the host application, also known as a container, contains only a reference to the object, but when embedded, the application contains an actual copy. OpenDoc is OLE's biggest competitor. It's a network-enabled compound document standard developed by Apple, IBM, Novell, and Xerox. OpenDoc reached the marketplace well after OLE.

OOP:

Object oriented programming. OOP is a different way for programmers to model the physical world—one claimed to be closer to reality. Many people think that OOP is just an extension to modular programming because it encourages the use of small chunks of code to define the objects and their associated methods. But OOP is more than that. It rests on three "principles": encapsulation (information hiding), inheritance, and polymorphism. One of the goals of OOP is to construct small, reusable pieces of software. To enforce this, the code used to define objects generally is not available to the outside world for review. This black-box approach encourages programmers to accept the object's contents and focus on how to interact with the object instead. That's what encapsulation is all about. Taking a real-world view, OOP also allows objects to inherit features from others they're related to. For example, a programmer could define a "car" and then create a specialization of that—sports car—that inherits all the attributes of the "parent."

Polymorphism is a little stranger than the other two OOP principles. We know that, again, in the real world, different "objects" do the same thing differently. How an object does what it does is left up to the object, but the message sent to the objects is the same. That's polymorphism.

Open look:

The graphical user interface acknowledged by AT&T, Sun Microsystems, and supporters of the now-defunct UNIX International. Sun, by the way, called its rendition of the GUI Open Windows. The company now has adopted the OSF's Motif as the standard GUI as part of the COSE movement.

OpenView:

Hewlett Packard's OpenView was the first network management platform to take an open, highly graphical approach. It set the pace for SNMP-based network management. Even IBM's NetView/6000 was based on it originally. HP is working to bring the many versions of OpenView (for Windows, for UNIX) under a single umbrella. Called OperationsCenter, efforts such as this hold the promise of enterprise-wide network management in the not-too-distant future.

OSF:

The Open Software Foundation. Formed in 1988, the OSF was a protest action against AT&T and Sun in response to what the rest of the UNIX industry saw as a disturbingly close relationship between the two. The protesters also weren't too pleased with revisions to licensing fees levied by AT&T for the System V core. The OSF has produced a graphical user interface, called Motif, now an industry standard; a new operating system, OSF/1, and the Distributed Computing Environment. In March 1994 the OSF unveiled a new business model that included one-time archrival Sun Microsystems. The OSF countergroup, known as UNIX International (headed by AT&T and Sun), folded soon after OSF's move. The new sponsors of the OSF are: AT&T, Bull Worldwide Information Systems, DEC, Fujitsu, Hewlett-Packard, IBM, International Computers Ltd., NEC, Novell, Olivetti, Siemens Nixdorf, Silicon Graphics, Sony, Sun Microsystems, and Transarc.

OSI seven-layer model:

The ISO/OSI model for data communication. The ISO examined the process of data communication and splits it up into seven discrete tasks. The bottom layer is the physical line itself. All the other layers are to be implemented in software. Few actual communications protocols follow this seven-layer model exactly.

P6:

A chip that is the successor to the Pentium. With more than 5 million onboard transistors, and some very aggressive designing, it can outpace the fastest Pentium by about 30 percent. It's expected to become available (for both workstations and servers) towards the end of 1995.

packet:

The group of bits assembled by the various pieces of software making up the transmitting node's communication protocol stack. Each layer of the stack contributes something to the overall packet. Packets have a set length. If the data to be sent plus header exceed that size, the data must be first re-packaged into pieces small enough to fit. The message is reconstituted on the receiving end.

packet-switching:

A method of digital communication in which data are broken up into "chunks" and are routed to their destinations over a number of different communication channels.

Pentium:

The latest in the hugely successful Intel 80 X 86 family of microprocessors. (The Pentium is the 80586.) Already in its second generation, the Pentium is a sophisticated CISC design able to keep pace with many RISC chips.

POSIX:

Portable Operating System Interface eXtensions. POSIX is a family of standards, proposed by the IEEE, to enhance application portability across platforms. POSIX strives to do this by defining the interface between applications and the operating system. POSIX was originally based on UNIX, but is no longer only restricted to that OS alone.

PowerBuilder:

Currently, the leading (low/medium-size) client/server development tool. PowerBuilder is a 4GL that can be used to "paint" end-user screens with graphics and data fields and then connect these fields up to any of a number of databases.

PowerPC:

A new RISC chip collectively designed by Motorola, Apple, and IBM. Its first commercial use was in an IBM RS/6000 250T. Shortly after, it debuted in Apple's new line of PowerMacs.

RAID:

Redundant Array of Independent Disks. A nonstandard set of levels for the use of multiple disks. It's a fault-tolerant scheme that tries to lessen the overhead of dedicating an entire second disk for the storage of data (RAID 1). There are at least six levels of RAID: 0 to 5 plus RAID 10 (sort of a cross between 1 and 0); but as it is nonstandard, vendors are completely free to call anything they like RAID or even to make up levels.

RDBMS:

Relational DataBase Management System. There are a few different ways in which data can be stored and accessed logically: the hierarchical model popular in bygone days, the network model, the object model, and the relational model. Relational database engines represent data as a series of two-dimensional tables. SQL is used to create, manipulate and extract data from these tables. Most industrial-strength database engines, such as DB2, Oracle, Sybase, Informix, InterBase, SQLBase, and Ingres, are relational.

RIP:

Routing Information Protocol. NetWare, TCP/IP, and XNS (a communication protocol stack designed by Xerox) all use RIP. It's a rather simple protocol that aids IPX, in NetWare's case, to come up with the "best" route from sender to receiver. It does this by using the hop count in a router's (NetWare file server's) routing table. Both NetWare and TCP/IP are replacing RIP with newer protocols that also account for the speed of data links between the sender and receiver. (If a 56 kbps line and a 1.5 Mbps line both led to the same collection point in a WAN, for example, these newer protocols can recognize that, and choose the fastest pathway.)

RISC:

Reduced Instruction Set Computing. DEC's Alpha and IBM/Motorola/Apple's PowerPC are the leading examples of RISC design. RISC chips do two things CISC (Intel 80 × 86-like) don't: They work with a smaller instruction set of chip-recognizable commands, and they tend to do most data manipulations right on the chip. Without having to worry as much about history as Intel has had to, with its 80 × 86 line, RISC designers generally have had a freer hand in their designs. This had led to some revolutionary chips.

RPC:

Remote Procedure Call. RPCs are just an extension to the standard, local, library, or subroutine call. The difference now is, that, as the name implies, the routines being called don't have to sit on the same host. RPCs often are used for remote data access. They are the most interesting when used in conjunction with a multithreaded operating system. Then the main body of the application can issue a number of RPCs and continue to work on something useful while it waits for the responses to return. This is parallel programming.

SATAN:

Security Administrator Tool for Analyzing Networks. SATAN is a highly graphical expert system designed to identify security risks in networks that is available free of charge over the Internet. (Even the source code is available.) Many people worry that SATAN will be used for nefarious activity. The solution is to act first. Get the program, use it, and act on its advice to close any openings.

Screen-scraping:

Using IBM's EHLLAPI mainframe application program interface to grab data fields off of 3270 green screens and representing these fields in a graphical format. Often this is an organization's first humble step toward client/server computing.

Service point:

An SNA node that acts as a bridge to non-SNA nodes for management purposes. This is IBM's primary means for growing NetView/390 control beyond traditional SNA networks. NetView/PC is the main service point product. It runs on a PC.

SMDS:

Switched Multimegabit Data Service. SMDS is a packet-switched service strongly supported by the telephone companies. It has a lot in common with ATM in that it too is a cell switching service. Cells are fixed-length data frames. SMDS came to market later than frame relay, and there are indications within the industry that it's in for a rough ride.

SMTP:

Simple Mail Transfer Protocol. One of five upper-layer TCP/IP protocols. SMTP is a basic e-mail facility that's used on the Internet. It also serves as the basis for more sophisticated packages.

SNA nodes:

Often, but not always, the actual devices composing an SNA/APPN network. There are four types: Type 5 (mainframe), Type 4 (communications controller), Type 2.0 (a hierarchical SNA node), and Type 2.1 (peer-to-peer peripheral node). Within the Type 2.1 grouping, there is further division; the most capable node of this type is the APPN network node. These nodes define the backbone of an APPN net-handling dynamic routing and route selection. Next in peer-to-peer capability, is the APPN end node. It possesses local (it independently recognizes local LUs) directory and routing functionality. Last in this hierarchy is the Low Entry Networking (LEN) node. LEN nodes exclusively function as end users in an APPN network. They have no dynamic routing capability. They can communicate only with physically adjacent nodes.

Sniffer:

Software that's used to monitor and analyze network traffic. Although often designed for legitimate purposes, system intruders use sniffers to trap user ids and passwords.

SNMP:

Simple Network Management Protocol. A polling protocol adopted into the TCP/IP suite of protocols. SNMP doesn't need to run over IP, however. Any connectionless protocol, such as Novell's IPX, for example, is just as good. SNMP has become very popular for the control of networked devices. The leading SNMP management platforms are IBM's NetView/6000, HP's Openview, and SunSoft's SunNet Manager.

SONET:

Synchronous Optical Network. More of a standard than a tangible technology, SONET is intended to aid in very high speed (international) optical communications. Sprint and AT&T currently are leading the charge toward SONET.

SPECmark:

Another one of those performance measures popularly bandied about in computer articles. This one makes a bit more sense than some, however. It's an average execution rating for a group of standard programs. There's a SPECfp (floating point) rating and a SPECint (integer) rating.

SPX:

Sequenced Packet Exchange. This is NetWare's OSI transport layer protocol. It is responsible for ensuring the delivery of data packets.

SQL:

Structured Query Language. SQL is a data-access language invented by IBM. It removes the navigational responsibilities from the user. (You don't have to know exactly where things are.) Most of the newer, larger database engines are SQL-based. A standard version of SQL set out by ANSI is available, but it is kind of limiting. It contains little in the way of data reporting, for instance. This means vendors need to add their own functionality to the base. Oracle, for example, calls its rendition of SQL SQL*Plus. It adds approximately 40 additional commands. SQL is commonly embedded in programs written in languages such as COBOL and C for database access.

SQL driver:

A piece of proprietary software that hooks up clients to database engines. The SQL driver takes care of much of the low-level stuff, such as the networking protocols. It also works at a higher level, linking the client application to the database. Every database has its own SQL driver, since every relational database has its own implementation of SQL.

SQLWindows:

A client/server development product, much like PowerBuilder. Although it doesn't have the same market penetration as PowerBuilder, many contend that it is a technically more sophisticated offering.

SunNet Manager:

The most widely used SNMP-based network management platform. Sun's product fell behind offerings from HP and IBM, but in a move to catch up, the company recently has released Encompass, a more comprehensive object-oriented management platform. It's too early to tell if it will turn the tide back in Sun's favor, however.

T-1/T-3:

Both T-1 and T-3 are part of the T-carrier facility. If you're wondering what ever happened to T-2, well, it exists—as part of T-3 services. T-1 is a digital multiplexed technology that's usually leased from telephone companies. It operates at 1.544 Mbps. In Europe, the T-1 equivalent is called E-1; it "runs" at a slightly higher speed (2.048 Mbps). T-3 is a newer technology but essentially takes up where T-1 leaves off. Its speed is approximately 44 Mbps. T-1 and now T-3 have a reputation for being expensive WAN options. This is why many telcos came up with fractional T-1, or FT-1. FT-1 lets you step up to full T-1 capability in 64 kbps increments. There's little or no mention of FT-3 yet.

TCP:

The Transmission Control Protocol. TCP sits at the transport-layer level of the OSI protocol. It ensures reliable delivery of packets. TCP creates a packet containing the data to be sent plus address information. It hands this off to IP, which envelops all this into an IP packet. Upon reaching its intended destination, the packet is disassembled.

Telnet:

An upper-layer TCP/IP protocol. Telnet is used for remote host logon.

3GL:

Third-generation language. In the beginning there was machine code: 1s and 0s. Not a lot of fun to work with. Then came assembler. It was an improvement but still left much to be desired. It was pretty terse stuff. The third generation introduced "languages." There are a lot of them around, but the most popular ones are Cobol, FORTRAN, C, and Pascal. The newer object-oriented languages, such as C++ and SmallTalk, generally are still considered to be 3GLs as well, but it might be fairer to call them 3.5GLs since they build on lower-level constructs. Computers still speak 1s and 0s, so compilers must step in to translate.

Token-ring:

A noncontentious style of networking invented by IBM. Token-ring uses a single "token" (an electrical pulse) for all data interchanges. When a node wishes to transmit a message to another on the LAN, it must first capture the token (if it's available). After the data has been received by the target node, the token returns to the sender. Only it can relinquish the token (under normal conditions). Token-ring has been adopted by the IEEE and is known as IEEE 802.5. Token-ring comes in two speeds: 4 Mbps and 16 Mbps. Like Ethernet, it too corresponds to the two bottom layers of the OSI model.

two-phase commit:

A synchronous data replication strategy. Whenever one data store is updated, a related one is too. During a two-phase commit, the database engines first confirm to each other that they're ready. If they are—and there can be more than two of them involved in this process—the data is officially modified. The problem with two-phase commit is that network latencies or all-out system failures can leave one (or more) of the parties waiting. Asynchronous replication is becoming popular because it avoids this problem.

UDP:

User Datagram Protocol. A low-overhead alternative to TCP that offers little beyond basic IP services.

UTP:

Unshielded twisted pair. UTP is the emerging cable of choice in the LAN world. It's inexpensive and easy to work with.

V series:

A set of modem standards created by the CCITT. The series covers modem speeds, signal modulations, and data compression. Within the series are V.32, a modulation standard for modems in the 4,800-to-9,600 bps range; V.42bis, a data compression standard for transmission speeds up to 38,000 bps; and now V.34, an emerging standard for modem communications at speeds that may someday reach 115 kbps.

VBX:

Visual Basic control. A small executable chunk of code conforming to Visual Basic's interface standards. Essentially, VBXs are clamp-on components that developers (often VB developers) add to Visual Basic in order to draw on their functionality as needed. To add an encryption routine, for example, a VB programmer could use (often for a fee) someone's VBX instead of writing his or her own from scratch. 4GLs such as PowerBuilder and SQLWindows can access and use VBXs too. The code inside the executable doesn't even need to be written in VB; some C++ compilers can generate VBXs.

Veronica:

A keyword search application designed to complement Gopherspace searches.

Visual Basic:

Microsoft's enormously popular Windows development tool that is easier to learn than PowerBuilder or SQLWindows and certainly easier to learn and use than C++. Many are turning to Visual Basic in order to develop small client/server applications.

VLM:

Virtual Loadable Module. Something new for NetWare 4.0, VLMs are similar in concept to NLMs, except that they reside on and provide the specialized functionality for the client.

WAIS:

Wide Area Information Server. Another Internet application, used to search databases attached to the Net.

Windows 95:

Unlike all previous versions of Windows, Windows 95 is a full operating system, very much like OS/2—not surprising, since Microsoft helped create it too. All agree that if it turns out to be even half as popular as Microsoft expects, OS/2 (and every other operating system vying for the desktop) is in trouble.

Windows NT Advanced Server:

A full-fledged, multitasking, multithreaded operating system from Microsoft. NT actually comes in two renditions: Advanced Server and Advanced Workstation. While sales of the workstation version are doing well, most see the server as the right platform for NT. It features the easiest installation of any network operating system and comes with a number of server management tools. User Manager is used to add and delete end users from the server. Disk Administrator is used for managing disk space, and Performance Manager gauges the performance of server components such as the CPU and disk. It's very scalable, coming with symmetric multiprocessing support for up to 32 processors. The NOS favors the TCP/IP protocol stack but comes with out-of-the-box support for SPX/IPX as well.

wireless LAN:

Wireless LAN technology is a fast-growing segment of the networking business. There are three styles: infrared, radio-frequency (also sometimes called "spread-spectrum"), and microwave. Infrared is the most limited of the group. It can't penetrate walls. Microwave can get up to Token-ring speeds but requires a license. Spread-spectrum is highly secure and can reach Ethernet speed. As it stays within the "civil band," it doesn't need to be licensed.

workflow management:

Many are pointing to this as the big application for client/server computing. Workflow management is middleware that knows how work moves around the workplace. Beyond being able to link up clients and servers and mainframes, it also can be programmed to route pieces of work. Some organizations are looking to workflow management to revolutionize their businesses. The leaders in this field are long-time information technology leaders such as Xerox, Wang, Digital, and IBM.

World Wide Web:

Like Gopherspace, the WWW is a virtual space created by thousands of Web servers. These servers all contain information that's associated by hypertext links. Once onto the Web, users can move from Web site to Web site by selecting these links with a mouse or other pointing device.

X:

A network-aware set of display-handling routines for UNIX. X was designed at MIT. Motif is built from X.

X.25:

Another set of recommendations by the CCITT. X.25 defines the connection between a terminal and a packet-switching network. X.25 is known for two things: It's dependable, and it's slow. Both of these are related, of course; X.25 expends a great deal of available bandwidth checking for transmission errors. It is generally expected that frame relay will succeed X.25. (It's a CCITT standard too, by the way.)

Index

A

ANSI, 4, 172
Apple, 136, 257
application partitioning, 157
ASCII, 13
Asynchronous Transfer Mode, 76–78
authentication service, 145

B

backbone, 13
baud-rate, 67
Bay Networks Inc., 242, 257
Borland, 172, 186, 258
byte, 13

C

C++, 167, 181, 204, 206
campus-sized network, 14
CCITT, 66
circuit switching, 64–65
Cisco Systems Inc., 242, 258
client/server:
    benefits of, 158
    defined, 153
    risks of, 160
    security, 232
        Computer Emergency Response
            Team (CERT), 241
        disk duplexing, 238
        disk mirroring, 238
        smart cards, 236
        sniffer, 241
    3-tier, 157, 206
Complex Instruction Set Computing
        (CISC), 132

CompuServe, 73, 98, 164, 259
concentrator, 22
CORBA, 187–188
COS, 4

D

data encryption, 242
    Clipper, 244
    cryptography, 248
    DES, 244–245
    Diffie and Hellman, 243
    public key encryption, 243
    RSA Data Security Inc., 243, 245
    SATAN, 245–246
    triple DESing, 244
data warehousing, 157
Datalink layer, 16
DataPac, 73
dial-up analog, 65
Digital, 130, 133, 259
Digital Alpha, 133, 147
Distributed Computing Environment
        (DCE), 142
Distributed File System (DFS), 146
DSU/CSU, 69

E

EBCDIC (Extended Binary Coded
        Decimal Interchange Code),
        16
EHLLAPI, 216
Ethernet:
    Carrier Sense with Multiple Access
        and Collision Detection
        (CSMA/CD), 21
    defined, 19

Ethernet (*cont.*)
  high-speed, 23
    100BASET, 24
    100VGAnyLAN, 24
  switching, 23
  10BASEx, 21
  versus Token-Ring, 28
Expanded Memory Specification
    (EMS), 173
extended memory, 173

F

Fiber Distributed Data Interface
    (FDDI):
  CDDI, 31
  defined, 29
  dual attached, 29
  FDDI II, 32
File Transfer Protocol (FTP), 100,
    102
4GL, 204, 207
frame relay, 75

G

Graphical User Interface (GUI), 172
groupware, 189, 195
Gupta, 210, 260

H

handshaking, 65
Hewlett Packard, 130, 231, 260

I

IBM, 112, 130, 136, 181, 224, 262
IDAPI, 172, 186
IEEE, 4, 141

Informix, 189, 191, 262
Insignia, 135, 262
Intel Pentium:
  defined, 137
  P6, 138
Internet, the:
  accessing, 98
    Point-to-Point Protocol (PPP), 98
    Serial Line Interface Protocol
      (SLIP), 98
    Winsock, 98
  addresses on, 96
  Archie, 103
  ARPANET, 87
  defined, 87
  doing business on, 108
    First Virtual Holding, 109
  Gopherspace, 88, 105
  Hypertext Transfer Protocol (HTTP),
    108
  JUGHEAD, 106
  Mosaic, 108
  Netscape, 108
  security, 110
    firewalls, 11, 242, 249
    IP-spoofing, 110
  service provider, 98
  Universal Resource Locator (URL),
    108
  VERONICA, 106
  WAIS, 105
  World Wide Web (WWW), 88, 106
    Secure-HTTP, 110
    Web pages, 108–109
internetworking, 14
ISDN:
  Basic Rate Interface (BRI), 69
  defined, 69
  Primary Rate Interface (PRI), 70

K

Kerberos, 144, 240

L

line conditioning, 68
Local Area Network (LAN):
  baseband, 36
  broadband, 36
  defined, 20
Lockheed, 166
Lotus Notes, 189

M

Microsoft, 52, 140, 172, 182, 263
middleware, 7, 186, 208
models of computing, 155
multiplexer (mux), 71
multi-protocol routers, 90
multi-threading, 143, 192

N

near-line storage, 52
NetTech Inc., 230, 263
NetView/6000, 231
NetView/390, 224–226
NetWare:
  file serving, 43, 157
  Internetwork Packet Exchange
    (IPX), 45, 162
  NetWare Core Protocol, 48
  NetWare 4.x, 50
    NetWare Directory Services
      (NDS), 50
  NetWare Link Services Protocol, 46
  NetWare Loadable Modules (NLMs),
    42, 53
    Database Management Systems,
      54
  Routing Information Protocol (RIP),
    46, 96
  Sequenced Package Exchange
    (SPX), 46

SPX/IPX and the OSI 7-layer model,
    46
  Virtual Loadable Module, 60
Network File System, 100, 103
Network Interface Card (NIC), 49
Network layer, 17
Neuberger and Berman Management
    Inc., 161
Neuron Data, 167, 264
  Open Interface Elements, 167, 207
NeXT Computer Inc., 131, 264
Novell, 41, 45, 50, 265

O

Object-Oriented Programming:
  class library and, 180
  classes in, 178
  message passing, 179
  object hierarchy, 179
  an object in, 178
  polymorphism, 180
  SmallTalk, 181, 204, 206
Object Request Broker (ORB),
    187–188
ODBC, 172, 185
off-line storage, 52
Open Datalink Interface (ODI), 49
Open Software Foundation (OSF),
    129, 131, 141–142
OpenView, 231
Oracle, 189, 191, 265
OSI 7-layer model, 15

P

packet-switching, 64, 72
Peregrine Systems Inc., 230, 266
pipelines, 132
PKZIP, 3
POSIX, 141
PowerBuilder, 161, 175, 209

PowerPC, 136
PowerSoft, 209, 266
protocol, 12, 15
Public Data Network (PDN), 73

R

RAID, 52, 239
Reduced Instruction Set Computing
    (RISC), 131
Relational DataBase Management
    System (RDBMS):
  asynchronous replication, 191
  Binary Large Objects (BLOBS), 191
  defined, 183
  stored procedures, 190–191
  symmetric multi-processing, 193
  triggers, 190
  two-phase commit, 191
relational (database) model:
  concurrency, 189
  consistency, 189
  data locking, 189
  defined, 171
  referential integrity, 190
Remote Procedure Calls (RPCs), 144,
    187
RemoteWare, 68

S

Santa Cruz Operation (SCO), 130, 267
screen painting, 205
Secure Dynamics, 236, 267
Simple Mail Transfer Protocol (SMTP),
    100
Simple Network Management Protocol
    (SMTP), 100, 102, 227
SNA (Systems Network Architecture):
  Advanced Peer-to-Peer Networking
    (APPN), 115, 226
  classical, 112

front-end processor (FEP), 112
  Logical Units (LUs), 116
  and the OSI 7-layer model, 18
  VTAM, 112
SONET, 78
SPECfp, 134
SPECint, 133
SprintNet, 73
star topology, 22
StarTrek, 103
SQLWindows, 210
Structured Query Language (SQL),
    172, 183
  SQL driver, 208
  SQL server, 184
Sun Microsystems, 130, 164, 230, 268
SunNet Manager, 230
Switch Megabit Data Service (SMDS),
    75
Sybase, 189, 191, 268
synchronous and asynchronous
    communications, 66

T

T-Carrier Facility
  defined, 70
  Fractional T-1, 72
  T-1, 71
  T-3, 72
TCP/IP:
  and its association with the Internet,
    87
  Internet Protocol (IP), 91
    IP addressing, 92
    Open Shortest Path First, 96
  and the OSI 7-layer model, 17
  Transmission Control Protocol
    (TCP), 99
  User Defined Protocol (UDP), 100
3GL, 204–207
Token-Ring:
  defined, 25

and Ethernet, 28
IEEE 802.5, 26
Multi-Station Access Unit (MSAU),
   26
trellis encoding, 66

U

UNIX:
   defined, 126
   file system, 128
   the shell, 127
      Bourne shell, 128
      C shell, 128
   file system, 128
UnixWare, 53
Unshielded Twisted Pair, 21

V

V-series:
   defined, 66
   V.Fast, 67
   V.32bis, 67
   V.34, 67
VISA, 245
Visual Basic:
   case study, 166
   defined, 211
   OCX, 212
   VBX, 212

W

Windows:
   Cairo, 140
   Dynamic Data Exchange (DDE), 175
   Dynamic Link Libraries (DLLs), 174
   emulation, 135
      SoftWindows, 135
   history of, 173
   NT Advanced Server (NTAS), 52
   NT Server, 140
   NT Workstation, 140
   Object Linking and Embedding
      (OLE), 176–181
   95, 182–183
Wireless LANS:
   defined, 33
   infrared, 33
   microwave, 33
   radio frequency, 33
   sun-and-moon topology, 34
workflow management, 188
WORM, 3

X

Xcellenet, 68, 269
X/Open Ltd., 2, 141
X-Windows:
   defined, 128
   Motif, 129
X.25, 73